# ANOTHER TIME,

# ANOTHER PLACE

## 1927—1947

### BY

### RAMON GREENWOOD

ISBN: 1-4033-1274-5 (Electronic)
ISBN: 1-4033-1275-3 (Softcover)
ISBN: 1-4033-1276-1 (Hardcover)

This book is printed on acid free paper.

First published in the United States of America in 2002 by Common Sense Publishing Company, 1920 North Evergreen Avenue, Arlington Heights, Illinois 60004

1stBooks - rev. 05/23/02

*This book is dedicated to my mother and father,*

**Ophie Mae and Carl Greenwood**

*who nurture me to this day*
*with memories of their love and care that knew no bounds.*

# WITH MANY THANKS

I owe my appreciation to many people who contributed to the writing of this book.

There are the untold number, some named and more not, who played their individual and collective roles in creating the experiences from which this book comes.

There are those who helped me fill in the blanks of my memories of that time and place. They include, but are not limited to, Pete Godwin, Shirley Broach Godwin, Pat Murry Walker, John Claude Greenwood, George Morgan, Joyce Godwin Moore, Noma Anderson Watkins and Bob Newton.

There's Martha, who had heard all of the stories more than once before, but nevertheless patiently read and reread the manuscript searching out mistakes of commission and omission.

There are our children who encouraged me to write the book.

There is Jean Flagg, my editor, who made helpful suggestions to improve my writing and helped me exterminate most of the bugs of misspelling and punctuation.

Finally, the shortcomings the book may have are all mine.

**Ramon Greenwood**

*"You knew that a record had to be kept,*
*or the world or you would disappear."*

**Betsy Lerner**
*The Forest For The Trees*

# TABLE OF CONTENTS

## THERE WAS SUCH A TIME AND PLACE

I have written the essays that comprise *Another Time, Another Place* out of a compulsion to record for my children and my grandchildern and their children what life was like in Warren, Arkansas from 1927 through the defining years of the Great Depression and World War II into the respite of global peace that followed.

Hopefully, my progenies will have a better understanding of who I am, and why, if they know these things about my beginnings.

Eric Zorn, a columnist for *The Chicago Tribune* explains: "We write to enlarge and preserve that which we know, that which we have felt. We write because organizing our jumbled impressions into sentences is sometimes the only way to figure out what we think. We write because words—inadequate as they always are—are the best and most lasting way to connect with ourselves and with others."

As improbable as it may seem such a time and place did once exist.

My memories are of another world so different from the one we inhabit now that it defies all logic to believe that my recollections are anything more than wisps of dreams and imaginations born of my yearning for a kinder and gentler time and place.

But I am reassured when I realize that my memories must be more than illusions created from the passage of the years and bittersweet longings for the past. If they are not real, how could my recollection of that time and that place be so vivid?

1

There was always time then—an endless, flowing stream, unbroken by deadlines, paychecks, meetings, counting the weeks until the next promotion, waiting for the results of a critical medical test to come from the doctor.

Time did not count back then because we did not count time. It was an inexhaustible commodity. Now the reality is that time is finite.

During the long, lazy days of spring and summer I had nothing more urgent to do than lie on my back on the soft grass and look into the depth of the sky where in my imagination I painted pictures in the billowing white clouds that rolled across the blue canvas—a camel here, an old man's face there, puffs of soft cotton. In the fall, we had the time to chase the falling leaves and rake them together for burning. When it snowed in the winter we were awed by the snowflakes and the sparkling crystals of ice on tree limbs.

The night skies were alive with bright stars forming a canopy stretching in all directions. We did not know enough then to be puzzled and frightened by thoughts of the cosmos. After all, we saw Flash Gordon conquer the Martians at the Saturday matinee.

We often saw shooting stars streaking across the heavens. The light of the full moon was so bright that it cast the night in a silver haze.

When dusk turned to night in the spring and early summer, a blizzard of lightning bugs came out from their hiding places, busily blinking their golden lights, adding magic to the world. Untroubled by ecological concerns, we captured the tiny, mystical creatures in Mason jars creating lanterns that cast off a golden glow. Sometimes we pinched off their lights and fashioned them into designs on our hands and arms.

Tree frogs, crickets and other creatures filled the night air with their urgent matings calls.

Now the ground lights and the fouled air have diminished the splendor of the night skies. Pesticides and other pollutants have decimated lightning bugs and other occupants of the night time.

We are no longer cooled by night breezes. Instead when night time comes we lock out the world so that we can sit inside in our overstuffed reclining chairs in rooms warmed by central heating and cooled by air conditioning, trading the splendor of moonlight and stars for the inanities paraded on our television sets.

Joy, love and anger were accepted without question. Joy, boundless in supply, would always come again; love would never leave; anger passed quickly and left no scars. Friendships were without subtleties or innuendoes. If they were fractured, it was only for a moment. The wounds of the flesh and heart healed quickly. Regrets were few and apologies hardly ever necessary. Friends understood.

There were dreams to enjoy. No one said they were impossible. In fact, as youngsters we believed that any and all things were possible. Often the dreams were more important than their realization. When dreams did not materialize, disappointments were brief, for we knew there were other, better dreams waiting to take their places. We believed the opportunities of life were boundless. Now, tempered by the realities of living, we find it harder to conjure up dreams; we reluctantly conclude there are fewer opportunities to achieve grand things.

I often ask myself how things could have changed so much in so short a time. I once wondered, wishfully, if a time and place so different, so simple and so gentle might ever return. Now I know they won't for me, or my children or their children's children. That time, that place have been taken away in the name of progress. Now, time counts, dreams are fewer, terror stalks our way of life and the world has lost its innocence.

Little is left from those years but memories and they must be preserved.

Jason Epstein made the case in his *Book of Business* when he declared that "…without a vivid link to the past, the present is chaos and the future unreadable."

ooooooooooooooo

Now Melissa and Mark have children of their own. At the slightest opportunity I tell my grandchildren many of the same stories I have told my children through the years. They declare they like to hear them and ask me to tell more. Sometimes their eyes glaze over. It is their way of letting me know that I have told that story before, perhaps several times.

Through the years the children have urged me to write a book so as to record my memories for them and others. Many of my contemporaries have suggested the same undertaking.

Flattered, I have always said, "Yes, I will do it," but I have put off the writing. Relating these stories around the family dinner table and over drinks at reunions with my friends has been easy to do. Writing a book is a more formidable task.

Finally, I came to grips with the fact that I have a responsibility to create a written record for it seems to me that those values, as I remember them, are in imminent danger of being lost. If they disappear, life will be diminished for all who come after me.

There are two compelling lines racing across the time chart of my life. One is my mortality. The other is that my recollections, which are so vivid today, are bound to fade and seem more improbable with time in a rapidly changing world that often seems alien and out of control—even insane. I have already waited too long to talk with many people whose memories I would like to have recorded to help me hone my own.

One day lifelines of mortality and fading recollections will cross. Then my memories will be in the hands of my children to nurture them as they see fit.

But when it came to putting my memories on paper, I encountered one mental block after another. I finally identified my problem. I was trying to put those thoughts into a tightly organized sequence, instead of letting them flow at random as they do when I am speaking about my recollections. Finally, I broke the block and I have let the memories unfold, as they would.

I sat at my computer and began to write with my mind freed to reminisce in snippets and blocks of time and experiences, randomly skipping from here to there, one memory leading to others like branches and twigs growing from the trunk of a tree. The book organized itself into essays about the people, the places and the experiences that were important to my growing up.

oooooooooooooooo

*Another Time, Another Place* is not intended to be a definitive history.

Rather, it is a recording based primarily on one man's recollections. No doubt my memories have been influenced by the passage of time and my experiences since those days. I have supplemented and tried to verify my recollections by listening to a great many people in informal conversations through the years and by way of formal interviews more recently. I have looked back through newspapers of the day, including issues of Warren's *Eagle Democrat*. I have also done research by reviewing many other publications and reading a great many books about those times.

Some readers will have differences with my recollections of those days. But I am satisfied that my book provides an accurate picture of what it was like to grow up in that time and that place. In striving for candor I have tried to avoid glossing over events. In most cases, I have used the names of real people in telling of real places and events. But in instances where I have felt that someone might be embarrassed or hurt if I used their actual names, I have avoided their identification where I could without doing harm to the story. I have reasoned that if the truth is not told, I will have wasted my time in writing this book and yours in reading it. In any case, no harm is intended to persons living or dead.

Still I may have hurt some feelings, either through commission or omission. If I have, I apologize.

ooooooooooooooo

I recognize there is a certain grimness in the undercurrent of my memories, particularly of the earliest days.

The fact is we did experience some hard times. Nevertheless, surrounded as I was by love and nurturing, my life in those days was a happy one. It might have been otherwise if I could have made comparisons between our lives and the lives of those with more privileges.

By the time I had finished the writing, I was comforted by the realization that there is very little I would change about my growing up even if I wanted to and had the power to revise history. The people and experiences of those times imbued in me a sustaining view of the possibilities of life that can be defined by ambition and realized through focused effort. I know that each generation has both the opportunity and the obligation to use what it has been given by those who came before to a

6

create a better life, one more productive and more prosperous, for themselves and those who follow.

So, these essays, dedicated to my mother and father, have been written for Melissa and Mark, Jeff and Cindy, their spouses, and our grandaughters Emily, Lauren, Katherine, Joanna and Melissa. It is my hope that this book will serve as a direct conduit of important lessons and reassurances so their lives, and the lives of all others who read it, will be made more enjoyable for the moment and richer for the future.

*Ramon Greenwood*

## *MY FAMILY*

The family in which I grew up surrounded me with caring love that knew no boundaries or conditions. It was a close-knit network made up of two grandmothers, my parents, aunts and uncles and cousins. Most of my family who didn't live in our home or next door was no farther away than a short walk across town. We only had one set of relatives living away from Warren.

My immediate family living in the house at 410 East Church Street was made up of my mother's mother, Melissa Catherine Ashcraft Reep; my mother, Ophie Mae Reep Greenwood; my father, Walton Carl Greenwood; and my uncle, Jewell Melrose Reep.

Although the writing of the story of the family of my youth provides me with many memories of lasting value, I also feel great regret that I did not make the small effort required to learn more about my ancestors while there were still those around me who could have shared their personal recollections.

ooooooooooooooooo

My grandmother Reep was a woman of sparse build and spirit.

She was probably no more than five foot three inches tall and as thin as a rail; her dark complexioned skin seemed barely adequate to cover her bones. There was a pronounced hump in her back. Her face was sharply sculptured, her eyes dark and piercing; her hair was jet black without a trace of gray; it was pulled back in severe sweeps to form a bun.

She rarely smiled; I don't remember that she ever laughed. Mostly she seemed removed, worried and moody. Her one concession to the pleasures of the flesh was that she dipped snuff. That was not an uncommon habit for women, as well as men, in those days.

But it is easy to see now that her personality was powerfully influenced by the hard knocks she endured.

Melissa Catherine Ashcraft was born near Rye just north of Warren the year the Civil War began. She was one of three daughters of William and Josephine Ashcraft. Her clan, some 19 of them, had moved en masse from South Carolina. Her immediate family was fairly prosperous during her childhood. Her father raised cotton, ran a livery and blacksmithing service and operated a mercantile business.

I know next to nothing about my grandmother's family. I did hear her tell that she had learned her grandfather had been murdered by a stranger who rode up on horseback to Mr. Ashcraft's blacksmith shop and shot him to death after a brief argument and then rode off undeterred.

My lack of information about my ancestors is exemplified by the fact that I have only two pieces of material evidence that my great grandfather existed.

One is his handwritten accounts book from the store he operated near Rye. The other is a short note written in pencil which he had enclosed in his ledger. The note reflects an educated man who had a flair for words as he expressed his sensitivities about the land where he lived. He wrote:

"I was raised in South Carolina. Emigrated to this state (Arkansas) soon after I was married. When I landed here where I am now living, I found this portion comparatively unsettled, except a few pioneers. The whole face of the country was then beautiful, the entire woods was very open with a dense growth of wild grass growing throughout the entire woods, in early spring. It had the appearance of the Carolinas or virgin wheat fields, with large quantities of wild flowers which was beautiful to behold, as nature had displayed it."

The accounts book from his store revealed an easy-going man who was quick to provide credit to his neighbors and family and reluctant to collect. My grandmother simply said he was "too good for his own good."

Accounts in the book reveal a lot about the man and the economies of the time. Charges ran page after page. "Charles Hunter, 20 cents, tobacco; C. Hunter, $1.50, shoes; L. C. Cooper, 65 cents balance due on shoes; Andy Cook, meal and tobacco, 30 cents; Ross and White, $8.00, 64 1/2 pounds of bulk pork; J. T. Ashcraft, 15 cents, 1 1/2 bushels of cotton seed; J. T. Ashcraft, 30 cents salt and quinine."

He loaned money from 50 cents to $18.00, traded in cotton and sold an occasional bottle of whiskey. A few patrons earned credit by picking cotton from my great grandfather's field.

The list of people who owed him money is heavily populated with Ashcraft relatives. One, J. T. Ashcraft, seems to have worked from time to time at the store, but his need for credit was constant. My great grandfather kept close track of J. T., perhaps with good reason. He recorded several instances where J.T. failed to show up for work because he was sick. On one occasion he entered a note in his ledger that J. T. took a half-day off to "go fishing."

Another relative was recorded as owing $505.28 for the years of 1885 through 1889.

The failure of my great grandfather's enterprise was, as they say, foretold "in the numbers."

oooooooooooooooo

My grandmother married Charles Strong Reep, who also lived in the Rye community.

The only photograph I have of him shows a thin man of medium height who wore a heavy black handlebar moustache. He worked in his in-laws' mercantile and livery stable business. But he proved to be no better businessman than his father-in-law, so the enterprise soon failed.

Melissa Catherine and her husband moved to Warren in the early 1900s. I think he tried to operate a livery stable without much success.

Charles Strong Reep died in 1913, at age 57, his face consumed by skin cancer that could not be turned back by the elementary radium treatments of the day. My grandmother was 52; my mother 14; her brothers were several years older.

I have always found it interesting to consider how and to what extent the decisions and actions of ancestors impact the lives of their progenies. I believe in the progression of the generations where given an even chance each person can improve on the lot of those who came before. But this begs the question. What kind of legacies of spirit and purse would Great Grandfather Ashcraft and Grandfather Reep have left had they been hard-nosed businessmen who demanded payment for credit extended? Would we be people of different personal values? Would we have been owners of property and people of wealth?

I never knew first hand any members of my grandmother's family, except for Mills Ashcraft, a cousin some four or five years her elder, who lived out in the country from Warren. His periodic visits to our home provided many interesting times for me. There were two distinguishing characteristics about him. One was his long white beard, which was stained just below his mouth by the chewing tobacco juice that dribbled over his lips when he spit. The other was that he loved to talk.

He and my grandmother would sit in the swing on our front porch talking by the hours. He chewed his tobacco and she dipped her snuff. It took little prompting from me to get Mr. Ashcraft to tell the stories of his growing up as a boy during the Civil War. My favorite of his tales was the one about the time the Union soldiers came to his house.

His father and older brothers had gone away to fight on the side of the Confederacy. Barely a teenager, he had been left at home to take care of his mother and sisters. His father had hidden a rifle in the peach orchard behind the house. He was to use the gun to kill wildlife for food and if called on to defend the home.

Soon after the men of the house left, a troop of Yankee soldiers came by and camped overnight in a nearby field. Before they decamped the next morning the officer in charge asked the lad if he had a gun. The young boy admitted that he did. The Yankee officers told him to keep it because he might need a weapon to ward off marauders passing themselves off as Northern troops. He warned that even Rebel soldiers might confiscate his weapon.

His story might or might not have been a fanciful recalling of his youth in the days of the Civil War. I have heard similar stories from other sources. In any case, his telling of it never varied in its detail or in the way it fascinated me.

ooooooooooooooo

My writing of this book has provided me with a new and growing appreciation of what a defining influence my mother had on my life.

As her only child, I was raised as a "mama's boy," according to the neighbors. She resented that characterization, but she did admit, with a sort of perverse pride, that I was "spoiled rotten." She had plenty of help in this dubious accomplishment from other members of the household.

I now know that my mother, whom I saw in a one-dimensional role, was in fact a complex person.

Mama was a pretty woman. About five-foot three or four inches in height, she had black hair without a trace of gray and dark eyes like her mother. Her complexion was free of blemishes.

For most of her life she was a strong, energetic, positive, out-going person. She was blessed with creative talents. Unfortunately, she never had the opportunity to really develop them. Still she showed an instinct for colors and painting and sewing and flower arranging. The fact that her grandchildren, our daughter Melissa and our son Mark, and I, to some extent, have thrived through creativity is testimony to the power of genes.

Gregarious, with a streak of aggressiveness about her, she exercised natural leadership skills. Even as a young boy I took pride in her being elected many times to head the ladies' auxiliary at the Woodmen of the World Lodge, which met amid the trappings of deep secrecy in their own building next door to the Coker Hotel. She also held the office of president of her Home Demonstration Club for several years.

At the same time, she often seemed to be conflicted about her happiness by an underlying sense of grim puritanism that called up questions about her right to enjoy life. She never recovered from the scars of growing up a poor child and then being knocked about by the Depression. It was always difficult for her to spend money for pleasure. Every dime should go to fit a need. Her credo was that needs should always supercede wants. Save, when you could, she admonished, against the rainy day that was certain to come.

She drilled the puritan lessons into me. When I was a child she woke me each morning with the recitation of a little poem. Regrettably, try as hard as I can, I can't remember the exact words. However, the message remains with me: gather fame and riches, all you can, but always be an honest man.

So I grew up with a sense of seriousness about me. She declared when I was 12 years old, "Ramon, you have been an old man all of your life."

oooooooooooooooo

Her reluctance to spend money was intensified if it meant going in debt or installment buying. If she had a choice she didn't want to buy anything until she could pay cash for it.

We never ran a charge account with any merchants in town except The Bradley Store where almost all of the business was done by the "company store" system of credit. I am not sure she was ever entirely at ease with the fact that we bought most of our groceries and household goods there, but that was the way it had to be.

For my father, and for others employed at the mill, that meant that time worked was credited to his account against which we could buy almost all the basics we needed so long as he had worked enough hours to cover the bill. For the working man credit was earned before it was granted, not extended on good faith. Credit was on a short leash for employees at the mill. No work, no credit.

15

An old man I worked with at the mill told me that he had married and raised all of his children without ever seeing a paycheck.

By contrast, the business and professional people in town were able to maintain charge accounts underwritten by good faith.

We heard that the charge accounts for several of the more prominent families in town were overdue by hundreds of dollars and growing. One of the town's leading attorneys was said to have owed The Bradley Store thousand of dollars when it closed. The gossips had a field day, and no small amount of satisfaction, with the stories of how the folks who lived on what they called "silk stocking row" couldn't or wouldn't pay their bills.

As a child I couldn't fathom the barter system—work for credit.

My father always bought a candy bar each for me and my mother on our Saturday night excursions uptown. One Snicker bar or a Baby Ruth rarely satisfied my craving, so I usually begged for more. When my parents said "no," I countered with what I thought was a perfectly logical argument: "Why can't I have another candy bar? It doesn't cost anything." After all, I hadn't seen any money change hands. That argument didn't get me very far. My parents explained that my father had to work to buy everything we had. However, they were kind not to tell me that he had to work longer to pay for the candy bar than it took me to eat it. It wasn't until I worked at the mill as a teenager for 35 cents per hour that I understood.

ooooooooooooooo

What little shopping our family did out of town was by means of the Sears Roebuck catalog.

We called it the Wishbook. We received a new copy at least once a year. Three or four inches thick, it was crammed cover to cover with every type of merchandise we could imagine: clothing for the entire family; automobile tires and replacement parts; baby chickens; fruit trees and garden seeds; bicycles, erector sets and all sorts of toys; guns and ammunitions; animal traps; boots and hunting jackets; cookware; furniture. It was even possible to buy a kit with pre-cut parts and instructions to build a house. Over 400 models were offered. One that could be turned into a house of two bedrooms, one and one-half baths, a gas-log fireplace and hardwood floors for $1,100. More expensive models could be had if a family desired a "stately" mansion with a solarium and servants' quarters.

In the poorest of times before most everyone had an indoor toilet, we, and a lot of other families, used the pages of the catalog as a replacement for toilet paper.

Mama finally broke her rule against going into debt when she opened a charge account at Sears Roebuck with a deposit of $5.00. This meant we could order things and pay for them on the installment plan. She never missed a month buying a money order at the post office and sending it off to Sears when there was a balance on our account.

I was embarrassed to have most of my school clothes bought from the Sears catalog. I don't know why. My parents always saw to it that I had good sensible clothes and shoes to wear, which is more than could be said about some of my classmates, who never had better than hand-me-downs. Others I went to school with wore clothes from the Wishbook or out of catalogs from Montgomery Ward or Spiegel. I guess some of them were as embarrassed as I was. It didn't help my feelings when Mama bought my clothes "plenty big." She always tried to convince me that I would "grow into them."

One of Mama's most prized purchases from Sears was a pressure cooker. We also bought baby chickens, which we raised in our chicken yard out back, and Christmas gifts from the Wishbook.

Toward the end of her life, my mother gave a bit of ground to the values of the emerging consumer society as she expressed regret that "we didn't buy more things on time, because we would have paid for them one way or another."

She always got great pleasure from making-over and making-do with those things that were in hand. Cotton sacks in which cooking flour was bought provided her with material for her sewing. I went away for my junior year at the University of Arkansas with some undershorts she had made from cotton sacks.

The scars of needing and not having had all but obscured the hopes of wanting in her life. But she never held back her love or her gifts for her children and grandchildren. She always gave generously from both of her heart and her purse to the best of her abilities.

Martha became the daughter she never had. Although I was known to be the apple of my mother's eye, when Martha and I had a disagreement it was as certain as the sun rising in the east that she would agree with her daughter-in-law whom she adored.

oooooooooooooooo

I learned a great deal about my mother's life when I was still short of my teenage years.

I had been allowed one of my privileges of spring, which was to skip school one afternoon to help plant the garden.

She and I were breaking up clods of damp dark dirt and forming rows when she dropped her hoe and hesitantly told me that she had had a husband before marrying my father. My first question, asked before she had barely finished her sentence, was "Is my daddy, my daddy?" To my great relief she went on to assure me that Carl Greenwood was my father and that they loved me more than anything in the world. She explained that they had decided she should tell me before I heard it from somebody else. She anticipated my second question when she told me that I didn't have any brothers or sisters.

She had married a Mr. Bunn at the age of 16. A kind man several years older than she, he was relatively prosperous from his part ownership of a dry cleaning business. He was good to her, and she respected him, she assured me. Her decision to marry, presumably blessed by her mother and brothers, was based on the need to get away from home and relieve the family of one more mouth to feed.

Mr. Bunn died of tuberculosis in a sanatorium in Texas a short time after their marriage. She came back home a widow still in her teens. She remained single until she and my father married.

Of course, she had to find employment as soon as possible. She did as a clerk in a local five and dime store. That was her occupation until she married my father.

She attributed the problems she suffered with her feet throughout her life to standing all of those hours clerking. A particular problem arose, she believed, from wearing a pair of shoes she had bought on sale despite the fact that they were significantly too small for her.

She found a niche for her talents when she worked at Morgan and Lindsay's five and dime during the holidays and took the lead in putting up the store's decorations for Christmas and Easter. However, her main job, which she enjoyed immensely, was in gift wrapping packages. Her creativity could flow there.

ooooooooooooooo

Happy memories of my mother prevail.

During the spring and summer, Mama was always up early, at work before the heat of the day set in. It was then, while the dew was still heavy, that she tended her flower garden where she grew flowers of all sorts; her specialty was nasturtiums and various kinds of lilies. While she worked she always sang her favorite hymns: "The Old Rugged Cross," "I Walk Through The Garden Alone," and "Sweet Hour of Prayer." She returned to the house with bouquets of blossoms for her vases.

One day a week was washday. That was quite an undertaking, but she never seemed to mind the chore. She had three large tin washtubs, which she placed on a bench that leaned against one of two large persimmon trees in our backyard. Her equipment was completed with a large iron washpot.

Her first task was to fill the washpot with several gallons of water she had drawn from the deep well that stood next to our back porch. It was cheaper than city water. Next she started a fire under the pot.

She went back to the well to draw more water to fill the washtubs. I was always fascinated to see her mix blueing in the water of one of the tubs. Despite its name and the fact that it turned the water a sapphire blue, it was meant to whiten the clothes.

While the water in the pot came to a boil she went about picking up eggs from our flock of chickens in the henhouse or gathering vegetables from the garden.

When the pot was up to a full boil she added slivers of soap to the cauldron. Sometimes the soap was pure white, bought from the store; other washdays she used a dark-brown soap she had made. It contained lye, and its odor promised it would clean away any dirt.

She dumped the pants, shirts, bed sheets, towels and washcloths (we called them washrags) made from flour sacks into the washpot and let them boil for a while under her frequent stirring with an old broomstick. When the clothes were boiled clean to her satisfaction she removed them with her stirring stick and carried them over to the first of her washtubs. Another batch would go in the washpot.

Each piece of washing was subjected to a vigorous attack on the rub board, a device made of ridged tin attached to a wooden rack. She spread out the cloth, rubbed in more soap and then scrubbed it up and down the tin ridges. Next, the laundry went into the second tub which was filled with clear water for rinsing and finally into the blueing tub.

Piece by piece the washing was taken separately from the last tub and twisted by hand until all of the water was wrung out. Sometimes she called me to help with the large pieces such as bed sheets. I held one end of a sheet, heavy with water, while she started twisting it from the other end, forcing out any remaining wetness.

The washing was hung out on clotheslines to dry. She could deftly drape a piece of washing over the line with one hand while pulling clothespins from her ample apron pockets with the other. Laundry today, no matter how fresh, never smells as good as that dried in the bright sunshine and warm breezes.

This was the laborious way she did the washing until after World War II when Uncle Howard, her prosperous brother who lived in Camden, gave her

21

a second-hand washing machine. It was a great advance over the washpot in the backyard, but still a far cry from the automatic machines of today.

Washing one day meant ironing the next. Ironing was a particularly unpleasant task on a hot summer day.

First, certain of the clothes, such as her dresses and those of my grandmother, had to be starched so that they could be dampened and then ironed, leaving them as stiff and crisp as cardboard. Once this was accomplished she built up a hot fire in the wood-burning kitchen stove. On the stovetop she heated two heavy flatirons. She used one until it cooled down, then placed it back on the stove and picked up the other, repeating the process until the ironing was done.

When the washing, ironing or other weekly routine tasks were completed, she turned to cleaning up the house. Sweeping and scubbing floors, making up beds, dusting furniture, fighting off various varmints that always seemed ready to take over. Housekeeping was a formidable task in an old house in a questionable condition.

Along the way she was cooking the two main meals of the day, which we knew as dinner at noon, and supper at night.

After we had eaten the noon meal she hand washed the dishes, pots and pans. This chore accomplished, it was then time for her to rest a bit and then clean herself up and put on one of her starched dresses over a corset that was as stiff and binding as a body cast. She wore dresses she had hand made from cotton material she had bought at the Bradley Store or from cloth sacks she had gotten with her purchase of flour.

She emerged from her daily toiletries bearing an aroma of talcum powder. All this was preparatory to visiting with the ladies of the neighborhood on our front porch or our sitting room. Occasionally she walked down to the corner grocery, stopping along the way to visit with neighbors.

As darkness fell, the men came in from work. Supper was put on the table right away. The kitchen was cleaned again from stem to stern before she could sit down to sew or listen to the radio.

ooooooooooooooo

My father, Walton Carl Greenwood, was a polar opposite from my mother in personality.

He was a man of quiet and meek demeanor. Life had taught him to accept things as they were. Yet there was a smoldering temper within him that could explode in an instance, especially if he sensed that someone was trying to make a fool of him. It was best not to be around him on these occasions. I only saw this happen once or twice and that was enough.

He stood about five feet ten inches of medium build. He never weighed more than 165 pounds. Not handsome, still he was a good-looking man of light complexion. He had turned bald at an early age and this troubled him considerably.

He had a little beer to drink now and then, but after their marriage my mother kept him on a short leash. He smoked cigarettes that he hand-rolled from Bull Durham tobacco that came from the store in small cotton sacks along with a packet of rolling paper. He said from time to time that he should quit, but he never did.

He was born December 22, 1886, at El Dorado, Arkansas.

The family soon moved across the Ouachita River to the south part of Bradley county, near the crossroads community of Jersey. He was the first of ten children born to Jennie Irene Stephens Greenwood and William Karl Greenwood.

William Karl Greenwood, my grandfather, seems to have been a man who harbored aspirations that were higher than his application of hand to work. There must have been quite a story behind his father, Dr. O. P. Greenwood, a well-to-do physician in El Dorado, leaving him only $5.00 as compared to willing the remainder of his sizeable estate to William's two sisters.

My grandfather was a hardscrabble one-mule farmer, whose major interests seem to have been serving as the census enumerator for his township in 1900 and as a member of the county's levying court that voted the tax in 1902-1903 to build the county courthouse that stands in Warren today. He experienced poor health as a young man and died in 1910 at age 53. By then the family consisted of my grandmother and ten children, plus a son-in-law and granddaughter.

My father was officially the man of the house at 24. This was a de facto responsibility he had been carrying since his early teens because of his father's questionable health.

His burdens didn't get lighter, because by 1920 there were 14 people in the household, including my grandmother, his nine brothers and sisters, one of whom was married, another of whom was divorced, and two nephews and a niece.

ooooooooooooooo

My father was well acquainted with hard work almost all of his life, but I never head him complain, not once, about his lot. He played the hand he had been dealt the best he could.

As a boy he began doing a man's chores on the family farm which by all accounts was failing. Some said the farm didn't prosper because of my grandfather's preference for courthouse politics over working in the fields.

Whatever the reasons for the failures at home, my father was forced to leave the farm to find what they called "public work" to make ends meet for the family. His best opportunity for work was to be found in Warren. The only way he could get to town, some 20 miles away, was to walk or hitch a ride on a passing wagon. Then only about 16 years of age, he was a shy boy who had had little contact with life outside his family and the farm.

No doubt apprehensive yet exhilarated, he set out before daylight on a summer morning, walking over the dirt road from Jersey to Warren. But by the time he had covered half or so of the distance without encountering another person, he had all but given up hope of catching a ride. Finally, he heard the sound of a team of horses coming from behind. An old man pulled up alongside him, reined to a stop and called out, "Son, you look mighty hot and tired. You want a ride to town?"

My father stood there drawing lines in the dirt with his toe while he contemplated the offer as if it had never occurred to him.

Finally, he was able to blurt out, "I don't know."

My father's timing was most unfortunate. The old man glared down at him, snapped the reins on his team of horses and called over his shoulders as he drove away, "Well, if you don't know, I don't know."

Welcomed to the world away from home, my father walked the rest of the way to town.

One of his first jobs off the farm was as a laborer on the crew building the Bradley county courthouse. It can be assumed that his father may have used some influence to help him get on the payroll.

oooooooooooooooo

After the courthouse job was completed, my father got his first sawmill job. Still short of his 20th birthday, it was there he was to find the trade that he would follow for well over 50 years.

The family responsibilities that he had been forced to accept at far too young an age caused him to endure a major disappointment. When World War I erupted he was caught up in the patriotic fever and yearning for adventure that gripped most young men, but he couldn't go to fight Kaiser Bill and the Huns. Instead he had to remain behind as head of the household.

The war had one other more immediate effect on him. In view of the strong anti-German sentiment in the country he elected to change the spelling of his name from the Germanic Karl to the more American version, Carl.

His brothers, Ned, Claude (Joshua) and Clarence, did serve in the Army. Ned, four years my father's junior, died in the great influenza epidemic just a month before the war ended in 1918. Claude survived the trenches in France to tell the story of falling asleep one night on the ground to awake hours later in a freezing rain with his hair frozen to the earth.

Family responsibilities also dictated that my father had little or no social life.

He couldn't have known much about courting a girl. When he was in his 20s, Sunday afternoon was the time of choice for most young couples to do their "sparkin'." It was then that they strolled about town and stopped to buy an ice cream cone or a phosphate at the soda fountain. Sometimes they visited in the girls' homes, hopefully, out of sight of ever-watchful parents.

He told me that while the other young men were courting the girls he went walking in the woods alone because he did not feel he had the proper clothes to wear or the money to spend on girls. In so many words, he explained that he didn't see much point in courting a girl because he couldn't leave his family to marry.

I do recall with great sorrow that in later years he told me that even if he could, he would not want to relive those years. They were too embarrassing.

ooooooooooooooo

I never heard my parents talk about their courtship and their marriage. From what I know of their early lives, they must have had a different kind of romance with limited dreams.

Their circumstances surely created special pressures. She was a young widow who worked to help support her mother; he was the breadwinner for his mother and siblings. Their marriage reordered the economics of two households. Then there was my grandmother Reep's harsh view toward the world and stern judgment of him. It's hard to see how they had much time or freedom to get to know each other before their marriage, or in the early years of their life together for that matter. But court, fall in love and marry they did despite the odds.

They married on New Year's Eve, 1923. He was 37 years of age; she was 24. She had been a widow for six or seven years. My father worked until noon their wedding day. After the ceremony, conducted by Elder G. L. Boles late in the afternoon, the newly weds celebrated by eating supper at a café in town. Their wedding night was spent at my grandmother's house, where they were to live almost all of their years together.

I can imagine that it was an uncomfortable time for my father. My grandmother always seemed to hold him at a cold distance, never appreciating him despite his easy nature and the fact that he was the principal breadwinner in the household for most of the years they coexisted under the same roof.

My mother and father lived together 41 years in a union that the outside world would never have rated high in the traditional trappings of romance. There was little time spent alone; no words of affection spoken aloud; no lovers' quarrels; no handholding or embraces; no flowers or gifts on birthdays and anniversaries. Just the steady business of getting on with life. Nevertheless, their marriage endured as a solid relationship of love and caring through good times and bad.

oooooooooooooooo

It was with deep regret, as I was to recognize later, that for any number of reasons I did not grow up feeling a very close relationship with my father.

Our relationship may have been shaped by the fact that he was nearly 40 when I was born; perhaps it was mother's strong personality that captivated my attention; it could have been my grandmother's influence.

There were no ill feelings between us. It was just that he was not able to express much affection and he was at a distance from most of my daily comings and goings. Neither of us recognized the void and if we had we would not have known what to do about it.

Now I know I was blessed to have had him as a father. I wish I had told him so and that I loved him.

Dad and I went on only one outing together during my youth. It was a rich experience for me, a time that I recall to this day with great affection and appreciation. We took a Saturday to go fishing on the Saline River. Leaving home at sunrise our fishing poles in hand, we walked to the river at the railroad bridge between Warren and Wilmar. Our tackle, consisting of lines, sinkers, corks and hooks, fit in a paper sack. We also carried an iron skillet, grease and cornmeal for frying the fish we were sure we would catch. My mother had packed sandwiches and homemade pickles for our lunch. She said she was sure we could catch fish, but just in case…

The roiling river had risen to the point that it was almost out of its banks. We headed south, stopping every now and then to try our luck at fishing. By the time we had hiked to Camp Mansfield we had only caught fingerlings no larger than sardines. We built a fire and fried our "fish" to eat with our sandwiches. Then we walked out to the highway at the Airport Inn and headed home. It was a great day!

ooooooooooooooo

Discipline was left to my mother who administered it with a stern voice and blazing dark eyes while applying a switch or paddle to my rear end and legs when I wore short pants.

When she gave me a tongue-lashing and I argued back, the session was always ended with her admonishment, "Do as I say, not as I do."

My father only spanked me once, and that was enough; the memory remains with me. I had sassed him while he sat resting on the back porch. Quick as lightning he flared up, jerked me to his side and whacked me once or twice across the butt while he declared, in a voice I had never heard from him before, that I was never to sass him again.

Given his personality and our relationship, it follows that he never sat me down for the storied "facts of life" discussion. He only touched on that subject once, the day I left for the Army at 18.

He came home from the sawmill for lunch. Between tears my mother had prepared a big lunch of my favorite foods—fried chicken, potato salad, lima beans and cornbread.

The meal finished, we sat in awkward silence until it was time to walk to the court square where I would catch the bus with the other inductees.

My mother stayed at home because, as she explained, she couldn't bear to see me get on the bus. Dad and I walked to Frank's soda fountain and poolhall across from the court square where he bought Coca Colas for us. We had little to say until finally he declared that we should talk.

"Ramon, you are going to meet a lot of women. You will find that some girls will and some girls won't. Take care of yourself." That said, he abruptly walked away, having completed the mission that I am sure my mother had laid out.

As we lined up to board the bus I spotted a man named Myers, several years my senior, who worked with my father at the Southern Lumber Company. He suggested that we sit together on the bus. By the time we had reached the North Steel Bridge on the way to Little Rock, Myers confessed that my father had asked him to look after me. As the bus pulled into the station in Pine Bluff for a rest stop, my newfound friend and mentor asked me if I ever drank whiskey. I said I had had a drink or two. When we reboarded the bus Myers pulled a pint of bourbon out of his pocket, took a big drink and offered the bottle to me. He and I finished the contents by the time we reached Camp Robinson in North Little Rock to become soldiers.

oooooooooooooooo

Thankfully, in later years after I had served in the army and had graduated from college, I came to understand and appreciate my father.

I learned that he was a man of infinite patience and gentleness. Yet there must have been an inner will of great strength for him to have persevered and won out in the daily business of living the life he lived. Most important, I came to know that he always loved and respected me, although frequently he did not understand the track that the ambitions of my life had put me on.

It is the way with life that as he and I grew older our roles were reversed. He turned to me for advice and help. I found great pleasure in being able to take him with me on several business trips.

We drove to New Orleans for one of my business meetings. There is no amount of money I would take for the memory of him getting out of my car at the Roosevelt Hotel and standing back as the bellhops picked up our luggage and led us inside. He and I ate raw oysters and walked down Bourbon Street, neither of us acknowledging that we saw or were interested in the striptease dancers at work and the busy bars we glimpsed as the hawkers swung open the doors and urged us to check out the action.

The anomalies in his life surprised me.

He could hardly carry a tune and I never heard him try to sing except at the Methodist Men's Sunday Class which he came to enjoy greatly in later years. Yet, somewhere along the way, he had taught himself to play one song, "Home Sweet Home," on the harmonica. I heard him play it only a half-dozen or so times.

When I was stationed in Greenland in the Army Air Force I was reduced to tears one night in the barracks when a G.I. pulled out his harmonica and played that song over and over again.

My father had two other talents that greatly impressed me and my playmates. He could cup his fists together and blow through a "mouthpiece" formed by the knuckles of his thumbs, producing a hollow whistle sound. He also could take a small section of a branch from a hickory tree at a time

31

of the year when the "bark was slipping" and using his pocketknife, fashion a whistle from it. Those whistles, which lasted only so long as the bark remained moist, were highly prized.

I only saw him truly enjoy one form of entertainment other than reading. He was fascinated by the wrestling matches that came to town under the sponsorship of the American Legion Post. He missed few if any of the Friday night matches, which featured such notables as Farmer Mack, Wild Red Berry and Gorgeous George.

ooooooooooooooo

So deeply ingrained were the lessons learned from the hard times of his youth that he rarely bought things for his personal pleasure.

The only notable exceptions in his way of life were when he acquired four items of personal jewelry during the time he worked at the Arkansas Lumber Company and the Fordyce Lumber Company.

I inherited all but one of those treasures. One is a classic Burlington gold pocket watch, which I glance at from time to time as I write these words. Another is a pair of gold cuff links. They tell me that he must have aspired to be a dandy, at least for a time, if he was wearing them.

I also inherited from him a monogrammed sterling silver belt buckle which is a source, for me, of sweet irony. For many years I had no way to put the buckle to use. Then I took it with me to London on a business trip. While there I went to one of the finest leather and saddle shops in that city and had the craftsmen make a belt to fit the buckle from a piece of leather of a quality regularly used for the custom tooling of English gentlemen's riding boots and shoes. Here I was, the son of Carl Greenwood, who would have loved to travel but never had the opportunity, in London having a belt fashioned for his buckle in a leather shop that served the aristocrats.

For many years he wore a monogrammed gold ring until it became so thin on the underside that he had to put it away and it was lost.

oooooooooooooooo

My father was to work at the sawmill trade until he was nearly 70 years of age.

In that over one-half century he never enjoyed a paid vacation or earned a penny in a retirement fund, other than Social Security.

He had worked beyond the normal retirement age because he needed the money and because the company needed him. When his working at the mill came to an end it was sudden and without ceremony. The foreman at the Southern Lumber Company came to him at the end of the day on Monday and declared, "Carl, we won't need you after Friday." That was it.

Inexplicably, he wore a service pin in the lapel of his jacket for the remainder of his life. I could not have been as loyal and forgiving after such shoddy treatment, although that was about the standard for those days.

That abrupt ending started a transition into what were probably the happiest days of his life. His principal occupation, in which he took great pride, was tending his garden with his prize tool, a tiller powered by a tiny gas engine.

He bought an old single-barrel shotgun which he took in hand to wander in the woods and fields over past Cemetery Hill hunting for squirrels or rabbits. I don't recall that he ever killed anything.

Improbably his personality underwent a decided change. Where once he had been rather shy and withdrawn, he turned out to be quite a "talker." He walked everyday to Wayne's soda fountain where he had a cup a coffee with a regular group of old men. They'd sit there smoking and sipping their coffee or coke, gossiping about the comings and goings in town. It was probably his first social circle. To greet him with the customary "How are you doing?" was to invited a detailed report on his health. It was his turn to talk; he had listened a lot in his lifetime.

ooooooooooooooo

All boys would benefit from growing up in a household including a bachelor uncle like Jewell Melrose Reep.

Uncle Jewell and I had a special kind of relationship. He was more my buddy than an adult relative. Never mind that he sometimes was gruff and impatient with me, he contributed at least his share, if not more, to my reputation for being "spoiled rotten."

He was a man of no more than five feet eight inches in height and of slim build with pronounced muscles. His hair was dark, heavy in growth, and curly. He smoked an occasional cigar, much to my grandmother's dismay, despite her habit with snuff.

His most apparent shortcoming in life was that he could not break the habit of swearing. "Cuss" words came from him regularly, in anger, frustration and sometimes just in animated casual conversation. It didn't seem to make much difference who heard him—his mother, my mother, me, the next-door neighbors.

Sometimes his swearing struck me as funny, but at the same time I worried about him because I heard the adults say that if you "cussed" you would go to hell and burn forever.

Uncle Jewell was a skilled carpenter and cabinetmaker. Despite those skills he never seemed to work very much at those trades. Mostly he found work as a common laborer off and on at the sawmill, a job he hated.

He earned quite a reputation for mastering the difficult task of building fishing boats, generally known as "John Boats." He didn't have the money to buy the fine cypress lumber, paint and hardware required to make boats. So he struck up partnerships with other fisherman who did. His sweat equity earned him the right to use the boats.

He built boats in the backyard on two sawhorses under the shade of the persimmon trees. I was his gofer, fetching tools and running errands.

When Jewell Reep started a project, he brought his full chest of woodworking tools into play. Those tools were things of beauty. He kept them—saws, hammers, levels, squares, and planers—in a large wooden chest that he had made. Each tool was heavily oiled and wrapped in tow sack material. Not a single spot of rust was tolerated.

He applied the same loving care to his splendid automatic shotgun that he kept wrapped in oil-soaked cloth in a wooden gun case he had made.

He used his handsaws to render the long boards of aromatic cypress into the sizes required for the boat pattern, which resided entirely in his mind. He employed various sizes of hand planers and sandpaper to work the wood into glasslike smoothness and precise shapes.

Then came the point of great tension. The long boards that were to be fashioned into the sides of the boat had to be brought into their graceful shape from their widest point in the middle to their somewhat narrower points at each end of the craft. This was accomplished by wetting the wood and pulling it in with vises and ropes. The problem was that despite the best of his efforts, a board would split now and then. It was hell to pay when a board did break. He went ballistic, throwing things and cursing at the top of

35

his lungs. I had sense enough to withdraw from the scene. Just as quickly as his temper flared, it subsided and he picked up a cypress board and started all over.

In addition to boats, he made iceboxes. Cypress was the preferred wood, but sometimes he substituted pine. He lined them with tin. Of course, they were terribly heavy, but they held ice.

Uncle Jewell was a devoted bass fisherman. Almost every Sunday morning during the spring, summer, and early fall he went to the Saline River with one of his friends who had transportation. He left home before daylight and came back late afternoon. Most often he returned with bass, which he dumped from his icebox out on the grass in the backyard. The silver fish amid the chunks of ice on the wet green grass made a classic picture.

He and my father cleaned the fish at the water faucet in the backyard. My mother fried them, only hours out of the river. She served the fish with potato salad, seasoned with lots of onion and bell pepper. Sometimes we also had a platter of sliced tomatoes, onions and radishes.

Uncle Jewell often did special favors for me. My mother took me as a lad of perhaps four years old to the Bradley Store to see Santa Claus, who was receiving lists of Christmas wishes from children and giving away candy. I watched the children ahead of me in line with great interest and impatience. When it came my turn, it became obvious to me and no doubt others that Santa Claus kept me on his lap longer than he had those who had gone before. When I left he gave me two bags of candy, not one as was standard. Naturally, I was wildly enthusiastic about Santa Claus and the favoritism I had been shown. My mother told me that it was probably because I had been such a good boy. It was not until much later when I stopped "believing" that I realized that Santa Claus had been Uncle Jewell.

Uncle Jewell provided me with another great treat, made doubly special because it happened within full view of my playmates and several adults in the neighborhood.

He was a member of Warren's Volunteer Fire Department. Periodically, with Fire Chief "Cab" Rowell at the wheel the crew took the lone fire truck on a test run to be sure that everything was in working order for the next emergency. It was also good for what we would now call "community relations," because taxpayers had an opportunity to see their fire department in action under happy conditions and be reassured they were ready. The truck was driven up one street and down the next with lights flashing and siren wailing. Citizens came out to stand on the sidewalk, watching the parade go by.

Sometimes the onlookers applauded and cheered. Children ran behind the sparkling clean truck. The crew riding the truck and acting as if they were celebrities waved to the crowds.

My day in the spotlight arrived when the firetruck came down East Church Street with Uncle Jewell standing on the back platform. The truck stopped in front of our house right where I was standing; Uncle Jewell climbed down to pick me up and place me by his side on the platform. We pulled away with all the whistles and bells going full blast. Transported to another realm, I waved to my audience as we made our way around the block.

A short time later Uncle Jewell had to retire from his duties as a volunteer firefighter when his foot was run over by the rear wheels of the truck.

Uncle Jewell from time to time took me to town at night to sit with him and his friends under the "Tree of Knowledge."

The tree, a substantial oak, stands today on the northeast corner of the court square just in front of the small brick building that served then as the library. Solid chairs of a style now known as "captain's chairs" surrounded the tree. Weather permitting, a cadre of five or six men gathered there at night to smoke, dip snuff or chew tobacco while discussing affairs of the town and swapping tall tales, intermingled with an occasional bit of gossip. No rules of hierarchy or protocol applied other than that the men gathered after supper and left for home when the clock in the courthouse began to strike nine. The cast of characters and the routine varied little each night Monday through Friday.

"The Tree of Knowledge" was a place of pure magic for me, made particularly special because I never saw another child privileged to be there. When I grew restless I was permitted to run back and forth to the limits of the court square. On rare occasion my uncle took me across the street to Glasgow's confectionery to buy a Coke. I appreciated those treats because I never expected them.

The men kept their conversation within proper bounds in my presence. About the naughtiest story I heard was the one about the old man who had been sitting under "The Tree of Knowledge" when a bird deposited a dropping on his cream-colored Sailor Bill straw hat. When his friends started to laugh at his predicament he calmly removed his hat, flicked off the offensive matter and declared, "Well, it's a good thing cows don't have wings."

Uncle Jewell aided and abetted me in my various entrepreneurial enterprises. He must have thought many of them to be farfetched; I know he often took them to be uproariously funny. But he never discouraged me.

I tried to sell vegetables door-to-door from our garden. Even with encouragement from family and friendly neighbors my efforts met with little success. After all, most everyone had a garden.

Once when there was nothing to pick from the garden, I gathered up a bucketful of green walnuts from the tree that grew in the lane between the Hammons and us. There is probably no item of food less desirable or useful than a green walnut. After offering my wares to most of the houses in the neighborhood, I returned home without a single sale. Uncle Jewell saw me coming home down in the mouth. When I told him what had happened he was so amused that he fell to the ground laughing so hard he could hardly catch his breath. Of course, I failed to see the humor in my situation, so my ego was wounded. I don't remember what he did to soothe my feelings, but I am sure he did something to distract me and regain my affection. He always did.

My brief experience as a goat driver also amused him greatly. One of my playmates, a boy from the black family that lived over on Cemetery Hill, had a goat which he had trained to pull a wagon. I greatly envied him and his working goat. It occurred to me that if I had a outfit like that I could make a great deal of money and have a lot of fun hiring my rig out to haul junk and to perform other chores.

My parents did not see any practical prospects in this venture, but I was relentless in my effort to convince them to buy a goat and wagon for me. Finally, we reached a compromise—I could rent the goat and wagon from my friend "just to see how I liked it." I agreed, confident that my scheme would work.

The boy turned the goat and wagon over to me with little or no instructions. I paid the rent, I think it was 25 cents, and I was in business.

My mother suggested that I start my enterprise by hauling away some tin cans and other trash from our own backyard.

I carefully loaded the wagon and headed down the sidewalk. The goat and I only made it only 15 or 20 yards before he started to act up. Matters only got worse when I tried to rein him in. The harder I pulled on the harness, the harder the goat jerked and thrashed about. Finally, inevitably the wagon turned over and the goat proceeded to drag it away, spewing cans and trash here and there. At that point the owner took charge of his animal and headed home. My career of driving a goat was ended. I was 25 cents poorer, but a great deal smarter.

ooooooooooooooo

We were closely bound as a family by mutual love and dependency expressed almost exclusively by our relationships at home.

We did not know about "togetherness," or "quality time," as family values are measured today, where so much of the lives of families revolves around parents involvement in their children's sports and school activities, travel and vacations.

Friends as couples rarely came to our house to visit; it was an unusual occasion for my parents to go out.

My parents saw me play in only one football game and no more than four or five basketball games. They came once to see me on stage performing a secondary role in a high school drama.

It was not that they did not care, because they did very much. It was simply the constraints of those times and their lifestyle. The families of most of our close acquaintances were in the same position.

My father, like most men who worked hard all day at the mill, had little energy left to walk home, clean up, eat his supper and walk back across town to see a ballgame with which he had little familiarity because he had never played such games.

ooooooooooooooo

My mother and father and I had one outing together on the Saline River.

I was perhaps 12 or 13 years of age. The trip to the river was made even more special because we were driven in a taxi to the Airport Inn. From that point on the Monticello highway we walked perhaps a mile and a half into Camp Mansfield where we stayed the day. I spent the time swimming in the river and playing in the ice-cold spring that emerged from the bottom of the high bank and ran across a sandbar into the river itself. I was amazed to see my mother and father frolic about in the river. My father demonstrated his ability to swim in a style he called the dog paddle. My mother waded into the water up to her knees.

No finer or more welcomed food was ever served than the picnic that my mother had packed for us.

Once most of the Greenwood clan went on an overnight camping/fishing trip to Moore's Mill on the Saline River. We carried a 100-pound block of ice to keep our food and drinks cool. The ice was wrapped in a burlap sack and buried in a hole in the ground filled with sawdust. We ate our meals and slept on pallets spread on the ground around a big campfire. During the night the men drifted off to run the trotline. They took turns drinking from a bottle of bourbon before and after each run.

They let me make one of the runs with them. It was then that the only fish was hooked. It was a large drum that managed to jump off the hook just

41

as my Uncle Claude was hauling it into the boat. I cried and the men in the boat cursed the luck of it all.

ooooooooooooooo

No family experience generates more intense memories of my youth than our celebrating together during the Christmas Season.

People didn't begin to focus on Christmas until well after Thanksgiving. A merchant decorating his store before December would have been thought to be odd. We began our celebration toward the end of the second week of December.

My parents and I always went for a walk in the woods on a Sunday afternoon looking for a cedar tree just the right size and shape to be taken home for our Christmas tree. Some years we found a holly tree from which we cut branches loaded with bright red berries. We always brought home a sack of dry pine cones. Mama was in her heyday as she took over decorating the tree and making a wreath with pine boughs, hollyberries and pine cones. I was her chief assistant.

A few days later she began baking-cakes, coconut and fruit filling; sugar cookies; taffy candy; date-nut bread; mincemeat pies. She started serving these delicacies a few days before Christmas.

It was at about that time that I could expect to receive my Christmas money, as much as $3.00, to buy gifts for the family and fireworks.

Christmas was the time for fireworks, rather than the Fourth of July. Every kid who could scrape together the money rushed to stock up with firecrackers, Roman candles, rockets and sparklers.

Uncle Jewell could hardly wait to join me in shooting fireworks the first year I had my own supply. Based on his experience from many years earlier, he assured me that I need not be afraid to hold the firecrackers while I lit them and threw them to explode a few feet away. Why, he explained, he could let a firecracker go off in his hand and not suffer any damage. My friends witnessing this bit of bravado and I urged him not to try it. With his usual string of cuss words, he declared that he would show us just how weak the firecrackers were. When the explosive went off, it just about tore his thumb off and left his hand badly burned.

I slept very little the night of Christmas Eve. By 3:30 or so Christmas morning I was calling out to my parents that it was time to get up. They urged me to try to sleep a while longer because they explained Santa Claus might not have had time to come. After all, they said, he has a lot of boys and girls to visit.

Finally, Dad would get a fire going in the heater. When we went to the tree I was never disappointed. I always found that Santa Claus had gone the distance my parents could afford in bringing me presents. Always there were goodies under the tree—fresh oranges, which we didn't see much of during the remainder of the year; a big red apple; a coconut; one or two candy bars; stick candy in a range of flavors including cinnamon, lemon, peppermint, grape.

One year I was given a little desk, which I learned later my mother had rescued from someone's attic and refinished a dark green with red trim. Other Christmases there was a BB gun and a .22 rifle, an erector and a chemistry set, games, hunting boots and other things to please a boy.

I was truly surprised when I was 11 or 12 years of age to receive a bicycle, because I wasn't sure my parents could afford one. It was a handsome maroon model with all sorts of shining trim, that I had wanted desperately.

The tires were low. I pushed it up the hill to town and the nearest filling station to get air in them. When I rolled the bike back to the top of the long hill on East Church Street that led to my house, I had to face the fact that I didn't know how to ride a bicycle. I had stubbornly refused to learn on someone else's because I didn't want to have the skill and not be able to exercise it without asking to borrow one.

My eagerness to ride my new bike overcame my trepidation. I mounted it and went careening down the hill. I made it to the town branch at the bottom before I fell off. I got back on and rode the rest of the way home as if I had been doing that all my life.

I usually gave Dad a carton of cigarettes or a bottle of shaving lotion. For my mother I almost always gave her a box of dusting powder or a handkerchief.

After we opened gifts we ate a huge breakfast of country fried steak and eggs with lots of brown gravy. Nevertheless, by noon we were ready for the Romanesque Christmas dinner Mama had prepared around baked chicken and cornbread dressing.

For a number of years we joined all the Greenwoods at my grandmother's house for a potluck Christmas dinner. We drew names for gift giving. My cousins Shirley Broach (Godwin) and Pat Murry (Walker) were in charge of passing out the presents. I was a little jealous of the attention they received, but I consoled myself with the thought that that was after all a girls' thing.

oooooooooooooooo

My mother's brother, my uncle Van Reep, and his family lived next door. He was an electrician and plumber who never held a job for very long during the hard times of the 1930s. He and my Aunt Myrtle had three children: Catherine, named for my grandmother Reep; Clifford, a very bright, but rather strange fellow, who went on to earn a degree in chemistry from Arkansas A & M College at Monticello soon after the start of World War II, thus becoming the first member of my family to graduate from college; and Bobby Van, a late-comer to the family.

My uncle had built a new home on land deeded to him by my grandmother from the plot she had acquired soon after she was widowed. Their house had hardwood floors throughout which were always polished, as was the very nice furniture. I envied their indoor plumbing, which included a flush toilet and a bathtub. There was a piano in the living room which Aunt Myrtle would play with the proper amount of encouragement. We sang the words we read from the sheets of music.

A large separate building with a tin roof behind the house served as a garage for Uncle Van's truck and his workshop. I would make a beeline for the shop when I saw him there working on one of his projects. On one of my visits I complained that I was about to lose a tooth, but that it was just hanging on. He said he could fix that for me, whereupon he took a pair of electrician's pliers and jerked out the stubborn molar. I ran home spitting blood and screaming to high heaven.

Despite the hard times and Uncle Van's sporadic employment the Reeps always seemed to live in good style. My mother often said, "Myrtle can stretch a dollar farther than anybody in the world."

Bobby Van came into the family when I was about five years old. I don't recall even recognizing that Aunt Myrtle was pregnant. I was surprised one morning with the news that Aunt Myrtle had borne a son. We saw the baby within hours of his birth in the front bedroom of the Reep's house.

45

The Reeps lost their house toward the end of the 1930s because they couldn't meet the mortgage payments. The foreclosure was a bitter experience, especially in view of the fact that it sat on land my grandmother had given to him.

The Reep family moved to a rented house across town. Their circumstances were bare, as my uncle could only pick up odds and ends of jobs. Soon after Pearl Harbor, Uncle Van moved to Camden to live with his brother, Howard, and family. When he was able to get a regular job at the local war arsenal he rented a house and moved his family to that nearby town where they prospered.

ooooooooooooooo

A lot of families claimed to have well-to-do relatives to whom they pointed with pride.

Usually, that kin had moved far away from Warren. The more glamorous stories were of those brave souls who had "gone to California to work." Our claim was Uncle Howard and his family who lived 50, miles away in Camden.

Uncle Howard was a handsome man of medium build with jet-black hair that tended to grow in waves. My mother doted on him. He had served in the National Guard during the trouble on the Mexican border with Pancho Villa. His dashing image was solidified in the family when he went into the Marine Corps during the First World War. A picture of him in uniform was an inspiration to me.

Sometime in the early 1930s he rejected the idea of working at the sawmills and moved with his family to Camden, where he became quite successful, by our standards, as a housepainter and paperhanger. My mother insisted that he was a decorator.

I was greatly impressed when I learned that he played in the Camden softball league. That seemed like a far stretch for an adult because the grown-ups I knew of whatever age were somehow too old to be playing in ball games.

It was a great occasion when their family came to visit us on a Sunday afternoon.

The adults sat around talking while Bob and I played outside. Later, in our mid-teen years, Bob drove me about in their car. He eventually taught me how to drive, but only on backcountry roads. I was grateful for his help, although I was somewhat embarrassed.

Uncle Howard always treated the family to an ice-cold watermelon when they came to visit during the summer. He drove us over to the icehouse at the cotton oil mill where we were allowed to go into the huge freezer and select the melon from a large assortment on display among the blocks of ice. The shock of the cold temperature and the giddy sense of the whole excursion provided us with a rare thrill.

oooooooooooooooo

On two or three occasions Bob stayed behind for a week's visit during the summer when Uncle Howard and Aunt Maude returned to Camden.

He was accustomed to having his own way in all matters in his home. My mother stopped short of using one of her favorite expressions, "spoiled rotten," when she spoke of him. She simply said, "He was a handful."

At an early age, Bob showed evidence of the professional career as a musician he would follow. At one period, in a vain hope that I might be

47

musically inclined, my parents encouraged me to take violin lessons. Little came from that venture. In any case, during one of his summer visits, Bob displayed considerable envy over the violin. He vented his feelings in a dramatic fashion, seizing the instrument and running out back to the chicken house. We all chased after him, urging that he lay down the instrument. Our calls only spurred him on to climb to the roof of the little building. There he struck an Olympian pose with the violin held high over his head. My mother demanded that he come down immediately. He declared that he would throw the violin to the ground if we didn't leave him alone. There was a tense standoff. Finally, my mother ordered us all back in the house, saying she would deal with Bob. Whether by threats or promises she talked him down from the roof.

Once a year my mother and I took the bus over the two-lane gravel road through Banks, Hampton and Harrell to Camden to visit the Reeps. The bus ride alone was a real adventure. We took a sack lunch even though it was a trip of only about two hours.

I was impressed with the Reep's house, which was solidly built and heated with open gas stoves. They had a bathtub.

Bob enhanced his reputation for being spoiled during one of our winter visits. Uncle Howard came in from work to report that he was running late because when he had crossed the railroad track he saw a campfire set a hobo's clothing on fire. Again the hero, he had stopped and smothered out the blaze. We were quite excited and impressed by the story. Bob declared that he wanted to see the man on fire. My uncle explained several times that he had put out the fire, but Bob pushed on, insisting finally that we all return to the site of the incident and that Uncle Howard set the man on fire again. For one of the few times in his life Bob met a firm wall of "no."

ooooooooooooooo

At a time in my life when my travels had been limited to a bus ride from Warren to Little Rock and back and two or three trips on the bus to Camden, Uncle Howard provided me and my mother with a trip to thrill any boy of my age and circumstances.

He and his family took my mother and me to the Gulf Coast and New Orleans.

The sight of the endless vista of the Gulf of Mexico mesmerized this boy who was probably nine or 10 years old. I saw men fishing from the piers. There were ocean-going ships passing in the distance. My imagination was deeply stirred. For some reason we weren't allowed to go swimming, but we were permitted to wade along the edge of the sandy beach, where we picked up tiny shells. I thought it was funny to see the grown-ups take off their shoes and join Bob and me in the water.

In New Orleans we walked through the French Quarter and marveled at the foreign look of it all. We stopped at an open-air coffee bar to eat delicate rolls covered with powered sugar.

We stayed in a private residence. Accommodations of this type, which were known as "tourist homes," were forerunners of today's motels. The room where my mother and I slept was clean and neat as a pin. We shared a bathroom with the owners who served us a hearty breakfast as part of the package. The orange juice was a special treat.

ooooooooooooooo

As we grew older, Bob and I drifted apart.

He became a sickly boy, thin in build and afflicted with a tic in his neck and shoulder. His parents sheltered him from the realities of the world. Music consumed him as he went on to earn a master's degree with a specialty in the pipe organ. Some said he was sissy. My interests turned to athletics and hanging out at the poolhall and on the court square.

In 1950, Uncle Howard was killed instantly by a drunk driver as he and Aunt Maude were driving to visit Bob at a college in Missouri. My aunt was severely injured physically and emotionally. It was a sign of the times that the drunk driver was jailed overnight until he sobered up. After months passed he stood for a hearing and was set free.

Aunt Maude was brought from the hospital in Little Rock to my parent's home, where once again my mother was called on to nurse a critically sick relative. The recuperation was long and painful, and although she was eventually able to return to her home in Camden, she never fully recovered. All this took a heavy toll on my mother, grieving as she was for a lost brother and dealing with the deep depression afflicting her sister-in-law. My father, always patient and understanding, never complained. Each night when he came from work he sat with Aunt Maude and made small talk as best he could.

Bob returned to college. I saw him only a few times after that traumatic. He died at age 49 of an ailment the nature of which we never knew.

ooooooooooooooo

My Greenwood relatives lived most of their lives in and around Warren.

Although I lived in a home more closely attached to the Reeps than to the Greenwoods, I know more about the history of my father's family than I do of my mother's, thanks largely to the research of the family tree by a cousin, John Claude Greenwood.

John Claude tells me that records show our roots trace back through our grandmother to a passenger on the Mayflower and subsequently to Presidents Zachary Taylor and Franklin D. Roosevelt.

My cousins, Shirley Broach (Godwin) Pat Murry (Walker) and John Claude, lived in much closer connections with the family and have more accurate memories and impressions than I do. Shirley's home for many years just a few houses away from our grandmother. Pat resided for some time with her divorced mother in the home with our grandmother, Aunt Grace King and Uncle Pete Greenwood. John Claude lived with his parents, Claude and Pearl, across the street from them.

The matriarch, my grandmother Jennie Irene Stephens Greenwood, "Mother Green" to me and "Burr" to my cousins.

I only remember Mother Green as an old lady, a figure of serenity and gentleness. She was always neatly dressed in a simple cotton dress. Her hair was a soft gray with waves held in place by small combs. We never heard her raise her voice or saw her act as if she was upset. Her special talent was growing beautiful flowers, especially carnations, which surrounded the various houses in which she lived. Anyone who came in her company recognized that she was a refined lady and loving grandmother. A casting director looking for a model to picture on a box of soothing warm oatmeal would select Mother Green.

Mother Green was born on February 15, 1866 and died on February 12, 1958 at age 92. Although there are no clear records, it is probable that she was born in Union County, Arkansas. Her father, Joshua W. Stephens, had married Ruth Dudgin the year the Civil War ended. Her mother was born in Ireland 34 years earlier. At age 42, Joshua came to Union County via

Alabama some two years before the start of the Civil War to farm land he had bought from the Federal Government.

Sometime after the end of the war the family moved to northern Indiana. It was there that Mother Green attended a private girls' school. Such an institution was commonly referred to as a "finishing school" because of its mission of "finishing" young women to make their way in the world as educated ladies.

There is no record of Mother Green and her family from this point until she married William Karl Greenwood back in Union County in 1886 at 20 years of age. Their marriage produced little prosperity, but a large family.

ooooooooooooooo

Decades removed from the scene, Mother Green's serene nature seems all the more remarkable.

She was widowed at age 44 after 24 years of marriage and the birth of 11 children, one of whom was stillborn. There were Carl, Ora, Ned, Clyde, Claude, Clarence (Pete), Martha Grace, Theodore (Jimmy), Louise and Dixie. My father was only two years older than the next oldest child, Ora, but 21 years the senior of the youngest of his siblings, Dixie. His brothers and sisters were to remember years later with respect and affection that he always made the last rounds at night to be sure that they were all tucked in bed. "He was just like a father to us," they would say later.

Mother Green dealt with many adversities in raising her children. Some of the difficulties arose from circumstances beyond their control. Other of Mother Green's trials with her children came from the choices they made in their lives. There were broken marriages with daughters returning home with their own children. There were daughters who tried to fly away from the family nest with their husbands only to crash and come limping back.

The second oldest son, Ned, died in the influenza epidemic of 1918 while serving in the Army in France.

Aunt Grace and her husband, Lester King, apparently a stable, hard-working man who followed the printer's trade, moved away to Arkansas City on the banks of the Mississippi River sometime in late 1926 or early 1927. By one means or another, they had put together enough money—probably a few hundred dollars—to buy a printing shop in that community. Just as they were getting on their feet the great floods of 1927 laid waste to the Mississippi River Valley. Their fledging business and the entire town of Arkansas City were wiped out. There were no disaster relief funds from the government to bail them out. They picked up the pieces of their lives and moved to Green Forest in north Arkansas and set out on another printing venture. Lester King died there in 1936. Aunt Grace had but one option; she returned to a household composed of Mother Green and Uncle Pete, plus various combination of kinfolks at any given time. She was dead broke financially and badly wounded in spirit.

Aunt Grace was to live there a childless widow the rest of her life. She became the primary caregiver for her mother and Uncle Pete in their final days.

Grace King had about her a no-nonsense view of life. Her sharp tongue never left any of us in doubt as to where she stood on any subject. She had no visible means of support except a minimum check from Social Security. In later years she earned some income as a baby-sitter, despite the fact that some young parents said she was a little too strict with their children.

She must have been a good manager of her money because she always had some cash in reserve which she could loan to various members of the family. When Martha and I decided we would marry, I borrowed fifty dollars from Aunt Grace in order to buy an engagement ring for my bride-to-be.

Aunt Ora married Lester "Watch" Tomlinson. He practiced the carpenter's trade when the stars were in proper alignment for him—that is, when work was available, he felt like it and he was sober. Quiet and sullen when he was sober, he turned argumentative and abusive as a drunk. He quit drinking as an old man. After that he spent his time in brooding silence broken only with snorts of derision and an occasional challenge to something Aunt Ora had said.

It fell to Aunt Ora to provide for the family's basic needs. This she did by becoming the premier seamstress in Warren who attracted steady clients in need of garments for parties, dances, graduations and weddings.

Aunt Clyde Broach was one of Warren's earliest career women. She made the grade after a rocky start. She was married early to a man named Councile with whom she had two sons, Clifford and Perry. That marriage ended in divorce when the boys were about 18 months old. She came back to Mother Green's home where my father was still the principal breadwinner. To her great credit she managed to graduate from what was known then as a "business school" in Little Rock. She made a career of working at the Merchant and Planters Bank and The Bradley Store. She married Harvey Broach and bore a daughter, Shirley.

Aunt Louise also married young and bore a daughter, Pat. When the couple divorced, Aunt Louise came back to Warren and moved for a time into the home already occupied by Uncle Pete, Mother Green and Aunt Grace. Aunt Louise made her way working in this and that office, including those of the county and circuit clerk at the court house.

Aunt Dixie married an itinerant printer, Neil Miller. He bounced from job to job. The family, including a daughter, Barbara, moved away to New York City. Miller had no more success there than he had in Arkansas. He abandoned his wife and their child soon after they came back home. He later served at least one term in prison. Aunt Dixie moved away from Warren and made her way in odd jobs, serving as a waitress, operating a liquor store and working as a sales clerk. She spent the latter years of her life raising a granddaughter after her only child, a daughter, died at any early age.

Although Uncle Claude most resembled my father physically, he was more outgoing in personality. He always held what by our standards was a substantial job at The Bradley. He was assistant manager of a department at the mill known as the box factory, a job popularly referred to as "straw boss." We all hoped that he would someday be promoted to manager when "The Old Man," Mr. Edeline, retired. As the years rolled by it was the judgment of the family that "The Old Man" would work until he dropped dead in his tracks. When he finally retired, the manager's job went to Doyle May instead of Uncle Claude. He just kept working as "straw boss."

ooooooooooooooo

The men in the family were heavy drinkers. I don't know whether it was in their genes or the circumstances that they grew up in or the mind-numbing monotony of their jobs in the mills that made the bottle irresistible. The "taste for the grape" was also indulged in on special occasions by some of the women. My mother, always a puritan at heart, viewed these practices with great disdain.

My father, who only drank an occasional beer, was an exception. I don't know whether he drank very little because he didn't have an overriding craving for alcohol or because my mother simply would not tolerate such behavior.

He and I learned just how hard her line was on a Fourth of July when I was probably eight or nine years old. It was the practice in those days for the Bradley Lumber Company to put on a barbecue for all of its white employees and their families. A smiliar event was staged for the blacks on June 19, Emancipation Day.

The Southern Lumber Company put on the same sort of spread. We heard that people who attended could ride from town to the site just west of the mill on the company railroad.

Volunteers from the mill crew showed up at the town park the night before the barbecue to dig long trenches in the ground in which they burned hickory wood into red-hot coals. Slabs of beef and pork, basted in pungent barbecue sauce, were suspended on webs of wire fencing over red-hot coals which were kept going throughout the night by the addition of chunks of hickory from the sawmill waste. The cooking took until noon on The Fourth.

The women and children and men, not helping with the cooking, began to show up by mid-morning. While they waited to eat, the adults visited and children played games. The Lumberjack band marched in and provided a program. By noon the excitement of it all along with the aroma of the cooking meat had everyone to the point of great anticipation.

It was a grand and glorious event, greatly enjoyed by all.

After the big feast, some of the men began to come and go from behind the cooks' tent. With each trip, things seemed to get funnier for them, while the women grew sterner.

By late afternoon the crowd began to drift away. My mother was in a huff, which she made no effort to hide, when she and I headed for home. Dad stayed behind with the other men to help clean up the park.

Night fell and bedtime came and still my father had not come home. My mother declared it was long past time when they should have had the place cleaned up and that we would go to bed. It was the first and only time I ever saw her lock the door.

It must have been about nine o'clock when there was a tentative knock at the back door. My mother could hardly have been surprised, but nevertheless she demanded to know who it was. My father identified himself and asked to be let in. My mother ruled that he would have to sleep outside, considering his condition.

He pled his case. I cried and begged her let him in. After awhile, satisfied that he had seen the error of his ways, my mother let him in the house, but banished him to an army cot on the porch.

There was very little conversation between the two for several days. Although I had enough sense not to speak up, I secretly took my father's side in the matter. Frankly, I guess I was somehow proud of him that for that one night he had "been one of the boys."

My father rarely took a drink after that.

oooooooooooooooo

Unfortunately, alcohol was a longer-lasting problem with more destructive results than my father's "escapade" with some other members of the family.

I rarely saw Uncle Theodore, better known as "Jimmy," a competent plumber and electrician, completely sober or free of a hangover. He was a smallish man of shy temperament except when he was three sheets in the wind on full cruise. Then he strutted, assuring everyone that he was one step away from a good job. When that came through he would straighten up, he declared, but it never happened. He died in 1955, just 54 years of age, leaving a widow, a son about my age and twin boys somewhat younger. We understood that he was a victim of his addiction.

Uncle Pete's drinking was of a different nature in the beginning. He worked all week at The Bradley, hour after hour, day after day, feeding strips of lumber into a sanding machine. The fact that his older brother, Claude, was his boss was both a blessing and a burden.

As regularly as the sun rises in the east Uncle Pete went to the mill on Monday morning, worked until noon on Saturday, came home, cleaned up and went to town. His first stop was "Peanut" Hughes's liquor store to buy a bottle of bourbon. He drank it all by sundown and bought another pint to carry him through the next day.

He usually spent Sunday afternoons napping and nipping from his emergency bottle hidden under the mattress on the single cot in the sparse room where he slept. That was his way of sobering up and getting ready to go back to the mill on Monday morning.

Uncle Pete and Uncle Jimmy made quite a pair when they ventured out together. With a snootfull they assumed an air of self-importance that I found to be rather funny. Both moved with a studied rigidity as if to steady both themselves and the world under foot.

Uncle Pete had acquired a Model A Ford automobile which was put in running condition by Uncle Jimmy. The family fondly named the car "Handy."

One Sunday afternoon a friend and I encountered them at the top of their form. We were walking along the Monticello highway coming home from the river. We had seen Uncle Pete's car parked at the Airport Inn, a convivial place where the drinking of a little beer on Sunday afternoon was ignored by the authorities.

We heard the gravel crunching behind us as a car approached and pulled alongside us. It was my uncles, "higher than kites," beaming from ear to ear in their state of bourbon-induced euphoria. Uncle Theodore was driving, in keeping with their agreement that he rather than Uncle Pete would drive when they were out on a spree.

"Hop in. We'll take you home," Uncle Pete invited with a sweep of magnanimity. When he was satisfied that we were safely seated and that the road ahead was clear he ordered, "Let's go, Jimmy."

None too steady at the wheel, Uncle Jimmy moved through the gears and got us up to perhaps 15 or 20 miles an hour. As he began to swerve from side to side across the narrow gravel road, Uncle Pete assumed command with a simple order: "Keep her between the ditches, Jimmy."

My friend and I thought it was great fun. That is more than I can say for my mother and father when we pulled up in front of our house.

In later years Uncle Pete increasingly couldn't make it to work on Mondays. Still hung over from the weekend he stayed in bed on Monday morning, explaining that he had to have time to get himself straightened out. Gradually his drinking started earlier in the week, sometimes on the job. Finally, inevitably, even his brother Claude couldn't save his job.

After losing his job, his drinking went in cycles of weeks, starting with a beer or two which he assured my father and others who expressed concern for him that he could handle it this time. Bourbon followed until he was too sick to go on. Members of the family took him in and nursed him back to health only to see him start the cycle of beer to bourbon again in a few weeks.

I was proud of my mother who in later years invited him into our home and took her turn at nursing him back to health despite her total dislike for his way of living.

He went away to the VA hospital more than once to be dried out, but the cures didn't last long.

Alcohol finally killed Uncle Pete in 1966 at age 70.

His nieces and nephews remember Uncle Pete with a particular fondness. My cousin Pat Murry Walker has perhaps the clearest memories of this kind and shy man who knew more than his share of demons. She was to say of Uncle Pete many years later, "He was a kind man with a good heart, who provided a home for my mother and me for many years. He never married, but he did have a namesake. I named my first child Charles in honor of Charles Clarence Greenwood."

ooooooooooooooo

The values of the family environment created by my Reep and Greenwood relatives cast the mold that made me the person I am today.

My children and grandchildren have in turn been influenced by them through me as to how they live their lives.

As I re-read what I have written I see that the reader might conclude that it was a grim and dysfunctional atmosphere in which I grew up. If it was, I didn't realize it then; I don't realize now. I was surrounded by a protective cover of love for which I am grateful.

My family was made up of good people who played the game of life as best they could in a tough environment.

# OUR HOUSE WAS A HOME

I grew up in the house at 410 East Church Street in which I was born. My grandmother Reep bought the property, which included the house, a barn and a pasture, and moved there with her brood shortly after she was widowed. She sold her cow and her house just across the street to make the deal.

No one seemed to know when the house was built or by whom. The age of the house was attested to by the fact that the nails used in its construction were square rather than the rounded ones that came along later. It stood pretty much as it was when she bought it until my family made some improvements after the Great Depression.

It was a relatively large wood-framed house with a roof of hand-hewn cedar shingles that leaked in heavy rains. Strangely enough, although I can see the house in my mind's eye now as if it were standing before me, I can't remember whether it was painted in the early days. Later, it was painted a light tan or cream color.

The basic construction must have been as solid as a rock because it housed our family for 36 years until it was wrecked along with many others, by the infamous tornado of 1949 that swept across the south and southeast sides of Warren. I know there is truth in the saying that "It's an ill wind that blows no good," because had that house not been destroyed, we would have had to completely overhaul or tear it down during my parents' lifetimes. Neither course would have been feasible.

The day after the tornado my mother took the lead in getting a new house. She made her case to the Red Cross and was granted money to rebuild, using a combination of lumber salvaged from the old house and new materials.

ooooooooooooooo

The old house was mounted on concrete pillars so that it stood two and one-half feet or so off the ground.

It was built according to a popular style of the day known as "shotgun" or "dogtrot," in which rooms branched off from each side of a wide central hallway. The "shotgun" layout was so named because it would have been possible to stand at the front door and fire a shotgun out through the back of the house without hitting anything. The alternate name "dogtrot" came from the idea that the dogs could trot through the front and out the back at their choosing.

A broad porch ran across a good part of the front of the house. The obligatory swing suspended on chains from the high ceiling occupied one end. Kudzu vines climbed rampantly up a wire lattice to the roof, shading the porch in the afternoons.

The "dogtrot" extended out on to a side porch. For many years it was open; later it was screened in and became a favorite place to sleep on those nights where the heat never broke.

Another open porch was next to the kitchen at the rear of the house. A closet adjoined the porch. This small, unheated room without running water served as our toilet in my early years.

Tall steps led down to the backyard. There was a deep well by the steps. It provided one way to reduce the bill from the city's water department. We drew gallons of water from it for drinking, washing clothes, sustaining the garden and chilling milk and an occasional watermelon. There was a purity of taste not available today even in fashionable bottled water.

There were five rooms extending off the "dogtrot" —a living room, which was rarely used except when visitors from outside the neighborhood came to call; two bedrooms, one for my grandmother, which also served as an everyday sitting room; and one for my parents and me; a dining room; and kitchen.

There was a room, not much larger than some modern walk-in closets, behind the living room at the northeast corner of the house. Furnished with a dresser and a cot, it served as Uncle Jewell's bedroom. It became our bathroom when we got indoor plumbing.

oooooooooooooooo

Looking back from the vantagepoint of today, I am amazed how we got by without indoor plumbing.

We just took it all in stride, except for the lack of a toilet, which was a plague and embarrassment for all of us.

During the winter we bathed once a week in number three tin washtubs placed in front of the kitchen cook stove, where bath water was heated in kettles and pans. The memories of those weekly baths are indelibly stamped in my brain. Each bath was quite a production. We carried water from the well to fill the tub. The trick, of course, was to get enough water heated and in the tub at one time. This done, there was the challenge of positioning oneself in the tub, legs hanging over one side and back pressing against the other. The side nearest the stove would get too hot for comfort.

As I grew older another problem developed. I didn't want to get naked in the kitchen while my mother and grandmother were scurrying about their chores. My mother seemed to be indifferent to my concerns. "Don't worry," she said, "if people haven't seen one they won't know what it is. If they have seen one, it won't make any difference."

Using just the right amount of soap was a challenge. Too much of the soap, which served all purposes from washing dishes to bathing, meant it was almost impossible to rinse off without the extra burden of bringing in and heating more water. Too little soap meant not getting cleaned and risking being scrubbed with a rough cotton cloth.

Baths were easier and a great deal more fun in the summer. We simply hooked up the garden hose and sprayed each other. The water was cold and refreshing, no matter how hot the temperature around us might be. Uncle Jewell rigged up a "showering" place just off the side porch. We had boards to stand on under the garden hose suspended from a hook on the wall. There was even a place to put a bar of soap. While we had to keep some clothes on for modesty's sake, we did manage to get clean.

oooooooooooooooo

Living in an old house enhanced our awareness of the changing seasons. There was no central heating to neutralize winters; no air-conditioning to abate the heat of summers.

As was customary for houses of that era there were 12-foot ceilings in all of the rooms. That space helped to ventilate the house in hot weather, but made it harder to keep warm in the winter.

A cavernous attic sat above the entire house. We stored all sorts of things up there. Someone said that if we looked close enough we could probably find everything from dead men to money.

It was an inviting place to play during the day, but it was foreboding at night or during a rainstorm.

It was always unsettling to encounter at close range the giant wharf rats or squeaking little mice that demanded to share the space. My memory tells me that the rats grew to the size of small squirrels; this must be an exaggeration, but not much of one.

Winters in the house were particularly memorable. Standing high off the ground the house created a sort of wind tunnel that brought the drafts of cold air up against the floor. The floors in most of the rooms were partially covered with linoleum, which was very effective in conducting cold. The problem was exacerbated by the fact that there were cracks between the boards. I could lie on the floor to peer through the cracks to watch the leaves being blown about and hear the wind howling beneath the house. During the summer, I could look through those cracks to watch chickens scratching the ground underneath the house searching for earthworms.

The wind, almost as strong, blew through the attic above.

We used wood-burning stoves made of cast iron and steel to heat the house. They were fueled with "cut-offs" of wood from the Bradley mill delivered in horse-drawn wagons.

On cold nights the heater in our sitting room was stoked to the point that by bedtime its sides and the tin chimney had turned bright orange-red and started making occasional popping sound. It was a thousand wonders that the house wasn't set on fire. Still, to move a few feet away from the stove was to find oneself too hot on one side, too cool on the other, much as with a roaring campfire. The trick was to turn sides from time to time.

As we neared bedtime my mother began to heat bricks on top of the stove. These were to be wrapped in cloths, preferably flannel, and placed in the bed to take the chill off and keep our feet warm.

My father's routine at bedtime was to lay a fire in the kitchen stove so that all he had to do when he got up the next morning was to set a match to paper and kindling. When he went to the kitchen it was not unusual for him to find ice standing in a pan that had been left to soak overnight. By the time the fire got going he had dressed, his pot of coffee had perked and he was ready to cook his breakfast.

Before he left for work he stoked the fires in the kitchen and started a fire in the sitting room stove so that the house would have warmed up some by the time the rest of the family stirred.

Years later when he and my mother came to visit our family in the winter, reacting to the wonders of central heating and cooling, he always declared that it didn't seem nearly as cold or as hot as the weather man reported.

ooooooooooooooo

Unspoiled by air-conditioning or numerous blow fans, we weren't bothered as much by the tropic-like temperatures of summer as we are now when we get out of the controlled atmosphere of our indoor living.

I don't remember ever hearing of anyone being brought down by a heat stroke.

Living was easier in summers than in winters in that old house. If there was any chance to be cool we would be. There were plenty of screen windows and doors and cracks in the house to admit the slightest breeze.

The only time we really suffered from the heat was when it didn't cool off appreciably after sundown. We called those nights "scorchers." The adults declared in somber terms, "There's not a leaf stirring." On the worst nights the sheets on our beds were hot to the touch. But there was a partial answer to that discomfort. We would sprinkle of water in generous amounts on the sheets to enhance the benefits of the slightest breeze. It was delicious to wake up at two or three o'clock in the morning and be so cool that a light blanket felt good. My father and uncle often retreated to the unscreened side porch to sleep on pallets spread on the floor. Mosquitoes were a pest, but there was some relief from the heat.

The kitchen was the hot spot in the house. It was there that my mother cooked three meals a day and canned endless jars of vegetables during the garden season. Matters were not helped when it was time to heat up the flat irons and to finish the weekly laundry.

ooooooooooooooo

My mother waged a never-ending battle to keep that old house livable. She simply would not let it be less than it could be.

She and the rats fought it out for several years to determine who would control our attic. While the rats bred prolifically, she trained every available weapon against them. Her arsenal included rat traps of various sizes to fit the prey. She scattered the bait covered with arsenic around the attic. When she found a nest of newborn vermin she killed them with a broom and dumped the carcasses in the field behind our house.

She finally won the war with the rats.

Mama also defeated the bedbugs which had somehow infested the beds in our house, despite her meticulous housekeeping. She won the battle with a relentless campaign including soaking the bed frame, railings and springs in kerosene and putting the metal pieces in a hot fire. She also boiled the mattress covers. She was ashamed to admit we had bedbugs in the house. I thought she should be proud that she drove them away.

She learned to hang wallpaper. The old house had settled on its foundation, leaving no room square, a nightmare for even professional paperhangers. Nevertheless, she stayed with the challenge on each job until the new paper suited her.

She also could paint with the skill that only full-time painters could match.

There came a time when she decided that the linoleum rugs looked worn and tacky. At a meeting of her home demonstration club she had learned how to refurbish such floor covering. The first step was to paint the entire base of the rug a solid color, say gray. Then she applied splashes of color on the base paint in patterns that were pleasing to her and covered the rug again with shellac to seal in her handiwork.

Finally, when things began to improve coming out of the Depression, some repairs were made on the house, including a paint job on the exterior. We got indoor plumbing including a flush toilet and a bathtub. Natural gas was brought in for cooking and heat when I was about 12 years old.

One thing that didn't change, whatever the condition of the house itself or other things that might have gone on in our lives, Mama kept our home spotlessly clean. She swept, dusted and polished every day. Beds were made early every morning. The curtains were always starched and ironed. She made pretty quilts and decorated pillowcases with delicate embroidery.

ooooooooooooooo

The house was surrounded by abundant shrubbery, set off during the spring and summer by flowering bushes and decorative flowers.

There were gardenias, wisteria and hydrangea. Violets and daffodils added highlights of color. Clumps of blue bonnets and other wild flowers grew in the yard. We didn't have roses because my mother decided she didn't have much of a touch with them.

Swarms of butterflies flitted about in graceful, colorful patterns. Birds in great variety played in the trees. Bumblebees hovered over the flowers. We captured some of them and tied a piece of thread to their leg so that we could control their flights around our heads.

Two chinaberry trees grew to the west of the house; two persimmons dominated the backyard. Those are species that seemed to have disappeared. A pecan tree produced faulted fruit in the side yard to the east. Apple and pear trees my father had planted grew out back in the chicken yard. They bore beautiful blooms in the spring, but very little edible fruit after the various infections and worms got through with them.

The chinaberries and persimmons provided many hours of fun for my friends and me. The persimmon trees begged to be climbed, sometimes to foolish heights. I wouldn't dare go up there now. But it was worth the risk to be able to look out over the neighbors' houses and down across the back fields from such a perch.

These trees also called out for tree houses. We started with great vigor, pulling boards up by rope and building a floor. We declared we would sleep in our houses high above ground. Our plans never fully materialized. But we kept trying, usually after we had seen a Tarzan movie.

Although the chinaberries weren't as attractive for climbing they made their contributions to our games. They produced a hard little berry a bit smaller than a marble. These berries were good ammunition for our slingshots. They could also be strung on strings to make beads.

We watched the persimmons progress from beautiful white blossoms to hard little green knots of a bitter taste in the spring to large soft orange colored fruit in the fall. They were delicious to eat at their peak which came with the first frost of the year.

It still astounds me to recall that my mother and grandmother permitted Uncle Jewell to try his hand at making persimmon beer. The recipe was simple. Fill a milk churn with the fruit at the overly ripe stage. Add sugar, close it off and wait a week or two. It was a good thing that all of this was accomplished on the back porch because the brew produced a terrible odor. I was permitted to taste the concoction, perhaps as a lesson in abstinence.

The persimmon trees created a real mess when their fruit passed its peak and fell to the ground to rot. It was not possible to walk out to the chicken house without going through the quagmire and coming back in the house with shoes covered with the dark orange skin, and brown seed of the fruit. There was one compensation, however; it was fun to watch the birds eat the fermenting persimmons until they staggered about drunk as a lord.

ooooooooooooooo

The houseplace was completed with a barn and chicken house.

The chicken house was built much later when my mother and father decided that it made sense to raise chickens. Uncle Jewell took the lead in building the structure, which probably measured no more than 12 by 15 feet.

Both the barn and the chicken house provided great places for my friends and me to play. The barn, which was never painted finally rotted down. After all, we had little need for it after Flossie was murdered. The chicken house was destroyed by a tornado.

Our house, meager in circumstance, was a home, large and nurturing, because it was filled with the love of my family through good times and bad.

.

# THE NEIGHBORHOOD THAT WAS

The old neighborhood ran west from our house across the town branch and up to the top of the hill, ending where the First Presbyterian Church stands today. It was bordered on the east by the start of the highway to Monticello at the corners of East Church Street and Cemetery Road. The people who lived on Gannaway Street up past the corner grocery were sort of annexed into the neighborhood.

It was a close community populated with interesting people, some of whom could have been called unique, or perhaps odd. Most were good neighbors, ready to protect an endangered child or chastise an errant one. East Church Street residents were always there to help a neighbor in need.

Neighborhoods of today may be populated with just as many interesting characters. People may be just as concerned and helpful. But we would not know that because we stay encapsulated in our individual air-conditioned cocoons, glued to our television sets and computers, communicating with the outside world by the Internet. When we do venture out, it is to dash to our cars to leave the neighborhood.

And anyway, precious little free time is left to interact with the neighbors after putting in a day working and dealing with an overabundance of organized activities. We are like ants running in all directions after the hill has been stirred up.

ooooooooooooooo

Miss Liza Brooks lived at the top of the hill. Her home looked like a haunted manor, right out of a mystery story. Legend was that her house had been used as a hospital for wounded soldiers of the Confederacy. Positioned at the end of a long gravel drive that made its way between giant oak trees, the house was surrounded by an unpainted picket fence. Just inside the gate, a walkway of red brick led to the front door. A lush garden occupied the front yard. The backyard was given over to another giant oak tree and several mimosas. There was a small chicken house where she raised "banty" chickens.

The front porch was decorated with hanging baskets filled with ferns. Various potted plants also flourished there.

It was dark and calm inside the house. A long stairway led off the entry hall. To the left was her sitting room where a single lamp burned beneath a fancy silk shade yellowed with age, casting a pale light on rocking chairs before the fireplace. Musty books resided on ornate shelves as if they had been in place forever.

Eliza Hughey was the first person from Arkansas to attend the renowned all-girl Vassar College, located north of New York City. She came home in 1874 to marry W. B. Brooks. She bore five children and lived the remainder of her life in the family home.

She was a tiny, elegant lady always attired in a long dress, high at the neck with a crocheted white lace collar and bib-like piece held in place with a broach. She moved and spoke in a quiet and genteel way.

She was always very nice to me. In fact, I had quite a crush on her. I was infuriated when my mother called her Liza because I thought that was an ugly name that did not suit such a lovely lady.

When she heard there was to be a parade featuring children and their pets she insisted that I take one of her "banty" roosters as my pet. We secured the frantic chicken to the end of a piece of cord and I marched along Main Street with other children leading dogs, goats, horses and assorted animals.

oooooooooooooooo

The Purcells lived on the same side of the street as Mrs. Brooks just down the hill.

There were grandparents, a young mother, either widowed or divorced, and three children, two boys and a girl. The family occupied an unsecured position on the fringes of town society. The boys were as different as daylight and dark. The older boy, Joe Ed, became a lawyer and went on to be elected Lieutenant governor of Arkansas. Later he came within a hair of being elected governor. His younger brother, Freddie, was something of a dandy. His various schemes created a tarnished reputation before he disappeared from the scene.

oooooooooooooooo

My childhood friend, John Guice, lived on the same side of the street, a way down the hill, in a somewhat puzzling family.

The household was headed by Mr. and Mrs. Belk, his grandparents. Suzie Belk, the Belk's daughter who taught school, acted as his mother. I never knew whether she was his aunt or, as some said, his real mother. Her profession did little to whet John's interest in education.

Mr. Belk was the character of that household. I remember him as a bull of a man always wearing overalls over BVDs with no shirt in the summer. He did not seem to hold a regular job, although he was qualified for some kind of skilled work at the sawmill. He spent most of his time maintaining a prolific garden and a flock of chickens. His fig bushes and grapevines were his pride and joy.

Once or twice when I had gone there to play with John, I was invited to eat dinner, as we called the noon meal, We drank buttermilk and ate vegetables and cornbread. Mr. Belk consumed a large onion as if it were an apple.

The family seemed to be wary of him and his moods.

oooooooooooooooo

Rex Vowell, a friend of early high school days, lived across the street from the Belks in a house with relatives.

We supposed that this shy boy was an orphan child. I would stop by his house so that we could walk together across town to school.

In the spring after Pearl Harbor I stopped by his house on the way to school. The lady of the house told me that Rex wasn't there. He had disappeared over night. She did not seem overly concerned. I would not have been more surprised if she had told me that the sun had set in the east the night before.

Several weeks later I received a picture post card from Rex in San Diego, California. He had enlisted in the Marine Corps. When I showed the card to my parents they hastened to caution me against such a bold act.

oooooooooooooooo

A sharper contrast in lifestyles couldn't have been found than in the second house down the hill from the Belks home.

Captain Claude Hawk and his wife, "Miss Birdie" Kight Hawk, lived there. Captain Hawk began his career in the military when he went with the National Guard to corral Pancho Villa, the Mexican bandit who had raised a ruckus on the border between Mexico and the United States. He entered the regular army when United States launched into World War I. It was then that he gained the rank of captain, which he carried proudly, all of his life.

The neighborhood gossip was that he had gotten a medical discharge and a pension for life after only a few months' service and just in time to avoid being shipped off to fight in France.

He and his wife operated a small millinery and dress shop on Main Street, in an unlikely location next to "Peanut" Hughes's liquor store.

Their presumption to an upscale social life kept them at a cool distance from the neighborhood. It was even said that they drank whiskey and "partied" on the weekends with Mrs. Hawk's sister, Mrs. Temple and her husband Barnett; and Mrs. Kight and her boyfriend, Nick Turner. Mr. Turner was quite a sport. I never saw him dressed in anything other than a starched shirt, set off with a somber tie and a large diamond stickpin. A confirmed bachelor, he came to call on Mrs. Kight almost every night, stayed until ten o'clock then drove to the house he shared with his old-maid sister, Miss Jesse Turner, a revered member of the teaching profession in Warren.

oooooooooooooooo

No family in our neighborhood held more fascination for me than the Croswells, who lived in a tiny shack of a house a stone's throw down the street from the Hawks.

Alex Croswell, the father, was a thin wisp of a man with a wry sense of humor. He worked from time to time at one of the sawmills; his main occupation in later years was digging graves.

Mr. Croswell built their house with whatever odds and ends of lumber he could lay his hands on. It sat far back from the street. Honeysuckle vines covered the front porch. Out front was a swing suspended from a frame made of cast-off pipe. An iron wash pot filled with blooming flowers stood next to it.

It was in that swing that I visited with Elva Croswell, the mother. It took some time to get comfortable with the fact that her left leg ended in a stump just above the knee. Some of the time she wore an awkward and ill-fitting prosthesis, but during hot weather, sore spots developed on what was left of her leg, forcing her to abandon the false limb and go to crutches.

She had lost her leg as a young girl when she and Alex were courting. It happened when he came calling at her home one Sunday afternoon. By way of teasing her he picked up her father's shotgun and playfully said he would shoot her pet kitten. She joined the game and stood in front of the cat to protect it. When he pulled the trigger he found to his surprise that the gun was loaded.

As soon as she had recovered they went ahead with their plans to marry.

They produced two children: Kenneth and Nell.

Ken was a tall youngster, perhaps six foot four in high school, which was unusual for those days. As skinny as a rail, he was known as "Skillet." It followed that he played basketball, a sport at which he excelled to the point that he became a local hero when he was named to the Little All-American team from St. Mary's University in San Antonio, Texas.

Even with an athletic scholarship and summer and holiday work at the Dr. Pepper Bottling Company in Warren it was hard sledding for him to make his way in college. His mother made and sold an endless number of patchwork quilts. The dollar or two she received for each one went mostly to the boy away in school. It was not unusual to see the ends of her fingers bleeding from the constant pushing and pulling of the sewing needle through the quilting material.

There was a particularly interesting facet in Mrs. Croswell's personality, recognized but rarely spoken about by the neighbors because it was "just Elva's way." She had great difficulty in distinguishing between truth and fiction. She told great entertaining stories that stretched the truth beyond the breaking point, but never harmed a soul. This side of her nature was probably what led me to visit her often because I liked to hear her stories.

Daughter Nell married a man named "Shorty" Arnold who died young, but not before fathering a child, Orville Arnold, one of my most interesting friends in high school. The girls said he was handsome in a swarthy sort of way. Orville had also inherited his grandmother's proclivity for making a good story better. More than most he loved a "dirty" joke or remark on the extreme side of risque. He was sometimes known appropriately enough by the nickname of "Snake."

Except in music Orville was a poor student. Some of this may have been due to the fact that he worked long hard hours as a "soda jerk" at Wayne's. He later qualified as a professional trombone player, a calling he followed part time in later years, playing at the casinos in Hot Springs. At the same time he worked as a lineman for the telephone company. Like his father he died young.

Ken became one of the most successful of the alumni from our neighborhood. In addition to his achievements in basketball, he gained a considerable degree of celebrity as a colonel serving in the Marine Corps in combat in both World War II and the Korean conflict. On one of his home leaves during World War II he held our attention with stories of his exploits, including one about having a date with a rising young singer in Hollywood by the name of Rosemary Clooney.

It was reported back in Warren that when he returned to civilian life he achieved substantial financial success in the California real estate market.

Ken had an extraordinary gift for burnishing his own image. Some said that following in his mother's footsteps he would embellish a point here and there as needed. It is in keeping with this talent for imagery that his tombstone in Greenwood Cemetery claims attention. His large black granite monument bearing the name Croswell in simple oversize letters stands out at the west entrance to the graveyard.

ooooooooooooooo

Parvin and Hattie Braswell lived on the south side of East Church Street in the second house west of us. Their sons, Leroy and Clarence, plus Leroy's wife, Eloise, shared the small white frame house with them.

A son was born to Eloise and Leroy a number of years after their marriage. His name was Alan, but my Uncle Van Reep, who lived in the house between the Braswells and us, insisted on calling the pudgy little fellow "Oolie." Uncle Van must have had a penchant for nicknames because he always referred to me as "Bill." I never knew why.

Parvin and Hattie made for a strange pair. Hattie was sparse and birdlike. Her hair was gray going to white all the years I knew her; she wore it pulled back into a tight bun, enhancing the rather mournful nature she projected. I never saw her smile or heard her laugh.

None of us ever witnessed Mr. and Mrs. Braswell engaged in conversation or for that matter exchanging a single word. However, she did open up a bit with the ladies in the neighborhood. She once confided to my mother that she knew when Parvin was romantically inclined because he always offered to fetch a glass of water for her.

Parvin was independent and fractious in manner. A different drummer provided his beat. We gave him a wide berth. He always wore blue denim overalls and high-top work shoes without socks. He worked on his own terms at some sort of menial job at the sawmill. While most of the men in the neighborhood were eager to work as many hours each week as they could, Mr. Braswell refused to go to the job on Mondays. A working man needed to be off at least three days a week, in his view.

We could count on seeing him on his special day off, except in the worst of weather. He hunkered down on his heels, leaning against the wall on the open deck attached by tall pilings to the back door of his house. That was his position for hour after hour, smoking his hand-rolled cigarettes, which he was not permitted to use inside the house.

He seemed to be occupied staring out across their small pasture, which was populated with numerous geese and chickens. We often played there under a large gum tree on the bank of the town branch. We always tried to steer clear of the geese. They were quarrelsome and threatening. But we could not avoid them completely, as one of my playmates was to learn painfully. He made the mistake of letting one of the geese walk up next to him. Unfortunately, he was wearing wide-legged short pants without the benefit of undershorts. As we told the story later, the goose looked up the leg of his pants, saw what it thought was a little worm and bit it.

Leroy was a highly skilled carpenter and cabinetmaker who had a very special job with the Bradley Lumber Company. He was occupied nearly full time applying his special talents to projects at the homes of Bob and Baker Fullerton, principal owners of the mill.

Rumors about Clarence, the younger son, and my cousin, Catherine Reep, caused quite a stir in our neighborhood when she reported that she had caught him peeking into her bedroom window. Uncle Van was outraged and threatened to do bodily harm to Clarence. Things calmed down after a few days, yet there was gossip that Catherine might have encouraged young Braswell's voyeurism by not being as careful as she could have been in pulling down her shades. Others suggested that Clarence might have started all of the talk just to draw attention to himself.

oooooooooooooooo

The Hickmans, Frank and Annie, lived across the street from the Braswells with their only son, Edwin.

To his great chagrin and our glee Edwin's mother always referred to him as Francis Edwin. This was especially noticeable when she stood on their front porch and called in a voice loud enough to be heard throughout the immediate neighborhood, "Francis Edwin, come home this minute." That affectation was a reflection of her pretensions to climb the social ladder of Warren, which in her judgment did not include East Church Street.

But it was clear that she was not to the manor born. The talk in the neighborhood was that she was not particularly proud of the branch of the Smith family from which she came.

The work habits of her brother caused some in the neighborhood to wag their heads in wonderment. Mr. Smith was a jackleg carpenter and roofer who worked only occasionally. His wife always accompanied him to the job where she would sit by the hours watching him peck away. Neighbors said she either didn't trust him out of her sight or that she was fascinated by what he did. A minority opinion with long odds held that she just couldn't stand to be away from him.

The most noticeable thing about Mrs. Hickman, aside from her social aspirations, was the fact that she bore a sharp crevice in the middle of her forehead. We were given to understand that her cranium was splitting open. Apparently that was incorrect because that never happened in the more than 25 years I knew her.

Mr. Hickman was a congenial man, big boned and somewhat awkward in his movements. One would not have wanted to leave him on his own in a cabinet of fine china.

The neighbors said that Mrs. Hickman pushed him constantly to reach for higher rungs in work and in society. They lived in a big, well-furnished house set back on a slight rise from the street, and owned a car. It was reported that she forced her husband into taking a job as manager of the local Morgan and Lindsey five and dime store. The consensus was that he was in way over his head and very unhappy with his position. Later, again at the urging of Mrs. Hickman, he ran for one of the county political offices and was soundly defeated.

But Mrs. Hickman, for all her trying, couldn't do much with Francis Edwin. He didn't take to music lessons, he was a lackluster student and he steadfastly refused to assume airs of refinement as she hoped. As far as I knew, he never read a book, not even a "funny book" or one of the "big little" books that were popular then. It is not surprising that he was an intimidating bully.

ooooooooooooooo

The Williams family lived next door to the Hickmans and just across the street from us.

Stanford, the father, worked on the maintenance crew at The Bradley. He was known in the neighborhood as "Sinbad," a fictional sailor distinguished by the "tall tales" he told of his adventures. To be more forthright about it, Mr. Williams lied, as one of the neighbors put it, when the truth would set him free.

He was also a stern and often cruel disciplinarian with his only son, Nolan. It was not unusual to see him beat the boy with a leather belt until he drew blood. I once saw him knock Nolan to the ground with his fist. It was only at Christmas that he showed his brand of affection for his son by lavishing gifts on the boy as if to wash away the memories of his cruelty.

Lena, the mother, was a dumpy, cheerful sort of lady. She didn't seem to object to her husband's treatment of their son.

Quite enterprising and inexhaustible, she offered potted plants and goldfish from her small hot house and in-ground pond for sale along with milk and eggs from a cow she kept and chickens she raised. She was known for having one of the best gardens in the neighborhood.

The Williams had a telephone in their house on which I received my first call. I was probably seven or eight years old. Mrs. Williams called across the street to tell me that I was wanted on the telephone. One of my playmates, Billy Gordon Blackwell, who lived a few blocks away, wanted to speak with me, she announced. I was afraid and refused to take the call without my mother being with me. When I worked up my nerve and picked up the telephone I learned that Billy Gordon Blackwell was inviting me to spend the night at his house. The fear of the telephone was replaced with terror at the thought of being away from home overnight. I stammered some excuse and ran back home. It was years before I ever used a telephone again.

Nolan didn't mix very well with the other boys in the neighborhood, although they could often count on him to buy soda pops for them with money he bragged he had snitched from the cash his mother put away from the sale of her plants, goldfish and produce. He irritated my mother and father greatly. He had inherited his father's talent for embellishing on the facts of a situation. My mother and father said he was a show-off, especially at Christmas time when he came to our house to display the gifts his parents had heaped on him. No one stopped to reason that this was his pathetic way to attract attention and respect, neither of which he received at home.

It could be said that I am here today, writing this book, in spite of Nolan. He and I were walking on the other side of town when we came upon a power line that had been broken by the weight of the ice accumulated during a storm. The bare wire was thrashing about on the ice-covered ground, throwing off fascinating sparks. Nolan repeatedly urged me to pick up the wire, assuring me that I would not be hurt. It has been said that the Lord takes care of fools and drunks. I guess He also sees after young boys. Instead of picking up the lethal wire, I ran back home, scared out of my wits.

Nolan entered the Army before Pearl Harbor. He was at Bataan at the time of the Japanese attack. He was captured there and forced into the infamous Death March. His father mourned often and conspicuously. Nolan survived the prison camp and a long stay in an Army hospital to come back to Warren with a bride, a young lady from Alabama who had been one of his nurses.

oooooooooooooooo

85

Contrary to our mobile society of today, it was a rare occasion when someone new came to live in the neighborhood.

Carl "Skeeter" Hughes and his bride, Elizabeth, a fragile and wan girl from Monticello, were such rarities.

The young couple moved across the street from us into one of the nicest houses on East Church Street.

We had "Skeeter" to thank for what had to be the single most exciting night in my memories of those days.

We were sleeping with all of the doors and windows open in order to cope with the summer heat. The moonlight made it almost as bright as day outside. The tranquility of the night was suddenly interrupted by the repeated sharp blast from what had to be an automatic shotgun. My father told me to get my .22 rifle, the only gun in our house.

When my mother, father and I went out on our front porch it was immediately apparent that the shooting came from "Skeeter's" house, where every light was turned on. In fact, we could see our neighbor racing about inside with his shotgun held at the ready. He fired two or three more times.

When "Skeeter" came to his front door he spotted us standing in our yard. He called out to my father, "Carl, Carl, come on. Bring all your guns. The Indians are all over my house. They've already killed my bird dog."

At about that time Tom Lowman, the night marshall, drove up, got out of his car and made his way cautiously toward the Hughes's house. When "Skeeter" saw him he aimed his shotgun and shouted, "I see you coming. Stop right there."

Marshall Lowman, a man of substantial girth, pulled his pistol and dropped to the ground. He began to call on "Skeeter" to lay down his gun "before things get out of hand." It seemed to us that they already had.

Finally, "Skeeter" surrendered and Marshall Lowman led him away to the city jail.

Within a day or two we heard that "Skeeter" had gone to a sanatorium to "dry out" from a habit of daily drinking that had brought on a severe attack of delirium tremens, popularly known in those days as "DTs" or "seeing pink elephants."

It was in the nature of the times, before someone invented the term "politically correct," that after "Skeeter" returned from being detoxed his friends good naturedly inquired of him, "'Skeeter' have you seen any Indians around your house lately?" We never saw him drunk again.

ooooooooooooooo

The Easterling family lived up the alley that intersected East Church Street in front of our house.

The father's arms were covered with tattoos from his wrists to his elbows. He had them done in the peacetime Navy where he had learned to be a baker, the trade that brought the family to Warren. Mrs. Easterling was a woman of dark complexion, suggesting she was of Mexican descent. No woman ever wore more makeup morning, noon and night. They had a house full of children, a wild bunch if one ever existed.

Mr. Easterling always brought home two or three loaves of "light" bread from his day at the bakery. This was before the days of sliced bread. Come suppertime Mrs. Easterling, who was not particularly given to spending time in the kitchen, put the loaves of unsliced bread on the table. The kids dug into the heart of the loaves with their bare hands and pulled out balls of bread.

ooooooooooooooooo

We probably had more interactions with the Hammons family than anyone else other than our kinfolk, the Reeps who lived next door on the west side.

The Hammons lived immediately to the east in a large white frame house separated from our place by a grassy lane where a big walnut tree grew.

Their household was presided over by the mother, Lummy. Her husband, a dentist, died quite young, leaving her alone to raise six children. They were Bob, Grace, Rex, Pat, Virginia and Jack.

Mrs. Hammons was a rather large-framed woman with gray hair, knotted into a bun, who had her hands more than full feeding and disciplining her brood.

Bob, the eldest son, was infected with tuberculosis as a grown man and had to be confined to the state sanatorium at Booneville, but he refused to stay there and soon came home to fight TB on his own terms. The doctors told him his only hope was complete bed rest.

One summer afternoon we heard Bob thrashing around and cursing, declaring he was not going to stay in bed for the rest of his life. He kicked out a screen window on the big side porch where his bed was located, climbed out and walked away. Months later his family got word from him through a lady friend that he had hoboed out to California and that she was going to join him.

Bob and his wife, Mary, both learned the carpenter's trade and prospered in California during the war years.

Grace, the older of two girls, was an elegant young lady, a real beauty. Somehow she had learned office skills and secured employment at the Bradley Lumber Company.

She turned out to be the leading lady in a true romance story. Grace and one of Judge Colvin's daughters managed to save enough money to go to New Orleans for a vacation. A highlight of one of their nights there was to change Grace's life. She and her friend went to the Roosevelt Hotel's Blue Room, a splendid place for dining and dancing, made famous by its being one of the venues from which orchestras broadcast nationally each night. That must have been quite an experience for a young lady from East Church Street.

The story that came back to the neighborhood was that Grace wore a bright red dress and attracted a lot of attention. Among her admirers was Bernard Oppenheimer, a young man who was prospering substantially from his food importing business. He had the orchestra play "The Lady In Red," a popular song of the day, and asked her to dance. He came to visit her in Warren a few months later. They were soon married.

Rex, another of the Hammons boys, was a "natural born" mechanic. On more than one occasion he built an operating automobile from little more than a pile of junk. His crowning achievement came when he and five of his friends took a car about ready for the scrap heap and put it in good enough shape to drive to and from California in 1939.

One of the adventurers, Pete Godwin, reported that they left home with about $35.00 each, drove to San Diego, turned around and headed home. Travelling on gas that cost 11 to 12 cents per gallon, they had one flat tire in 4,682 miles. The trip lasted two weeks, during which they spent only two nights in tourists homes and ate only a handful of meals in cafes. Otherwise they slept in the open on a tarpaulin and ate from a larder of canned food they had brought from home and fresh fruit and vegetables they bought at roadside stands.

One of the boys, John Harvey, stayed behind in California to learn how to make movies. His ambitions didn't quite pan out. He settled for coming back to Arkansas to own and operate a movie theater in a small town near Warren.

Soon after the California trip, Rex used a picture and a few drawings from *Popular Mechanics* magazine as his guide to build a vehicle the likes of which I have not seen, before or since. It was conventional in all regards except he had installed a platform on the back of it where he mounted a large wooden propeller that Clarence Braswell had made by hand. The motor drove the propeller by means of a complicated system of belts, creating an air draft which pushed the car ahead. Rex's car didn't set any records for speed, but it did move forward and attracted a great deal of attention. Of course, there was no reverse, but that didn't distract from the genius of it all.

Pat, the third son, was a true rebel who gained hero status among the young people for one of his escapades.

He was not what you would call a student. It was almost certain that he would run into trouble at school. He did and it came over his refusal to agree with a biology teacher that it was proper to call a crayfish a crayfish and not a crawfish or crawdad. We heard that the debate came to an abrupt end when Pat dragged the teacher out of the classroom to the banister at the head of the stairway where he threatened to drop the hapless man to the ground floor. He was stopped when Mr. Grigsby, the school principal, hurried up and pulled Pat off his intended victim.

"You are through with school, Pat," he declared. Pat allowed as how he didn't care.

Sometime later, Pat left home to hitchhike south. When he ran out of money he stopped off in a small town in southern Louisiana and went to work in a sawmill.

The story had a happy ending right out of a romance novel. Pat married Doris, the pretty and charming young daughter of the owner of the mill. He worked his way up to be the manager. Later he owned a butane distribution plant and became a substantial citizen of the community.

Virginia, the younger girl, was an outstanding sandlot athlete, a tomboy through and through. She played tackle football with the boys. One of her best sports was baseball, where she pitched and hit left-handed. She was fearless at "shinny," a rough game somewhat like ice hockey in which we hit a tin can back and forth with heavy sticks.

She even dared one of the Stell boys to put on the boxing gloves that he had received as a Christmas gift. He stepped up to the challenge, but soon gave up under her pounding. As a teenager, she often won wrestling matches against boys.

Jack, the youngest boy, was one of my main running buddies for a long time. We claimed the open fields behind our houses as our domain. It was there that we built a tiny shack of castoff auto body parts and scraps of wood over a hole we had dug in the ground.

Jack was a hard worker who was to earn the position as foreman of the Potlatch Lumber Company's Bradley sawmill.

Mrs. Hammons became estranged from the adults in our home. My parents said they never knew what caused the rift. In any case, the grown-ups didn't speak to each other for several years. But we youngsters never missed a beat playing together. As suddenly as the estrangement had begun, the adults became friends again.

ooooooooooooooo

The Moseley family was different from the rest of the neighborhood.

Theirs was a neat house, painted a sparkling white, standing behind a concrete fence, decorated with iron piping, in a carefully kept yard with neatly trimmed shrubbery. The fence was more symbolic than utilitarian because it stood no more than three feet tall. The frame house never seemed to lose the sheen of its white paint. The inside was furnished to the nth degree, which is not surprising since Mr. Moseley had been a partner in Martin and Moseley's hardware and furniture store, after which he "traveled" for a furniture wholesaler.

The Moseleys had one child, a boy with the unlikely name of Winfred. Of course, we called him "Weenie." A slender boy, he didn't play much in the neighborhood. However, he did capture our attention and envy when he received a .410 caliber shotgun for Christmas. His favorite pastime appeared to be standing in his backyard and firing away with that gun to stir up the flocks of blackbirds which were always clacking about in the spring.

ooooooooooooooo

The Stells, who operated the Corner Grocery at the intersection of Gannaway and East Church Street, brought international attention to Warren.

One of their sons, Cone, a graduate of Ouachita College, had become an ordained minister. Soon after the Japanese attack on Pearl Harbor he volunteered for the Air Force and chose to become a bomber pilot rather than a chaplain. He was shot down in action after only a few months of flying in the Pacific Theater. His fame spread when the national news media dubbed him "The Flying Parson." We kids were thrilled when his story was told in a widely distributed "comic" book. Some said that his exploits were the inspiration for the patriotic song, "Praise the Lord and Pass the Ammunition."

His body was not recovered, but a monument stands in Warren's Greenwood Cemetery. An inscription on its granite face bears a quotation from one of his letters or perhaps a sermon which sets out his belief: "War is definitely wrong, but we are all in this together and the man who pulls the trigger is no worse off or better than the taxpayer who finances it."

The Corner Grocery was the focal point of our neighborhood. Most housewives went there to buy the odds and ends of their grocery needs to supplement what they had gotten from the company stores operated by the Bradley and the Southern lumber companies.

Some of the young people from the neighborhood congregated there had a penny or two to spend for a wad of chewing gum or a nickel for a soda pop or a candy bar. Sometimes the choice was a big dill pickle speared out of a dark wooden barrel. There was a wide selection of cold soda pops: orange, strawberry, cream, chocolate and my favorite, Grapette.

Those who didn't have any money hoped they could share a bite of candy or a swallow of a soda pop with someone who had bought a confection. It didn't take very long to discover who took an extra large bite or swig.

Some of the older boys had perfected a scam they pulled on the drivers of the trucks that delivered soda pop. The bottles of "pop" were carried in wooden cases, set in open racks on the trucks. As soon as the driver carried his first cases into the store, the boys would run by the far side of the truck and pluck off one or two drinks from the racks and throw them into the empty field across the street. As soon as the driver finished his delivery and pulled away the boys raced to the field with much whooping and hollering to retrieve their loot.

ooooooooooooooo

The Reynolds family is worth an entire book of its own.

They lived up Gannaway Street in an ancient two-story frame house. If the exterior had ever been painted, the paint had long since disappeared, leaving it as a mottled gray and black. To a stranger in town, unaware of the compelling people and objects that filled it, the house would still have appeared appealingly, perhaps forebodingly, reminiscent of the old house in "The Addams Family" television series.

Professor Reynolds headed the household. We never knew whether the title was one he earned in academia or one bestowed upon him like a nickname because of his many obvious intellectual interests.

The professor was a dedicated scholar and bibliophile, a professional photographer, an accomplished artist, a naturalist, a taxidermist, a collector of all sorts of oddities and valuables. He was 180 degrees out of step with the neighborhood and the town for that matter. His only source of income appeared to be the paintings he sold infrequently and the occasional commission he received for photographing a family or a bride. My mother paid him a small sum to paint a milk churn with multi-colored pastoral vistas. He also painted a small vase with a similar scene for her.

He may have sold items from his collections, but that seems doubtful since his eclectic exhibits continued to grow, overflowing a house that was already full to running over:

His oil paintings. A giant bee hive. Memorabilia from the Civil War and World War I. Arrow heads, Indian pottery and a headdress. Old guns and knives. Crystallized rocks. Antique bottles. Pine knots and cypress knees. Petals of flowers pressed under glass. Butterflies mounted on delicate pins under glass covers. Chinaware and crystal glasses. Antiquarian books and magazines. A wide variety of "stuffed" animals, including an alligator and an eagle, testified to his skills at taxidermy.

There were always several snakes in wire cages in the backyard. Other cages held birds, squirrels, raccoons and rabbits. Exotic chickens of various sizes and colors along with a peacock scurried about searching for worms in the yard and in a small garden. There was a thriving vineyard where he gathered grapes to make wine.

One of the most interesting items in the professor's accumulation was a long tress of dark red hair displayed behind glass in a picture frame. The hair had belonged to James "Red" Reynolds, the younger son. At his father's insistence, the boy did not have his hair cut until he was 16 years of age.

"Red" Reynolds was himself different. He delighted in walking around with one of the snakes from his father's menagerie curled around his neck. Another of his tricks, which he alone found to be amusing, was to curl a snake around his arm, under a long-sleeved shirt, so that the reptile's head was in his hand. Thus prepared, he would offer to shake hands with young and old alike.

Regrettably, "Red" led a tragic life. Neighborhood gossips said that mourning a lost teenage love, he attempted suicide. During World War II he survived a prison of war camp.

The Professor and "Red" were not the only interesting characters in the family. The older son, William, an artist in his own right, traveled around the world as one of the features of Buffalo Bill's Wild West Show.

The story of Professor Reynolds and his family in our neighborhood came to an abrupt and tragic end one night when their house was consumed in a raging fire. Feeding on his collections of a lifetime the house was consumed in a few minutes.

oooooooooooooooo

The neighborhood was populated with many other notable personalities.

Owen Saunders, who lived three-quarters of a mile or so out on the Monticello highway, was another one of the rare birds. He was a master craftsman with a specialty in gunsmithing, a trade he had learned in Germany from which he had immigrated after World War I.

His workshop was a magical place for me. It was a narrow building with sides and roof of tin. The floor was bare dirt. It contained a crowded, but neat array of lathes, tools and a forge where he could heat metal to a red-hot state in order to shape it to his designs. Guns in various states of assembly and repair were always present. This collection usually contained at least one rifle he was making from raw metal and wood.

He kept beehives and a thriving garden. Several fig trees in his backyard produced bumper crops.

Mr. Saunders was a shy man, small and bony, who was rarely seen outside his workshop. On those occasions when he ventured out it was to drive to town to buy groceries and attend to business such as was required at the post office and the courthouse.

His infrequent trips attracted a great deal of attention because he traveled in a Model A Ford that was in mint condition, from its shinning black body to the engine that hummed along like a fine Swiss watch. His automobile was made all the more interesting by the story of its origin. He had literally dug it out of a heap of wrecks at the city junkyard and restored it to a better condition than when it rolled off the assembly line.

Miss Pearl Heatherington was another character who became a legend in our neighborhood. Her identity in life was that of "Old Maid School Teacher." It was not meant to be prejudicial; it was just a statement of fact.

Miss Pearl's story was a classic romantic tragedy. She became engaged to be married soon after she returned home from college. When her father, a doctor, died a short time later, her mother, who had always opposed the match, put her foot down, demanding that the marriage plans be cancelled or at least delayed to allow time for proper mourning. Miss Pearl gave in to her mother and the thwarted young man went away.

Miss Pearl was to spend the rest of her mother's life taking care of the old lady. The neighbors said her heart was broken and that she never was interested in another man.

She didn't venture out very much beyond teaching her classes in elementary school. A kindly, but no-nonsense woman, she dressed in a rather severe style, a longish black or gray dress with a high collar and broach. Somewhere in an obscure corner of my memories I seem to recall that she participated in the musical program at one of the churches.

Her only concession to the progress of the times was to drive her own automobile, a Model A Ford. We saw her driving to and from school. She maintained a stern position behind the steering wheel. Her back and head were held in a posture as stiff as a poker; her arms stayed straight forward with her elbows locked in position. She looked neither to the left nor to the right, never acknowledging other drivers or pedestrians. Her objective appeared to be to get wherever she was going in the most direct route possible with no diversions.

She died alone.

oooooooooooooooo

A family of blacks lived up on cemetery hill on a gravel and red clay road that was to become the street that now runs in front of the Bradley County Memorial Hospital.

There was no permanent father in the house. A woman we knew as Weeda was the mother of "a house full of kids." She and the children were afraid of the man who stayed there off and on because he administered severe punishment for the slightest infraction of his rules. Their house was little more than a wooden roof and four walls; no screens on the windows, no indoor plumbing.

We played with "Weeda's Boys" on the branch that ran from over toward the Bradley mill. We caught crawdads with chunks of fat meat tied to strings. Sometimes we cooked the meat from the tail of the crawdads in a skillet over an open fire and tried to convince ourselves that it was good. Our menu was expanded by our frying the meat of birds one of the boys had killed with his slingshot.

We swam in the branch when a heavy rain came. We made waterwheels, mounting them so that their paddle wheels turned with the current and sailed toy boats. Occasionally, we took clay from the banks of the branch and tried to mold it into bowls. We had little success with that undertaking because the clay cracked when we baked it.

ooooooooooooooo

Most of the houses still stand in what was my neighborhood, but few who live in them now can trace their roots to those days.

Nor do they know the stories of the lives of the families who preceded them—the good times and the bad, the successes and the tragedies, all those things that seemed so crucial and permanent to us then.

*Ramon Greenwood*

# THE BEST HOME TOWN

There must have been thousands of small towns like Warren scattered across America during the 1930s and into the mid-1940s. But in our insular lives we gave little thought to that probability. To have done so would have been almost as foreign to us as the idea that life existed on other planets. We just knew for a fact that Warren, inhabited by about 5,000 souls, was the best hometown ever, and we thought it would always be so.

Ours was a secure island connected to the rest of the world by two-lane gravel roads that were our causeways through farm fields and dense stands of pine and hardwood timber to a bigger world. One road led 50 miles north across the Saline River at the North Steel Bridge, through Rye, on to Pine Bluff, which at a population of 30,000 or so we considered to be a big town. Another route headed west across creeks and lowlands to Banks, Hampton, Harrell and finally to Camden. To the south the road made its way to Hermitage and on to Moro Bay, where a ferry powered by the current, carried cars and sometimes horse-drawn wagons across the Ouachita River to connect with the road to El Dorado. Highway 4 went east through Wilmar and on to Monticello. Along the way it crossed the Saline River on a one-lane steel bridge and made its way past the turnoffs to Possum Valley and the Prairie, an anomalistic site where Spanish Daggers and various types of cacti and other strange vegetation grew in unlikely sandy soil. The legend was that it was spotted with quicksand in to which a man or beast could disappear.

Missouri-Pacific busses came through Warren twice a day going north to Pine Bluff and Little Rock in the morning and returning in the afternoon. Earl Reynolds, who had stayed home during the war, got rich partly by operating a bus that made a daily round trip to Camden.

The Missouri-Pacific ran a regular train, carrying freight and occasional passengers, between McGehee and Warren once a day. The Warren and Ouachita Valley Railroad ran west daily beyond Tinsman to connect with the main line that ran south through Hampton.

While the W&OV mostly carried logs and freight to the sawmills it also pulled a caboose, complete with passenger seats about as comfortable as sitting on a pile of rocks. This car was warmed by a pot-bellied, wood-burning stove in the winter. Passengers cooled off in the heat of summer simply by raising the windows, which brought in a good breeze ladled with soot and dust. Mr. Frank Carmical presided over this domain dressed year-round in his black suit, white shirt, narrow black tie and high-top shoes. He wore a severely shaped blackbilled cap bearing brass letters that declared him to be The Conductor.

ooooooooooooooo

We had little need to go into the world outside Warren because we had everything we needed there to live our idyllic lives in a capsule of happiness suspended in time.

Warren looked like a Hollywood setting for Smalltown, U. S. A. The broad streets that circled the court square and served the main business district were paved with red bricks laid down in the early 1920s.

We didn't appreciate it then, but we had an beautiful court square on which sat a classic court house with a tower, housing a clock with faces on four sides and a bell that rang on the hour, loud enough to be heard all over town.

The town marshall looked the other way when adventurous boys went into the court house to climb the ladder in the tower. We timed it so we could stand next to the bell when it struck for the hour.

The bell tower provided a panoramic view of our town. Beyond the business district there was a well-ordered pattern of tree-lined streets, populated by small frame homes, with a few brick residences here and there. A walk through those streets was a trip past well-kept yards with flowerbeds and decorative shrubbery clustered around tidy front porches where swings hung from the ceilings.

ooooooooooooooooo

The particular sights, sounds and aromas of our town are deeply etched in my memory.

Roosters crowing at daybreak. Whistles from the sawmills joining in a duet to wake up the town to get to work. Later, the chugging sound of the air-powered equipment and screaming saws and planing machines at the mill. The reassuring sound of the town clock striking, particularly in the lonely hours of after midnight.

The wailing sirens of the town's fire alarm waking the town at night. The sky turned red and orange, laced with sparkles of white soot and trash lifted to the sky by the wind drafts from the fire ravaging a home or a business. The sounds of the crowd gathered at the site of the fire no matter the time or the weather. The excited chatter of the spectators as they watched members of the family and friends race in and out of the burning structure carrying valuables they salvaged. Commands of the fire chief to volunteer firefighters barely heard over the roar of oxygen being consumed by the flames.

Fall leaves in vibrant shades of orange and gold decorating the view in every direction. Later the smoke from their burning hanging low to the ground, filling the air with a rich aroma not yet matched by the finest perfumeries.

The crackling heat of bonfires, made of old tires and scrap lumber, to play by in the chill of the night air. The laughter and shouts of joy of youngsters at play, ignoring the insistent calls of mothers who had dinner on the table: "Your Daddy is home from work. Time to come in and clean up so we can eat supper."

The distant thuds of the bass drum and melodies of instruments of the Lumberjack band drilling to perfect its halftime show for the Friday night football game.

The once-a-year snow that was always enough to close the schools for a day or two. Ice storms that turned every tree and bush into an artistry of glasslike sculpture. Rain to play in during the summer days and to listen to as it pounded the house all night long and sent the adults scurrying for pans and buckets to catch the water that made its way through faults in the roof. Thunder and lightning that lit up the sky.

The sweet smell from the Cape Jasmine blossoms that grew outside our sitting room and from honeysuckle that covered the garden fence. Mama singing while she picked the flowers in her garden amidst the silent elegance of butterflies and the buzz of bumblebees. Songbirds chattering and whistling with sweet voices. Pesky bluejays creating a cacophony as they fussed among themselves in nearby trees.

The sound of an airplane flying low and slow enough over the neighborhood so that we could see the daredevil at the controls as he waved a friendly greeting to his admirers below.

The aromas of hamburgers and onions frying at the carnival. Popcorn at the Pastime Theater. Chicken frying. A pot of soup simmering on the cookstove on a cold day; a cake baking. The oily odor of a kerosene lamp lighting the sitting room when the power went out and pine kindling beginning to burn around firewood to get a stove going. The pungency of lye soap in the washpot.

oooooooooooooooo

Warren was a living example of the adage from the folklore of Africa: it takes a village to raise a child.

Few mothers worked outside of the home. With families composed of aunts, uncles, cousins, and grandparents, in addition to the parents, it was a rare occasion when there wasn't a grown-up around the house to keep an eye on the youngsters.

When young people went about town they were in a community of adults who knew them and assumed some responsibility for their safety and well-being. The streets were safe day and night for youngsters, singles and courting couples to walk about.

It was harder for us to veer from the straight and narrow when we aware that adults, who knew us by name and our families' histories, were watching us with eyes of concern and curiosity. When we got out of line they were not reluctant to pull us aside for an earful of earnest advice. There was also a strong probability that word of our misdoings would get back to our parents.

The parents we knew were glad for the reports and took swift action to punish those of us who strayed.

Most businessmen took a particular interest in high school athletes. Those who had played on high school teams, and a few who had competed at college, were eager to talk about how it was in their day and give coaching tips. Lack of athletic experience didn't hold others back.

Businessmen in the town were ready to go the extra mile in providing jobs for youngsters as well as supporting a list of school causes.

Some of us were fortunate to have the benefit of a special mentor. In my case, it was Jim Hurley Sr., the father of my good friend and teammate, Jimmy Hurley.

Mr. Hurley had more influence on me than anyone else outside my family.

I admired his success in business. When he lost out to Dick Warner, Sr., a man from Minnesota, in the competition to become boss at the Southern Lumber Company, Mr. Hurley immediately turned his experience in sales at the company to become immensely successful as a broker who supplied millions of feet of lumber to build military bases across the South. Later he became mayor of Warren and operated prosperous dealerships for automobiles and farm machinery.

He and I enjoyed a great friendship, built, I believe, on mutual respect and his sense that I might have some promise. I became almost like a member of his family. He was always ready with advice and on at least two occasions, significant financial support, where he saw an opportunity for me to better my circumstances.

He died in 1957 at the age of 55, a victim of a congenital heart disease. After his first heart attack, which occurred appropriately enough while he was watching a high school football game, I had the opportunity to thank him for his friendship and to tell him that I owed him a great debt of gratitude for showing me how things could be.

ooooooooooooooo

The streets of "uptown" were busy most every day of the week with the activity reaching its peak on Saturday.

Main Street was congested with people and vehicles from the railroad tracks on the north end of the main business district to the busy intersection of Church Street on the south end where the post office and three filling stations did thriving businesses.

Families from the surrounding farm country and small communities came to town to do their trading and to take care of business with bankers and officials at the seat of Bradley County government. Some just came to visit with friends and get caught up on the gossip.

Many country folks still traveled by horse-drawn wagons. They tied up in a wagon yard where a livery stable and mule barn had once flourished on the alley that ran behind Ederington's Cash Store past the back of Warren Savings and Loan, Martin-Moseley's hardware and furniture store and The Bradley Store.

Farmers shopped for at least a week's supply of the staples they couldn't grow on their own land. They bought large sacks of flour and cornmeal for cooking and oats and other feed for their farm animals. Kerosene was on most everyone's shopping list. Buyers brought their own cans to be filled from a large barrel by a clerk turning a handpump. A raw Irish potato sealed off the spout of the can.

Families gathered back at their wagons around noon where the mother laid out a lunch. The more prosperous ones ate treats which had just been

107

bought at the store—heavy slices of baloney, a hunk of rat cheese, crackers and candy bars—to be washed down with soda pops.

In the fall when their crops were laid by, those who had had a good year bought new overalls and shirts for their boys and material to make dresses for the girls. Youngsters, who were not consigned to wear hand-me-downs, got new shoes.

ooooooooooooooo

Townspeople usually didn't come to town until Saturday afternoon.

Some of those who owned cars arrived by mid-afternoon to get good parking places on Main Street so they could sit in their vehicles to see and be seen by the people walking by. These vantagepoints provided opportunities to visit with friends and gossip between forays into the stores.

Not all of the action was on Main Street. Plenty was going on along the block of Myrtle Street that ran along the east side of the Southern Hotel. Myrtle was just as busy as Main Street, but the panache wasn't there. Among the attractions were a beer joint and poolhall, a liquor store and a café. Burns grocery store stood on the southeast corner of the block. A service station anchored the northeast end.

Deserved or not, this part of town took on the reputation as the rougher side. Some people referred to it as "Little Chicago."

ooooooooooooooo

Shoppers could find all of the necessities and many of the luxuries of life right at home in Warren.

With few exceptions, these enterprises were owned and operated by local families. Often there were interlocking ownerships and perhaps conflicts of interests. Merchants and owners of large business enterprises often sat on boards of directors of two banks, which in turned financed their businesses, sometimes including their side interests in farming and cattle raising.

We did most of our family buying at The Bradley Store.

With a veritable cornucopia of wares on display on the sprawling ground floor and a balcony on the second floor, The Bradley was the anchor store in the town's main shopping area. There was a shop for men's clothing managed by Lovette Reaves. Joining it in the rear was a department for shoes for the entire family managed by Larkin Gray, a skinny little man who was a pillar of the First Baptist Church, and a Mr. Savage.

Ladies shopped in a large section for ready-to-wear clothing presided over by Verna Galloway. There were also all sorts of fabrics, patterns and sewing supplies for those who wanted or needed to make their own clothing at home.

The big store featured a grocery department offering everything from soup to nuts and a meat market where slabs of pork and beef were brought from walk-in refrigerators to be cut to order; there were raw oysters and beef liver for those who had a taste for such things.

Furniture, appliances and some hardware were found on the balcony.

The east side of the balcony was given over to the accounting office, the center of activity since almost all of the store's business was done on credit. A number of men and women sat at desks grinding away on their adding machines and entering transactions by hand in large ledgers. Mr. Harley oversaw the accounting most of the time from behind a bank teller's sort of cage down on the first floor.

Mr. J. E. Stewart, the store manager, could be found in the office upstairs. We understood that he had been brought to Warren by the Fullertons, who owned the establishment, from a big emporium in either St. Louis or Kansas City to assure a first-rate store and profitable business.

ooooooooooooooo

There were enough characters living in Warren in those days to populate an entire shelf of Damon Runyonesque novels.

We encountered them everywhere around town, forming such a busy mosaic of memories that they can't all be mentioned here.

Pete Morgan was a tiny man, severely retarded, who sold parched peanuts on the corner at the Merchant and Planters Bank. His face was always smeared with the overflow of a heavy dip of snuff. Voices that only he could hear constantly tormented him. To our everlasting shame, we youngsters mocked him just to see his preoccupations with his inner demons turn to outward fury.

Bo Weiss, optometrist and jeweler, could be seen behind the counter of Weiss's Jewelry Store, with his father, Albert, a classic Teutonic figure, who had immigrated to Warren from St. Louis. Bo, not a handsome man, was a fashion plate. He wore trousers with deep pleats, emphasized by a handsome gold watch chain. His summer shoes were highly polished "spectators" of the brown and white design. He was the first man I had ever heard of in Warren who played golf over at Fordyce. As regular as clockwork, he could be found at mid-mornings and mid-afternoons at the soda fountain enjoying a cup of coffee and holding forth on any topic related to sports.

Judge (and *The Eagle Democrat* publisher) Duvall L. Purkins, thin as a rail, was another dapper character. In the summer, he wore seersucker suits with starched white shirts and bow ties. He smoked cigars. Despite the fact that he never quite seemed to achieve lasting professional or commercial success, it was our impression that he was the resident everyman's intellectual. He did nothing to discourage that image. He could be seen frequently at "Shorty" Montgomery's barbershop improving his looks with a shampoo and shave. Two other barber shops on Main Street, operated by "Shorty" Finney and Mr. Sharp and Mr. Johnson, were also popular gathering places. A one-lane bowling alley gave Finney's a competitive edge for a time.

Walter Moseley and Elzie Bryant, brothers-in-laws, ran a meat market on the north end of Main Street, just two or three storefronts from the railroad tracks. One of their relatives, an engaging young man who worked in the market, suffered from epileptic "fits." Stories of these seizures held a morbid interest for the youngsters of town. My fascination came to an abrupt halt when I saw him fall to the sidewalk suffering one of the seizures. Another relative of the owners moved to Greenville, Mississippi, where he prospered as a pioneer in the large scale processing of chickens.

Fay Woods, who worked as a clerk at Adam's grocery store adjacent to the railroad track, was one of the town's most graceful athletes and he was ready to let it be known at the drop of a hat. He had come to town to play semi-pro baseball, as did a number of young men in the 1920s. A sort of roly-poly man, with a totally bald pate, somewhat of a show-off, Fay Woods claimed the spotlight each year when the skating rink came to town. People went to watch him glide around the portable hardwood floor, backward, forward, in graceful sweeps, bowing here and there, arms spread winglike. His admirers said he was for certain a professional skater.

Carl Davis owned and operated, with his mother, a shoe repair shop across from The Bradley Store. The fact that Carl had been badly crippled by polio as a youngster and wore heavy iron braces on his legs didn't keep him from earning a reputation as one of the town sports. He drove a big convertible automobile and flew his own airplane out of Griffin's pasture.

Some of the more adventurous young people went flying with him. Tragedy struck on a bright summer Sunday afternoon for Carl and the county sheriff's daughter, Mary Emma Hickman, one of the prettiest girls in town. She had just graduated from high school and was preparing to go away to college. Something failed, man or mechanics, as Carl's plane took off from the grass runway only to hurtle to the ground, instantly killing two of Warren's very popular young people.

oooooooooooooooo

Most of Warren's characters could be seen frequently at the local soda fountains, cafes and poolhalls.

The two places owned and operated by Wayne Wisener at different times were the epicenters for the social life of Warren. Wayne had acquired Glasgow's soda fountain and poolhall on the west side of Main Street across from the court square just prior to the beginning of World War II and ran it until he was called into the Army. After the war he bought the confectionery and poolhall Frank Culbertson had established between Hankins' Hardware and Ederington's store on the south side of the square.

I suppose we took the uniqueness of those places for granted, but it was the rare visitor to Warren who didn't go away talking about their ambience.

Where else could one find a poolhall separated from a soda fountains by only an unmarked line everyone understood to be anchored by a juke box and two or three pinball machines?

The poolhall was sedate when measured against the image of poolhalls of that day. Gambling was limited. No card games, no dominoes. There was some swearing, but it was drowned out by the laughter and hard kidding that winners heaped on losers.

The poolhall and the pinball machines were kept busy by a mixture of players—teenagers, old men, gentlemen, hustlers, full-time idlers, bosses from the sawmills, tradesmen, professionals, merchants and at least one member of the clergy. Women never played.

There was no more unlikely character to frequent the poolhall than Brother Bruce Boney. An aesthete, sparse in appearance and spartan in demeanor, with a degree from Princeton University, he was pastor of the First Presbyterian Church. He wore glasses with wire rims and a tentative smile. In the fall and winter he dressed in a severe black suit, complete with vest and a white shirt starched as stiff as a board, set off with a dark tie. A watch chain of gold, embellished with a Phi Beta Kappa key, adorned his midriff. His black shoes were always polished to a high sheen. In the heat of summer the somber winter suit was replaced by a white-with-blue pinstripe seersucker.

Somewhere along the way, perhaps at Princeton University, he had developed a lifelong passion for snooker and learned to play an accomplished game. His parishioners and the town took the strange idea of a preacher in the poolhall in stride. The consensus was that he needed some respite from the pressures of his pastoral duties and the demands of caring for a sickly wife.

Still, Brother Boney's arrivals at the poolhall caused something of a stir. The language was cleaned up and the noise dropped off a decibel or two when he came for his weekly session. He was always given a place at the table as soon as the game in progress came to an end. Out of respect for the pastor, the rules of the game were changed so that instead of the losers paying it was "Dutch treat."

After three or four games, Brother Boney shook hands around the table, carefully washed the cue powder and chalk from his hands, donned his suit coat and left as quietly as he had arrived.

Pool and snooker players performed before a gallery of spectators.

Seated in armed wooden chairs on a slightly raised platform along the wall the on-lookers reminded me of so many birds perching on a powerline. The regulars came early and stayed until they drifted home for lunch only to return at mid-afternoon to stay until suppertime. There often was a waiting line for seats on Saturdays.

Mr. Joiner was one of those regulars. He was of an uncertain age; we just knew he was elderly. Inevitably, he was known to one and all as Old Man Joiner. No one seemed to recall the last time he had been gainfully employed, other than occasionally to "rack" balls at the poolhall.

He regularly wore a full suit, frayed at the cuffs, and a high-collared white dress shirt, yellowed with age. Incongruously, he affected an accent somewhere between an Ivy League college and London when he made pronouncements on the skills of various pool players and other matters he considered to be important.

His whole image was one of dishevelment.

One of my friends, "Garmouth" Frazier, discovered the hard way that Old Man Joiner's eyesight was failing. The amenities of Wayne's poolhall were limited to a single urinal in a closet barely wide enough for one man to stand and lighted by a single lightbulb of no more than 40 watts hanging from the ceiling.

'Garmouth" had gone there to answer a call of nature. Unfortunately, the old man had the same calling at the same time. He, too, entered the closet to do his business. Unfortunately, he didn't see Frazier standing ahead of him and urinated down the back of his leg. The offended fellow called out, "Damn, old man, what are you doing?" His dignity always in place, "Old Man" Joiner went immediately to his affected accent to declare, "Ah, pissed upon you, didn't I, lad."

At least two regulars at snooker were qualified as professionals. They were also the best at playing the pinball machines.

By professional I mean they could beat the best of the competition for wagers ranging from a quarter in the corner pocket up to serious folding money. Both of them were also tops when it came to beating the pinball machines. It was a bad day for either one if they had to put more than two or three nickels in the machines to win enough games to play all day.

One of the pros was my boyhood friend, Jimmy "Sleek" Dowell, so named for his physique.

He was also quite a character beyond the poolhall. After we made it into high school, he had access to his mother's automobile, a black Ford vintage about 1938 or 1939. Almost every night, he drove with his friends around town, over and over on a fixed route anchored by the court square—up and down Main Street, over behind the high school and through the parking lot at The Topper, our in-town drive-in and beer joint, and out by Bill's drive-in. The mission was simple: see and be seen.

We would sometimes chip in to buy gas at about 25 or 30 cents a gallon, but mostly we were freeloaders. "Sleek" said he had a simple subterfuge by which he could mislead his mother about how many miles he was covering at night—simply drive in reverse so as not to roll over the speedometer.

One of his favorite stunts when driving the downtown streets at night when traffic was sparse was to make it appear that no one was steering the car. The trick was to attach his belt to the bottom of the steering wheel. He would then slide over toward the passengers side, reach over with his left leg to press the gas pedal and with his arm and hand out of sight, turn the steering wheel by pulling on the belt.

It was during these night hours that he spent a great deal of time and many gallons of gas trying to master another stunt. He vowed that some night he would start at the corner of the J. T. Ederington Store and make it all the way around the court square without moving the steering wheel. Such were the impossible challenges considered to be so important in those times.

"Rip" Johns, another of the snooker pros, was a roofer by trade, but his clear preference was for the games at Wayne's. The rumor was that he made a lot more money betting on his game when he left town for a month or two now and then than he did at his trade of roofing.

Harry Wilfong was another player good enough to be called a "shark" who appeared from time to time at Wayne's. The story was that he had gone away from Warren during the early days of the war to work in defense plants in California. He had saved enough money to come home and live what many of us thought was the ideal life.

His home was a fishing camp in the "big woods" in the Ouachita River bottoms in south Bradley County. There he trapped fur-bearing animals, hunted ducks, deer and squirrels, fished commercially and lived a solitary life. Wearing a ducksback coat, flannel shirts and knee-high boots he would appear in town from time to time to sell his furs, buy supplies and shoot a few games of snooker. His image as a frontiersman was enhanced by this silent, stoic façade.

Another of my friends qualified as a character because of his addiction to women. Rumor had it that he was so attracted to two particular women that he married and divorced one of them twice and married the other two or three times and divorced her once or twice before he reached thirty years of age.

I was a witness when he confirmed one of his marriages. It was the morning after he had invited several of us from our football team to a Saturday night fish fry his father was hosting. Beer was served out of a washtub full of ice, off the tailgate of a pickup truck to go with the fried catfish and hush puppies. In order to make it to the midnight movie, we high schoolers left just as the crap game got going and the pace of the party picked up.

I saw my friend the next morning at Wayne's soda fountain where I had stopped for a Coke after Sunday school. He called me aside and said, "I think I got married last night and I need you to go with me to her house to see if I did."

We got in his pickup truck and made a short nervous drive to her house. I stayed in the truck across the street while my friend knocked at the young lady's front door. She appeared in her chenille robe, looking somewhat the worse for wear. They talked intently for a few minutes before my friend returned to the truck. I asked, "Did you?" His response was to the point, "I did."

After a bit, he explained that they had been married by Justice of the Peace Baker in the men's room in the basement of courthouse.

Although slight of build and somewhat sickly by nature, he was a fiery competitor in sports of all kind. His support of our high school teams included his furnishing us with cigarettes from his father's grocery store.

When arthritis crippled him badly in later years, his upbeat attitude toward life never changed The legend of my friend was underscored when the story got out about his encounter at Wayne's with a local undertaker shortly before his death. He was making his way in the front door when he

117

turned to see one of the owners of Frazer's funeral home walking behind him. "Hell, John," he said, "you don't have to follow me around; they will call you when I die."

ooooooooooooooo

The soda fountain, just a few steps away from the poolhall, was an entirely different world.

There were booths mostly occupied by young people who came after school and on Saturday afternoons to laze away the hours, stretching a fountain Coke or maybe a milkshake beyond the last drop and stirring up their hormones with bouts of flirtation. Individual tables with wireback chairs, favored by adults, were set up around tables in the center of the black-and-white tile floor from near the front doors back to the entrance of the poolhall.

Other patrons sat swivel on stools mounted on pedestals at a marble-topped counter that ran from the booths almost to the two front doors. The soda fountain was stocked with the ingredients for a wide selection of concoctions—carbonated drinks, malted milks, cones and dishes of ice cream and ice cream sodas. Short orders of sandwiches, fried or scrambled eggs, French fries and bowls of chili were turned out with great efficiency and much chatter by the "soda skeets" at a griddle and over a gas jet.

A wide selection of magazines, from comics to pulps, was displayed along with newspapers on a rack that ran around the bottom of the plate glass windows at the front. There were usually people loitering about, browsing the publications. Every now and then Wayne or one of his helpers would call out, "Library closed." They had little lasting effect.

Curb service was available from three or four places marked off on the street at the front.

Sally Dixon and her mother, Annie Mack Courtney Johnston, two of Warren's wealthiest ladies, according to commonly accepted wisdom, were regulars for the drive-up service. The duo could be seen regularly driving around town in their luxury automobile. Mrs. Dixon, at the wheel, dressed as if she were on the way to high tea and made up with an extraordinary amounts of rouge, powder and all sorts of cosmetics. Her mother, a smallish lady who had suffered a stroke, rode beside her, looking at the same town scenes on every tour as if they were newly discovered.

The ladies ended their drive about four o'clock with a stop at Wayne's for their afternoon Cokes or ice cream cones and to watch townspeople come and go. Friends, young and old alike, would stop for a chat with them.

Sally Dixon's husband, Sam, was one of our local celebrities. An engineer with the state highway department, he had come to Warren with his family from West Virginia in the late 1920s to oversee the building of the North Steel Bridge. The gist of the gossip was that somewhere along the way Sam and Sally fell in love; his family left town; they were married.

Legend, true or false, further held that he had married the comely lady for her money so that he could start his own construction business which he did soon after their wedding. But the truth was that a substantial local businessman-banker had financed Mr. Dixon through one bankruptcy until he was on his feet and headed toward a highly lucrative career building highways and bridges, manufacturing hardwood flooring and serving as a director of a major bank in Little Rock.

Not surprisingly, Sam Dixon was one of our heroes. His mystique was enhanced by the fact that he was rarely seen around town. We heard that he gave a lot of money to the YMCA. He and his wife lived in her mother's home, an imposing two-story colonial house surrounded by huge Magnolia trees on Myrtle Street. As far as we knew, his social life was limited to attending the Sunday night movie with Mrs. Dixon. Even then, they contrived to arrive late, sit in the back of the theater and leave early.

Mr. Dixon looked the part of a dashing entrepreneur. A handsome man, he was thin and well dressed; he wore a neat, pencil thin moustache and slicked back hair. He was the first businessman any of us had heard of who flew his own airplane. In all he reminded one of the billionaire Howard Hughes.

oooooooooooooooo

Wayne's was a beehive of good fellowship, gossip, talk about sports and the latest jokes.

Some merchants and professional people, along with an assortment of insomniacs and loners who lived in rooming houses, came there soon after daybreak to eat their breakfast or at least drink a cup of coffee.

Owners and salespeople from uptown stores, lawyers, politicians and clerks from the courthouse, managers from the Bradley and Southern Lumber companies and full-time loafers crowded the counter and tables at mid-morning for their coffee break. Some took the occasion to play a game or two of pool.

There was bumper crowd at lunch time. I had the impression that having lunch at Wayne's was a distinction that set a few people apart from the majority of those who worked in town and brought their noon meal to work or walked home to eat.

Wayne's took on a different tone in the afternoons. It was then that some of the finest ladies, who were in town to shop, joined the mid-afternoon coffee-break regulars. Fountain Cokes were the drinks of choice. Some were flavored with cherry, lemon or vanilla. The ladies were not bothered by the games in the poolhall and at the pinball machines.

ooooooooooooooo

Wayne and his staff were regular catalysts that kept the cast of characters in a steady boil.

Wayne had two main men who ran the business over two shifts a day: Paul Whitaker and Jimmy Russell. We just sort of assumed that Paul was the lead soda skeet. We called him "Peanut." He was justly proud of having defeated a serious challenge from the bottle and was quick to chastise in a good natured way anyone who appeared to stray from the straight and narrow path. Garrulous, he kept up a constant flow of jibes, some as sharp and pointed as a pin, with customers of all ages, sexes and stations. He poked fun at himself and the business.

He had a standard offer for anyone who ordered a bowl of chili: "Suck it through a soda straw; if there's anything big enough to stick in the straw you get a second bowl for free."

Bill Love, publisher of the weekly *The Eagle Democrat* was one of "Peanut's" favorite targets. With Mr. Love at the counter, Paul delighted in announcing that the best way to get a good night's sleep was to "eat a bowl of corn flakes and read *The Eagle* just before going to bed." That way, he said, "you won't have anything on your brain or your stomach either to keep you awake."

It was the brave patron who chose to challenge "Peanut." One would-be wit set out to needle him in a loud voice about his lack of prowess as a lover. "Peanut's" response was quick and equally loud: "Damn, fellow, your wife tells you everything."

The other shift boss, Jimmy Russell, had a mouth just as fast as "Peanut," but he lacked his sharp wit. Jimmy's obsession was sports, a subject on which he held forth at great length.

His short, thin build at 130 pounds or a bit more did not suggest an athlete. Nevertheless, he let it be known that he had quite a record in baseball and other sports from his earlier days in nearby Monticello. Fact was he made up for his lack of physical attributes with a fierce competitiveness.

Jimmy apparently cared more about sports than he did his personal appearance. He had to have all of his teeth removed at an early age, but he doggedly refused to wear false ones. Someone said that Jimmy flapped his lips when he talked.

A cadre of youngsters completed the cast. Orville Arnold, a friend of mine with roots in our neighborhood always had a tale to tell about his latest romantic conquest. We never knew whether he was just creating these scenarios or whether he in fact was that irresistible to women. There was a Jones boy we knew as "Cigar," a nickname he had been assigned because someone unkindly declared that his nose looked like one. Wendell Gambill, who came to town from over near Possum Valley to finish high school, was a favorite of Wayne's. With a quick wit of his own, he was a ready straight man, for "Peanut" and Wayne. Jimmy, Wayne's son, an aggressive young fellow with his father's winning personality, was "skeeting" sodas by the time he could see over the counter.

Wayne had other regular employees. Several ladies came in to wait on tables. There was a "colored" boy to wash dishes, sweep up and haul out trash. Art Jones and Fowler Claytor ran the poolhall. It was ironic that both men were badly crippled—Mr. Jones by a stroke and Mr. Claytor by an extreme case of arthritis which turned his hands into gnarled clumps of exaggerated knuckles. They seldom moved fast enough to satisfy the players, who didn't hesitate to demand that the balls be "racked" immediately after they finished a game.

Wayne presided over this menagerie from his stand-up desk situated on the border between the poolhall and the confectionary. He would leave his managerial post to help fill orders when customers were backed up for service up front. He kept his extra operating money in a cigar box, secured in a large safe under his desk, until he found time to make a run to the bank.

A friendly, easy-going man, Wayne was still as tough as nails. He kept the big half end of a pool cue under his desk just in case anyone was foolish enough to challenge him as to who was in charge.

The Wayne Wisener I remember from our first meeting in the late 1930s was the same Wayne Wisener I knew at our last meeting. If you saw him once a day, or once a year, he was always the same. The conversation, the openheartedness and the warmth of friendship continued as if there had been no separation, no passage of time.

Life was not always easy for Wayne, but he never complained. When things did not go to suit him, he just worked harder with dignity and optimism.

Wayne was constant in his support of his friends, and many times strangers, who needed help. We were always certain that if we called on him from anywhere, at anytime, help would come. He would never question why help was needed; he would only ask what he could do.

He'd offer a word of encouragement, give a pat on the back or loan money to those in need. The loan might be a quarter to finance a movie date at the Pastime or really serious money to help someone bail out of a bad situation. His assistance might be a job, a good word, money for schoolbooks or decent clothes. Sometimes it was a free meal at his soda fountain. And his giving was without public notice and self-aggrandizement. At his wake, a young woman known to few of the other mourners told with tears in her eyes how Wayne had encouraged her to continue in high school, and provided the necessary money to buy clothes and books. She was but one of many who had better lives because of Wayne Wisener.

He told me that of all the thousands of dollars he had loaned out of his cash box, only one person had ever failed to pay him back. True to his fashion, he didn't reveal the name.

It was ironic in the extreme that Wayne died unexpectedly in late middle age, alone in his home.

ooooooooooooooo

Warren in those times was a typical town in at least one regard—gossip was a mainstay of life. In fact, it seemed to be the chosen avocation of most folks.

Few admitted they participated, but the fact was that everyone, men and women of all ages and on all rungs of the social ladder, engaged in the lively art of spreading rumors and talking about the doings of their neighbors as well as of the people across town.

The content of gossip has changed since those days. Conduct accepted now without a turn of the head was high-octane fuel for the gossip mill in those days. Now the President of the United States can act in the most sordid of ways, even in the Oval Office, and still receive a majority approval rating.

Most people my age well remember that Ingrid Bergman's career took a nosedive when she became pregnant with her Italian lover's child while she was still married to another man.

Gossip always had a sharp edge to it, although most of the gossipers adapted a pious air as they expressed their regret at having to pass along bad news. The providers of the latest stories sat for the moment in the catbird seat, cluck, clucking away in faux sympathy while decrying the fate of their fellowman. "What will the world come to?" they sighed.

The gossip might well have had some basis in facts. But those facts were almost always embellished upon, colored and shaped in versions altered by the teller's vivid imagination, misunderstandings and even meanness. No one seemed to take the time to question how the gossipers knew in detail what actually happened between two people when there were no uninvolved witnesses.

Such was the case with a juicy bit of gossip about a torrid affair between the wife of a local attorney and a small business operator.

It was widely recognized that the two couples had a close friendship, which some speculated might have gone beyond the borders of propriety. The gossip raced through town that the affair had come to an end when the attorney invited the suspected lover to "come go for a ride with me." Once out of town and on a country road, the attorney supposedly picked up his hat from the seat between him and his former friend to reveal a pistol. Without touching the weapon, he suggested that it was time for the man to leave town.

Who knew whether this story was true? All that the town really knew was that the merchant sold his business and left town with his own wife soon after the story surfaced.

ooooooooooooooo

Rumors about pregnancies among the unwed were prime fodder for gossip.

The gossip mill ran at full blast for days over the disappearance of a prominent young couple in town. Fired by the speculation, posses were formed to search for them. Some said that the young man and woman had run off to get married and were afraid to come home to face their parents. Others reported that the girl had been taken to the insane asylum. The more aggressive gossips "knew for a fact" that the girl had been sent away to live with a relative in California to have a baby out of wedlock. Further, it was said, that the young man had been paid off by her parents to leave town. The baby would be adopted by the aunt up north. There was even talk of kidnapping.

The gruesome truth was soon revealed. The lovers were found dead in their car parked on a woods road near the Airport Inn. The sheriff ruled that it was murder and suicide by shots fired from a pistol found in the young man's hand. A note left behind explained that the girl was pregnant and that she and her lover could not face the shame.

ooooooooooooooo

Gossip often started with outsiders who came to town.

We woke on a late summer morning in 1941 to the incredible sight of Army troops riding what seemed like an endless parade of military vehicles going by our house. The soldiers, bivouacked just outside of town, were on the historic Louisiana maneuvers that everyone understood were preparatory to the coming war.

There was much excitement, especially when the soldiers came into town on passes. A lot of jealousies flared when they flirted with the young ladies who were permitted by their parents to venture up to Glasgow's soda fountain.

The gossips predicted that "no good will come of this." And they were right. Still, the town could hardly believe it when a report circulated that one of the soldiers had been shot dead as he tried to climb through the window of a young lady's bedroom.

Feelings ran high in town about the "invasion" of the troops. After all "Nobody invited them; and to make matters worse, most of them are from up North," many of the city fathers declared, but merchants were pleased to take in the unexpected influx of cash the soldiers spent.

The father of the invaded home, showing a great deal of outrage and no little bravado, held that he was "just defending my daughter and my house, like any man would do." The legal proceedings, held within the next few days, were over in short order. No charges were brought against the father. He was ruled to have been acting in self-defense. The gossipers had a field day speculating as to why the soldier had come to the house.

Of course, top-of-the-line sensations such as that did not come along every day. But there was an endless stream of stories about young couples getting "just too familiar." These stories usually concluded with the conveyors of the tale declaring, "Well, there's one thing about it. When they get married there won't be anything new but the licenses." Or they might say, "That's the worse thing I ever heard of out from under the bed sheets."

oooooooooooooooo

There was gossip to spare about the lady who lived up the alley in front of our house who was "kept" by her lover, a man she had married and divorced twice, and other men.

Uncle Jewell was one of her "friends."

Another woman who lived nearby was said to be the mistress of a man who made a home with his wife and children across town near the Bradley mill. Most days his car was parked in front of his alleged lover's house. Her children were always playing outside when he was there. My mother ordered me to steer clear of the house.

Even as youngsters we knew and talked about—as did the adults—the rumor that various merchants were "ladies' men." The gossips "knew" that one of the more prominent merchants maintained a lady friend in her own house. The story was that when he closed his store at the end of the day he went directly to his lover's home, ate supper with her, visited awhile and then went on home to his regular family.

It seemed strange that preachers were often hot subjects for the gossip mill. Perhaps it was the irony of a man of the cloth having feet of clay. Maybe it was the drama of a woman seeking solace in the church and finding it in the arms of the pastor. Or it could have been the unadmitted attractiveness of sins of the flesh.

People in Warren were shocked when a local preacher resigned along with his secretary. Both left town. He was an intense, nearly handsome man. His demeanor, which was marked by severe piousness, was unsettling, particularly to the young people in the church. The secretary was not what anyone would describe as a "siren."

The gossipers reported that the preacher's wife found a letter on her husband's desk from the young secretary declaring that their love affair, which she reminded him had been a lusty one, had no future. She was leaving Warren, she said, so that he could further his ministry, which she assured him would right itself and enable him to continue the work of The Lord even more successfully, without the diversion of their passion.

A few months later the story resurfaced with the news that the preacher had divorced his wife and that the lovers had gotten married.

ooooooooooooooo

Much to Mama's chagrin, one of our distant relatives regularly provided grist for the gossip mill.

Hollywood handsome, Fay was given to dressing like a gentleman of leisure. One of his favorite costumes (and I think he thought of his clothing as just that) was comprised of highly polished riding boots and jodhpurs, topped off with a tweed jacket and a rakish felt hat, complete with feather. He rarely held a regular job, but when he did work it was as a land surveyor. It was said that the ladies provided him with spending money and otherwise took care of him in return for his favors.

Fay eventually married a lady who lived in a small town in the southwestern part of the state where he had worked at one of his occasional jobs. People marveled that she had captured such a handsome playboy. It was not surprising that she held a job that paid a nice salary.

It was said that Fay continued to play the field. He favored an unmarried lady who worked as a clerk in a local store for his extracurricular meanderings. The daughter of a prominent professional family, she had reached the stage of being referred to as an old maid.

"She's old enough to know better, she should be ashamed, but she can't help it," the gossipers declared. Despite his wife's repeated warnings, Fay continued to see his favored paramour. The gossips said no one should be surprised, least of all his wife, who must have seen what she was getting into when she married the man with the roving eye.

Fay and his wife were back in Warren visiting his widowed father. The story was that after Saturday night supper, he told his wife and his father that he had to run uptown to get a package of cigarettes. He didn't make it home by bedtime.

He pulled in the driveway in the wee hours of the morning, loaded to the gills with strong drink. When he awoke the next morning, no doubt his first thought was that he had gotten by with his dalliance. But his delusion of safety quickly came to an end when he looked up to see his wife towering over his bed, holding a ladies silk undergarment. She declared that she had found the evidence in the backseat of Fay's car and that they were not hers.

She made her errant husband get up and follow her out into the backyard where she proceeded to pour acid on the incriminating lingerie.

"Now," she ordered, "take these back to that hussy. Then come straight back here. We are going home."

Fay and his wife left Warren before sundown. The other woman was back at her sales job on Monday. The gossips said she was "as cool as a cucumber." Some said she was heartbroken; others said she was brazen.

The gossip was all over town. Anyone who stopped to think about it must have wondered how the story got out, since only Fay and his enraged wife were there when the matter came to a head.

oooooooooooooooo

Warren was known to harbor one homosexual, although given the statistics in such matters, there must have been others hidden deep in the closets of the town.

Despite much talk about what he had done and what he might do, Mr. X. was accepted in his church and the community. The small grocery store he operated with his twin brother prospered, although things did begin to come apart for him and his family when he was sent away to prison for the second time for molesting a young man.

He was a "groupie" who hung around our athletic teams at the YMCA and high school. We boys talked about him among ourselves. We knew to avoid being alone with him for fear of his flirtations and the gossip that might get started.

Still, there were a few boys who were willing to work at his store and drive his car. It was assumed they paid a price.

Mr. X. could always be counted on to haul us back and forth to out-of-town ball games in his car. He was known to let his hand wander a bit when he was manipulating the gearshift on the floor. It must have been obvious to him that we fought among ourselves to avoid sitting next to him.

It was my mother who took it upon herself to warn me from time to time to be careful around Mr. X.

"Ramon, I don't want you to ever get in the car with him alone," she declared. "And don't sit next to him when he drives on the ball trips."

It was cruel on my part, but I thought it was fun to tease her by asking for an explanation as to why I should avoid Mr. X. She'd close the conversation by simply declaring, "Because I said so."

oooooooooooooo

There was always plenty to gossip about some of it was amusing, some of it was tragic.

There were at least two middle-aged bachelors in town who put a different spin on gossip. They encouraged stories about themselves so as to create their own legends as Lotharios.

One of the young swains went to great lengths to execute his strategy. He made a point to be seen driving around town almost every night in his sporty convertible. Before the night was over his automobile could be seen at the Airport Inn and later at The Topper. Then he dropped by Waynes's soda fountain for a Coke and a sandwich before going home alone. He was always alone. We high school boys thought he was just about as suave as it was possible for a man to be. Kidding him about his romantic life and pleading for juicy details provided us with vicarious delights. He simply suggested that while he would like to tell us all, he was too much of a gentleman to kiss and tell.

We were left to speculate. It was not until years later that I figured out that he had little or no love life and that his thrills came from fabricating and acting out his legend.

Although verification seemed scanty, it was reported that just before daylight on a Sunday morning the son of a prominent official of The Bradley and a mill employee had had an unlikely automobile accident on Main Street at the courthouse intersection. One car was headed south and the other steered north on the otherwise deserted street. Somehow they managed to have a head-on collision. Neither man was hurt, but the street was littered with beer bottles thrown clear with the impact. Considering the identify of one of the participants in the bizarre event, the night marshal told them to clean up the mess, go home, sleep it off and be more careful in the future.

There were frequent stories of drunken husbands staggering into the wrong homes after a Saturday afternoon and night of drinking on Main Street.

The gossip mill was fed by reports that a young girl had been molested by a local businessman who left town. Two sons were alleged to have killed their abusive father. Husbands were convicted in the court of gossip for beating their wives and letting their children go hungry. Members of the "floating" crap game that moved from location to location in the woods around town were said to have been robbed by bandits who swept through town.

Few people were immune from the machinations of the busy gossip mill. Young people, adults, married, single, everyone seemed to participate as a purveyor or a target. With or without cause, reputations of some girls in high school were tarnished by gossip that they were "loose." It seemed to make little difference that sometimes the gossip was true, sometimes it was false. Frequently the talk was no more than benign chatter to fill idle minds. Other times it was malicious and destructive of reputations.

One thing was absolutely true. No one ever gossiped about the secret virtues of other people or good news of any sort.

Warren may not have been Shangrila, but we were blessed to have grown up in such a community of caring and very human people who left us with colorful memories as they enriched our lives.

# *SCARS FROM THE GREAT DEPRESSION*

I was a mere slip of a boy when the Great Depression hit and only in my pre-teens when it began to end as the country started to gear up for the Second World War. No one I have ever known who lived through those times survived the experience without suffering scars that they bore all of their life.

It was not until years later that we could comprehend the extent of the crisis for the nation and the lifelong impact that our own experiences would have on our thinking about virtually every issue from the way we raise our children to how we cast our ballots. The crisis and its resolution set our country on a course of government involvement in our personal lives that defines the political and social structure of our nation today. Certainly, we who remember have a different view of the meaning of security than do those who have lived only in the mostly good times since then.

The Depression was the subject of constant discussion and worry in the home where I was growing up. My parents didn't spare me from the facts and their fears. They couldn't have. Signs of poverty were everywhere, casting a pervasive dark cloud over all of us. We knew deep in our bones that we were living on the ragged edge of a disaster.

Most people in Warren worried about the Great Depression in micro-terms—the impact on their families, their neighbors and their town. The personal effects were measured in such immediate concerns as scrounging for work, putting meals on the table, scraping up money to make payments on the house to save it from foreclosure and to pay the bills so the lights and water wouldn't be cut off, putting do-it-yourself half-soles on a pair of shoes, patching clothes to get another few months of wear out of them.

ooooooooooooooo

The floodgates of misery opened on "Black Monday," October 29, 1929, when the stock market crashed. At year-end, the government reported that the stock collapse had cost investors $40 billion. Even then things stayed on a fairly even keel for the next few months. Some said the crisis would pass.

But banks across the country continued to fail—about 3,500 of them before it was over—crippling the economic backbone of the country. In 1930 and 1931, some 54,000 businesses closed their doors. One-fourth of the workforce was unemployed. About the only people who managed to get along in relatively good shape were those who had "old money" from their families and those who held public office, such as the postmaster, county and city officials and those working under them.

Lines began to form outside the "soup kitchens" where the hungry could get a free meal. Former bankers were selling apples on the street corners of New York City. Hobos, riding the rails seeking change and hope, showed up at backdoors begging for food.

An army of 20,000 men calling themselves The Bonus Expeditionary Force descended on Washington, D. C. Their announced mission was to get early payment of the bonuses of $1.00 a day they had been promised for their service in World War I. Hoover and the Congress refused to hear their plea. The president insisted that "good times are just around the corner." When the force would not disband and go home as ordered, they were routed with tear gas by U. S. Army troops.

It was about this time that 3,000 factory workers marched on Ford Motor Company's plant in Dearborn, Michigan. Henry Ford's private police force turned back the crowd, leaving four protestors dead and some 60 wounded.

Five hundred people in nearby England, Arkansas rioted in a demand for food. "We are not beggars," the rioters shouted at the mayor and sheriff who tried to send them home. "We are willing to work for fifty cents a day, but we're not going to let our families starve."

ooooooooooooooo

The country was teetering on the edge of anarchy as it approached the presidential election of 1932.

People talked about President Herbert Hoover, the sitting president, as if he was the devil incarnate.

Many blamed him for causing the depression by being in bed with the "Wall Street gang." The stiff and standoffish president, who was always seen dressed in a dark suit and high starched collar, demonstrated his lack of understanding and sensitivity when he declared: "What the country needs is a good big laugh. There seems to be a condition of hysteria. If someone could get off a good joke every ten days I think our troubles would be over." He couldn't have done more to enrage people if he had tried.

The grown-ups talked about Hoover's challenger, a man with the strange name of Roosevelt. Some said that with such a strange name he had to be a Jew or a foreigner of some kind. They said he was running for president against the much-despised Hoover.

We saw photographs of Roosevelt in various poses—sitting in front of a radio microphone delivering a "fireside chat," or waving to the crowds from the caboose of a campaign train or riding in a big convertible. There was a father-like look in his wide-open smile that made his friendly, cheerful demeanor totally believable. But we didn't know he was bound in heavy leg braces, crippled by polio.

We went to my uncle's house next door to listen to his radio carrying Roosevelt's encouraging promises. They were delivered in a voice of buoyancy and self-confidence that left no doubt he would save the country.

Roosevelt advocated an agenda of radical ideas. Some people said he was a socialist. In any case, he was a symbol of hope to most people that we knew. He was elected overwhelmingly by a frightened and discouraged people who would have voted for Satan himself if he offered a way out of their misery. We never knew anyone personally who voted against FDR. It may well have been an exaggeration, but we only heard of one or two families in Warren who belonged to the dreaded Republican Party.

In his inaugural address Roosevelt declared, "The only thing we have to fear is fear itself—nameless, unreasoning, unjustified terror which paralyzes efforts to convert retreat into advance." And the people believed him. They were happy with the country's choice. All the same I remember some apprehensive talk. Would he move too far too fast?

Things began to happen immediately after the election. Congress granted to him "broad executive power to wage a war against this emergency as great as the power that would be given to him if we were in fact invaded by a foreign foe."

Once he took office he launched a blizzard of initiatives, generally known as the New Deal. Many of these programs were thought to be radical in the context of the times.

The Works Progress Administration (WPA) employed an average of 2,000,000 men annually from 1935 to 1941. Its mission was to provide jobs on public-works projects for out-of-work persons while improving the infrastructure of the country. They erected post offices, schools and all sorts of public buildings.

At about the same time between 1933 and 1942, another 2,000,000 young men were provided with employment in the Civilian Conservation Corps (CCC). They conserved and developed natural resources through such activities as building roads and bridges in rural areas, planting trees, creating parks and fighting forest fires.

The Tennessee Valley Authority came into being. It brought a vast supply of electric power, flood control and work for thousands to the hillbilly country of eastern Tennessee and turned it into one of the soundest financial regions of the country.

There was talk later that the gigantic public works program could have come to Arkansas had not the state's congressional delegation struck a cozy political deal with the Arkansas Power and Light Company to keep it out of the state in order to protect the power monopoly held by the company. Such actions consigned Arkansas to the economic cellar of the nation.

ooooooooooooooo

People in some parts of the country were singing, "Happy Days Are Here Again." Many pundits were saying the New Deal saved the country from collapse and anarchy.

Still there were pockets of apprehension, fear and even hatred. Was Roosevelt moving too fast? Was it all a plot to overthrow democracy? Many businessmen, the landed gentry and those with "old family" money spoke darkly of impending Communism. Many well-to-do citizens were horrified that the federal government was borrowing incredible amounts of money to finance the New Deal. Total financial collapse was just around the corner, in their opinion.

We heard a lot about Huey "The Kingfish" Long, U.S. Senator from Louisiana. Some people from Warren drove over to Fordyce to hear him speak about his scheme to confiscate all estates over $1 million and redivide the money in a Share-The-Wealth Club. He said that way everyone in America would own a home, a car and a radio, along with a guaranteed $2,500 income per year.

Father Charles Coughlin, a Catholic cleric from Detroit, declared to some 40 million listeners on CBS radio that Roosevelt was a "betrayer" and a "liar."

ooooooooooooooo

When the country prospered during the late 1920s and early months of the 1930s my father held what were up to that point the best jobs of his life.

He was the "third sawyer" behind the lead men, the brothers Charlie and Wiley O'Rear, at the Arkansas Lumber Company. It was to be a point of pride with our family when my father appeared in a group picture taken at a dinner for the top employees of "The Arkansas," as it was known.

But then a catastrophe came into our lives. "The Arkansas" had begun logging its 80,000 of acres of prime south Arkansas timberland in the early days of the 1900s. No thought was given to selective harvesting; it was logging for immediate profit. Cut everything in sight that was big enough to be processed into lumber. Only the visionaries among the lumber companies gave any thought to selective cutting and reforestation. The result was inevitable. By 1928, the company had "cut out," which is to say it had removed all of the merchantable timber from its land. The Bradley and

Southern lumber companies and a few other big interests owned most of the remaining merchantable timber left in and around Bradley County. There were scattered small stands of timber on private lands, but "Tree Farmers" didn't exist. There was no steady supply of timber to keep The Arkansas running. The owners had no choice; they shut down. My father, along with several hundred others, was out of a job.

Fortunately, my father soon got an offer for an even better job with the Fordyce Lumber Company. He could become one of the two lead sawyers. It must have been the kind job he had always wanted.

It was a time of mixed and traumatic emotions in our home.

My father now had his big opportunity to have a home of his own for the first time in his life. But my mother was being asked to move 30 miles away from the house in which she grew up and her mother and two of her brothers. She would be taking me out of the family nest where I was, as they said, "spoiled rotten." At the same time, my father would be leaving his mother and brothers and sisters who lived just across town, as they always had.

Despite the family trauma, reason prevailed and we moved to Fordyce.

With the new job our family enjoyed a level of prosperity and independence we had never known before. My mother and father owned their first and only automobile. It was a tan Model A Ford roadster. It is revealing of my mother's personality and of the relationship between my parents that my mother learned to drive the car. That was somewhat rare for those days, when men were the bosses at home and in all such matters. I don't recall ever seeing my father behind the wheel. I don't know whether he never learned to drive or they decided it was better for my mother to do the driving.

We rented a house in Fordyce near the railroad track that ran to the mill. I can remember the fascinating sound of the train chugging by with its load of huge logs taken from the virgin forest.

None of the Warren relatives ever came to visit us. However, my mother and I went back "home" many times. She drove the Model A Roadster over the sparsely traveled gravel road down through New Edinburgh to Warren. It was a joyous time for me. I remember that as we drove out of Fordyce on one of our trips to Warren I saw people in another automobile laughing and having a good time. I told my mother that they must be going to Warren to see their grandmother.

My parents and I took the only trip just the three of us ever made together. We drove some 60 or 70 miles from Fordyce over to Hot Springs for a weekend. We stayed overnight in a tourist cottage. The highlight was a visit to the alligator farm.

When "the crash" came and plunged the country into the Great Depression, the market for lumber all but evaporated. It followed that my father lost his job at the Fordyce Lumber Company. We had no choice but to return to Warren to live again under my grandmother's roof.

My mother and father had tried to fly away, but they came home with their wings clipped. I don't recall that my father ever mentioned the experience. However, my parents must have felt a great sense of defeat. That feeling was no doubt symbolically underscored when they soon had to sell their few shares of American Telephone and Telegraph stock, the only equities they ever owned.

oooooooooooooooo

I cannot think of anything more indicative of the desperation that our family felt than the time my father tried to sell furniture polish door-to-door.

One of my father's brothers-in-law, Thomas Murry, was producing furniture polish in his garage. Mr. Murry said that housewives were clamoring to buy all he could turn out. No selling was required, he insisted; a salesman simply made the product available door-to-door and it sold like hotcakes.

From the vantage point of later years it was clear that selling furniture polish door-to-door to housewives, most of whom were more worried about feeding their families than they were about keeping a shine on their furniture, was about the last thing my father could do, given his introverted personality.

He must have hated the idea, but no opportunity to earn money could be overlooked. I imagine that my mother, an outgoing person who had some experience at selling from her days of working at retail stores in town, must have urged that they give the venture a try.

My mother and father launched the sales campaign in a most unlikely way. We loaded up in the Model A and drove to Greenville, Mississippi. We crossed the Mississippi River on a ferry. It seemed as if we were on the water for hours, but of course we weren't.

Our stay in Greenville was short, no longer than one day and one night in a tourist court. My mother and I waited in the car, watching my father go door-to-door. He spent only a few minutes at each stop. I can't imagine that he was very aggressive with his sales pitches. After knocking on doors all day, he had not sold a single bottle of polish. I have never been able to fully comprehend the sense of failure and humiliation my parents must have felt.

(With so many men out of their regular jobs, door-to-door selling was a popular form of merchandising during the depression years. Oscar Haygood sold life insurance that way, then made personal visits to collect the premiums. In our case, he took in a nickel a week on a policy for a thousand dollars that was to send me to college. My family had to cash in the policy. A thousand dollars wouldn't have made much difference anyway when I went to college in the late 1940s. Others came calling trying to sell cookware, cure-all medicine, world books and vacuum cleaners.)

ooooooooooooooo

One of the most visible signs of the hard times was the almost daily occurrence of men stopping at our back door to ask for food in return for any work they could do around the place.

They were the hobos, men riding the rails and wandering on foot across the country, looking for work and escape from the grinding poverty.

The hobos came in all varieties. Most of them were relatively clean. They were humbled. Some were obviously embarrassed by their circumstances. These lost men did not cause any trouble. They insisted that they wanted to earn their handouts, but with my father and uncle out of work and with not much to do but putter around the house and yard, there was little need for extra hands.

We seemed to get more of the hobos at our house than did the neighbors. The word got out that the drifters had placed a secret mark on the homes where a man had a good chance of getting food. True, my mother never turned anyone away. Uncle Jewell and I searched the front of our house and the sidewalk for the mark but we could never find it.

The memory of one man in particular remains with me. He was slight of stature and meek in demeanor. His snow white shoulder-length hair, neatly combed, was a rare sight in those days. His clothes were neat and clean, although tattered. While my mother fixed something for him to eat he sat and talked with me on the side porch. I wish I could remember what he told me. But I do recall there was something profoundly different about him, the way he spoke in a calming tone.

When my mother brought the food, which was probably a plate of beans and fatback with cornbread and molasses, we sat in silence for awhile. He ate hungrily, but with dignity. When he finished his food, he offered again to work around the yard. When my mother told him there was nothing for him to do he left as quietly as he had come.

There was something different about our house after he left. I asked my mother if he could have been Jesus. She said that he might have been.

A short time later we had an experience of a totally different kind when a black youth, probably 16 or 17 years of age, came asking for food.

He was the very definition of politeness, ready to work for food, quick with the "yes, mam" and "yes, sir," neat in appearance. My mother responded as she always did. She fixed a sack of food—cornbread with molasses and fatback.

Uncle Jewell sat on the backporch watching all of this. He declared he was suspicious of the boy so we followed him at a distance as he hurried around the house with his sack of food. The youngster walked across the street where he stopped and began pawing through the sack. Instead of eating what he had been given he was throwing it away. He must have hoped for fancier fare.

My uncle dashed back in the house, grabbed up his automatic shotgun, charged out the front door and ran after the boy, "cussing" at the top of his lungs and firing his gun in the air. I have yet to see anyone run as fast as that young fellow did.

I later heard my mother and uncle reason that the boy had been looking for "sweets." He dumped the ordinary food, scarce as it was, when he was disappointed.

ooooooooooooooo

Finally, President Roosevelt's recovery programs began to make their presence felt in Warren.

The Work Projects Administration (WPA) was one of the most notable of them because it not only provided jobs, it made Warren a better place in which to live.

Local laborers on the WPA constructed a new high school building on Pine Street in 1932. A new post office at the corner of Main and Church Streets was finished in 1935.

Men in another of FDR's programs were set to work growing garden vegetables to feed themselves and their families and to be distributed to the most needy who could not work. People around town provided plots to be cultivated in return for some of the food. The remainder was sent to community canning "plants" to be processed and stored by men like my father and Uncle Jewell for use during the winter months.

One of the most memorable sights of those days occurred on small piece of our unturned land situated behind our house.

Standing on our back porch we watched men hitched to harnesses like horses so they could pull plows to break up the rough ground.

My mother said it was terrible to make men work like animals.

(This sorry episode was recalled vividly for me in the 1990s when Carole Moseley Braun, the U. S. Senator from Illinois, rose on the floor of the Senate to declare that it was socialistic to expect residents of public housing to clean up trash around their homes in return for food stamps and other public assistance.)

There were a number of WPA projects under way out beyond our house on the graveled road to Wilmar and Monticello.

There is a snapshot in my mind as clear now as it was when it was imprinted there those many years ago.

It was an early hour on a clear, bitterly cold day. I was looking out the window from our front room, watching men walking by on their way to work. They were a solemn lot, trudging along in groups of three and four. Most wore overalls. The heads of some were covered with felt dress hats that had seen better days; others wore wool or duckback caps. Few had gloves. They had on an endless variety of bedraggled jackets, suitcoats, sweaters and worn-out overcoats.

A bareheaded man walked alone at the end of the procession. He wasn't wearing a jacket. Instead, he wore what looked like a denim shirt with the sleeves rolled up. The cold had turned his arms and face various hues of red, white and a grayish blue. I asked my mother why he wasn't wearing a jacket and why he had his sleeves rolled up. He was not wearing a jacket, she said, because he didn't have one and that his sleeves were rolled up because he didn't want to admit that he was cold.

It was only a few weeks later that my understanding of his embarrassment was greatly enhanced.

I was walking to school on another cold and miserable day. I was bundled up warmly enough, but I wasn't wearing gloves. Just as I reached the corner of Main and East Church Streets, I encountered one of my teachers, Miss McKimmey. She saw my bare hands as red and dry as beets fresh out of the ground. No doubt with the best of intentions she asked with a great show of sympathy, "Don't you have any gloves?"

147

I don't remember my answer, because I don't know to this day why I wasn't wearing gloves. Was it because I didn't have any or that I didn't want to wear them?

I do remember running away from the teacher, embarrassed almost to tears.

My mother was furious when I told her about the incident. The next day I wore brown cotton gloves to school.

We saw a great deal of the Civilian Conservation Corps (CCC) around Warren. In fact, we had two encampments. One was several miles south of town on the Hermitage highway; the other was located just beyond the site of the Southern Lumber Company where the city park is now located. The men came into town dressed in their khaki uniforms. The young men, most of whom seemed well-mannered, were particularly welcomed by the operators of the soda fountains, beer joints and other establishments because they had a bit of pocket change to spend, even after sending money home to their needy families. Many of the town's mothers were less happy. They were afraid their daughters would become involved with these boys from out of town, especially since they were obviously from poor backgrounds.

As the threat of war began to heat up, many of the men began to leave the CCC to take jobs in the shipyards and other defense industries. Others volunteered for the armed forces, where their CCC training stood them in good stead.

By the time the CCC was terminated in 1942, some of them had married Warren girls and our town had become home for them.

ooooooooooooooo

By 1935, nearly one-half of the families on relief in Bradley County had been dropped from the public works rolls to, as one newspaper put it, "to work out their own salvation."

Still, the Depression hung on. The economy as a whole was not much better than it was when Roosevelt took office in 1933.

When FDR was reelected in a landslide in 1936 he declared that he was "presiding over a nation where one out of three people are "ill-housed, ill-clad" and "ill-nourished." About 15 percent of the work force—some 10 million people—was still out of work.

Able-bodied men in Warren were desperate to find work where no opportunities existed. Decent food and respectable clothing were not available to hordes of people.

One farmer calculated that he worked for 25 cents per day.

The common wage at the Bradley Lumber Company brought in $9.60 a week.

However, these wages, as pitiful as they were, fall into perspective when we look at the newspaper advertisements of the day. J. T. Ederington Company offered men's work shirts at 55 cents each; work pants were $1.29. Lard could be bought for 98 cents per six-pound bucket. Six ounces of snuff cost 30 cents.

A pound jar of peanut butter sold for 19 cents. It was not homogenized, which meant that an inch or two of pure peanut oil stood at the top of each jar. The challenge was to be sure that all the oil got mixed into the peanut paste. The Bradley Store was proud to sell ladies hats from 98 cents to "$1.95 and up." Blankenship Motor Company offered Ford V-8 for $495 and up.

A column in *The Eagle Democrat* cautioned against any idea that prosperity had returned as if any reminder was necessary. Along about that

149

time, another column concluded that the social security program being discussed in Congress would put the country on the road to socialism or maybe even fascism.

ooooooooooooooo

My father and uncle got up before daylight to go over to the sawmill where they joined the long lines of men waiting there, hoping they would get work for the day.

More often than not they came back home at mid-morning. They were subdued, silent with the burden of rejection and worry.

We began to hear the grown-ups talking about labor unions and the threat of strikes.

There were stories about how owners and managers used brute force to resist the efforts to organize the work force into unions. Other forms of intimidation were used such as firing those leading the campaigns and even closing factories.

Workers fought back with a new strategy known as "sit-down" strikes. The number of union members increased quickly across the nation.

Warren was not to escape the trauma of unionization.

The July 25, 1935 issue of *The Eagle Democrat* reported that a meeting had been held at the courthouse to discuss the formation of a union by the Lumber and Sawmill Workers Local of the United Carpenters and Joiners of America.

R. W. Fullerton, head of the Bradley Lumber Company, issued a statement to *The Eagle* in which he explained that the minimum wage would be raised to $12.00 per week from the existing $9.60. Each man would be allowed to work fewer hours in a week so that more men could earn some money.

The company fired a number of workers who were leaders in the organizing effort. Representatives of the National Labor Relations Board, only recently created by Congress, showed up to investigate the situation.

The Bradley Lumber Company's operation was shut down by a strike in mid-summer of 1935, worsening the already dreadful economic conditions in Warren.

We began to hear scattered reports of violence in town. There were tales of strong-arm enforcers being brought in by the company. At the same time, officials of The Bradley charged that outsiders were disrupting the peace and tranquility of the town. They were, of course, referring to union organizers.

Local law enforcement officers were said to be under the control of the company. On the other hand, a black man who did some yard work for my Uncle Claude Greenwood, a member of middle management at The Bradley, was beaten by men sympathetic to the unionizing effort and warned never to go near my uncle's house again.

The Fullerton families went away to their vacation homes in Florida. They were reported to have said they'd just as soon stay in Florida; furthermore, they didn't care whether the mill ever operated again.

Finally, under strong pressure from the National Labor Relations Board, and facing up to the toll the strike was taking on their pocketbooks and those of merchants who saw their businesses crashing, the owners capitulated and the union was accepted. The strike ended in mid-September and the mill resumed operations in Warren. Other, smaller sawmills in the region that provided The Bradley with rough pine and hardwood lumber were able to go back to work.

Feelings were still strong on both sides. Work continued to be scarce. The Depression persisted in and around Warren. In retrospect it is remarkable that the wounds between the owners and managers of the mill and in the community of workers healed as quickly as they did.

ooooooooooooooo

There was a lot of discussion in our home about bad luck dogging the family.

That dire outlook was fulfilled when Uncle Jewell missed winning the jackpot at the Pastime Theater.

The Wharton family, owners of the Pastime, sponsored a once-a-week sell-out attraction known as "Bank Night." People became eligible for the cash prize when they bought a ticket on Tuesday night and showed up for the drawing right after the movie. If the person whose name was drawn was not there with a ticket stub in hand the prize money was left in the jackpot and increased by perhaps five or ten dollars each week until there was a winner.

I think the tickets were 25 cents each. Uncle Jewell was a regular. He would go to town and sit with his cronies around The "Tree of Knowledge" on the court square, then amble over to the theater just before the movie ended to buy his ticket. A large crowd gathered in the street in front of the theater, waiting with high excitement for the drawing of the wining number.

What my family thought of as the dark hand of fate intruded in our lives one of those Tuesday nights. Uncle Jewell was suffering from a painful boil on his backside. It was so bad that he didn't feel like walking uptown for Bank Night.

Soon after nine o'clock someone from the neighborhood came by our house to deliver the dreadful news. Uncle Jewell's name had been drawn. The pot was $85.00. But for the curse of the carbuncle he would have won an enormous amount of money.

My mother cried as if her heart would break. My grandmother sat stoically as if bad news was nothing new to her. She declared that he never should have signed up for the drawings. My father had nothing to say; this was just the latest visitation of misfortune. Uncle Jewell swore worse than any sailor ever had. I was sad for a time because everyone else was.

Neighbors stopped by the next day to express their sympathy as if a death had occurred in the family. My mother was to say for the remainder of her life, "I never won anything."

ooooooooooooooo

Finally, as the country prepared to get involved in the war already raging in Europe and the Far East, the economy began to change for the better in Warren and the world looked bigger and more promising.

As if to underscore the globalization of our concerns and opportunities, The Bradley became a prime supplier of hickory stock that would be milled elsewhere into skies for the snow troops in Finland in their fight against Russia. Later some of these skis also went to snow troops in the United States Army.

My father was hired as the lead sawyer and logscaler at this new mill. This meant he moved from sporadic work at or near the bottom of the payscale to steady employment in one of the top-paying skilled jobs at the mill. Our family began to participate in the prosperity being generated by the war.

I saw pictures in the newspapers and newsreels at the movies of the snow troops, so I was able to romanticize about where the skis that came from the hickory logs my father sawed might end up. I was proud of him. I regret I didn't tell him so, but I did ride my bicycle to the mill out south of town on the road to Hermitage to watch him work.

It was the first time I had ever seen by father in charge of anything. He was responsible for seeing that each of the large hickory logs that he brought into the mill by means of a moving chain was converted into the most profitable cuts for ski stock. I was fascinated to see him manipulate sift-gear sorts of devices and pedals to load the logs on a steam driven carriage, turn the logs over to various angles as he moved them back and forth through the band saw. He did this with authority, without hesitation.

When the noon whistle blew we went out back of the mill where we sat on a big hickory log and ate our lunches of pimento cheese sandwiches and pieces of cake out of his lunch pail. After we had finished, he drank black coffee from his themos bottle and smoked his Camel cigarette.

It pleased me greatly when his fellow workers stopped by to joke with me because I knew it meant they liked and respected him.

## *FOOD FOR BODY AND SPIRIT*

Even in the worst days of the Depression our family always had plenty to eat. It was simple fare, but there was enough for ample meals three times each day. I don't know how my family managed that feat because neither my father nor Uncle Jewell had regular work.

However, it was not unusual to hear the adults talking among themselves about what we could afford to eat. How much food did we have in the house? How much money did we have to buy the staples—flour, lard, salt—and some meat to go with the homegrown vegetables so that we would have a full meal? I heard talk late one afternoon that they could only scrape together 35 cents to make out the rest of the week. But I didn't worry; I felt sure that my family would take care of the matter.

We were fortunate because there were many families that had to scrimp by hand to mouth, on the simplest of diets—mostly peas or beans—or whatever they could take from their gardens. They ate those staples with hot-water cornbread which they made because they didn't have lard to make the regular kind. Times were especially desperate for many people during the winter months when their garden plots lay fallow.

Preoccupation with food remains with me to this day. My continuing concern that there will always be more than enough food on the table, especially if we are entertaining guests, has come to be a joke within our family. I am sure that my children cannot fathom why I am horrified at the idea of running out of food. It is not so much that I am afraid that I will go hungry. It is that we might be seen as unable to afford plenty of food. The same compulsion is probably what drives me to always want to pick up the check when I am eating out with other people.

○○○○○○○○○○○○○○

The appetites in our family no doubt were encouraged by the fact that my mother was an excellent cook.

Nothing particularly fancy, mind you, just good basic food, seasoned just right and cooked fresh daily.

There were no light snacks for us. There were three square meals a day. All of them were cooked on a wood-burning stove that made the entire kitchen feel like an oven in the hot months of summer.

The men of the house made their own breakfast when they were working at the mill—usually eggs, fatback and biscuits left over from the night before, and a pot of coffee. My mother and I ate freshly cooked oatmeal or scrambled eggs and toast after they left the house.

The men packed their noon meal in paper sacks or metal lunch boxes. There was little variety to their lunch—cold vegetables from supper the night before and biscuits or cornbread with a piece of fatback or ladled with molasses. Sometimes there might be a piece or two of chicken left over. In later, more prosperous, times, my father always packed a triple-decker pimiento cheese sandwich.

Dinner (lunch) at home was most often a full meal for whoever was on hand. We usually ate freshly cooked vegetables and cornbread and maybe some kind of meat.

For supper everyone sat down together in the dining room. We sat in straightback wooden chairs and ate off a table cover made of oilcloth. The floor of the room, which slanted downhill from east to west, was covered with a linoleum "rug" over course boards with cracks between them. No pictures adorned the walls which were covered with fading wallpaper. A bare light bulb hung from the ceiling made of beaded wood slats 12 feet above the table.

No TV or radio blared in the background. There wasn't much conversation, just, "Please pass the beans," and "Mama, this is mighty good."

Sunday dinner was always special. We had chicken, fried or baked with dressing, and a full array of vegetables and rolls most times. Occasionally, we had a pot roast, heavily seasoned with garlic, served with mashed potatoes and other vegetables.

No one complained about what we had to eat, even if some days it was not exactly what we wanted. Usually someone at the table, most often Mama, declared that we were lucky to have another meal of plenty. Her admonition was to "take all you want, but eat all you take." Then to underscore her point, she would add, "We should always remember that thousands of Chinese children are starving to death every day."

As I got older, I wondered how that related to the story we heard so often that there were so many Chinese they could march 12 abreast into the sea to drown everyday for the next 100 years and there would be still be Chinese left. It was accepted as fact that they would overrun the earth someday and all of us would starve. Some people, except the most devout churchgoers who supported the missionaries, said the world might be better off if a lot of Chinese did starve because there would be fewer of them to fight in the big war that was bound to come sooner or later.

When we finished the Sunday noon meal Mama took away the cutlery and dishes to be washed by hand right away. She left the serving dishes with the leftover food in place and covered them with a white tablecloth. This was a very inviting situation for a mid-afternoon snack.

ooooooooooooooo

Mama brought all of her considerable talents as a cook to bear full force when she prepared our dinners on Thanksgiving and Christmas.

We encouraged her not to change a thing from one special day to the next or from one year to another. There was baked chicken (we didn't know anyone who had turkey). The best dish on the table was a large pan of dressing she made of crumbled cornbread baked the day before, leavened with a few heels of light bread she had been saving and eggs. It was seasoned with a generous helping of chopped onions and chopped celery and hearty doses of sage, black pepper and salt. We bedeviled her by asking if she was sure she had cooked enough. She made a rich gravy, laden with giblets from the chicken and sliced hardboiled eggs, for the dressing. There were big bowls of dried lima beans and candied sweet potatoes, topped with marshmallows turned brown in the baking process. Garnishes of homemade cranberry sauce and sweet pickles added zest to the meal. There were always pumpkin or sweet potato pies and one or more cakes, including a fruit filling one that my Grandmother Greenwood had taught Mama to make.

Our menus for those two special days changed only in one regard. On Christma mornings there was a special treat at breakfast of a big platter of country fried round steak along with fried eggs and toast.

The big meal was always eaten at noon; warmed up left-overs were for another full meal at sundown. We enjoyed the remains of the dressing and desserts for several days following Thanksgiving and Christmas.

ooooooooooooooo

Our food came from many sources. I doubt that some of them would ever pass the sanitation tests of today.

But I was grown before I ever heard of botulism or salmonella. Maybe a few people suffered from these maladies, but doctors must have thought they were some other ailments.

Housewives faced a particular challenge keeping fresh foods, especially meat, from spoiling. Although some people on the other side of town were said to have electric refrigerators, we did not actually know anyone so fortunate. But most everyone, except the very poorest, had an icebox of some form or another. Many of them were handmade of cypress wood and lined with tin. Some people had deep wells where the cold water in the earth provided cooling for some foods, such as milk and butter.

Mr. E. L. Wise had a thriving business in the sale of block ice along with coal and the products from his cottonseed oil mill over near the Bradley mill.

Ice was available by home delivery for a few cents a pound. The man who peddled it on our side of town was a smallish, humpbacked black man by the name of Henry. He hauled his ice in a horse-drawn wagon, painted a high gloss dark green that reflected the sunbeams. The ice in the bed of the wagon was covered with a heavy, dark olive canvas blanket to retard melting. Despite his diminutive stature and quiet manner there was a certain air of commanding dignity about him that earned the respect of his customers and the youngsters who followed him.

Customers were provided with a cardboard sign about 12 inches square, divided into four triangles to hang in a prominent spot on their front porches. The four triangles bore numbers, 25, 50, 75 and 100. The customer designated the amount of ice needed on a given day by turning the sign so that the appropriate number was at the top.

The ice wagon attracted a lot of attention from the kids. As soon as we heard Henry calling "Iceman, Iceman" we rushed out to the street curb. When he stopped we stood around as supplicants and watched him follow his ritual—slowly climbing down and going to the tailgate where he threw back the blanket that covered the big blocks of ice. With a few deft strokes of his icepick he chipped out the required amount of ice. If we were lucky, shards of ice fell from his chipping. When we behaved, that is when we didn't push and shove, he let us scoop up handsfull of these slivers of ice. They sparkled in the sunshine as if they were gems. What a great treat on a hot day.

He carried the block of ice in a canvas sling or in the grip of heavy iron tongs to the backdoor of his customer. Some of the more daring of the older boys might sneak a small piece or two of ice while he was away from the wagon.

Mama protected our block of ice as if it were so much gold. Woe be to the one who left the door of the icebox open. She had her own icepick, which she used with great skill to take off just the right amount of ice for a glass of tea lemonade. She could make 50 pounds last up to three days.

Even years later when she had a refrigerator in her kitchen and could make her own ice cubes—as many as she wanted—she was troubled if so much as a sliver of ice was thrown away after someone finished a glass of tea.

ooooooooooooooo

We produced a lot of our food at home.

It would be hard to overstate the importance of the garden to our getting by. We expected that small plot behind our house to produce a rich and varied supply of vegetables year-round. Much of it we ate fresh the day it was picked, enjoying a crispness and richness of flavor I have never known since. Anything produced in excess of the daily needs was canned, or given to neighbors who for one reason or another were unable to raise their own.

Our garden was usually put in by late April when it seemed reasonably certain that there would not be any more heavy frosts or freezes.

A black man was hired to come with his horse to plow up the plot. There was great excitement the day he arrived. With much ado, he unhooked his horse from the wagon and arranged the maze of plowing harness on the docile beast. All the while he carried on a one-way conversation with the horse and anyone else within earshot. A large muscular man, he easily lifted the big plow out of the bed of the wagon and attached it to the horse's harness.

Once an agreement was reached with my mother on the exact limits of the job to be done and the charge, probably no more than a dollar, the plowman lined up his horse, firmly planted the sharp point of the plow in the soil and called out his own special command to the animal to move forward. His order was emphasized with a flick of the reins on the horse's side.

I tagged along, round after round, up and down what would soon be neat rows. The plow blade looked like the bow of a ship, pushing through a sea of black soil, moist and cool to the touch. The turned-up earth revealed a universe of earthworms and grubs that had been feeding over the winter on the roots of weeds and grass.

Some years we collected enough worms to make a worm bed. We created the bed by partially filling an old tin washtub with dirt, then "planting" the worms we had gathered. We kept the bed damp with greasy dishwater and scraps of food. We always hoped to sell the worms for fishing bait. I don't recall much ever came of these ventures.

Midway in the plowing my mother brought out a pitcher of water for the plowman, who by that time had broken out into a sweat. As he gulped the water, cold from our well at the back door of our house, he and Mama discussed when it would be best to plant the various vegetables according to the signs of the moon.

Once the ground had been broken, the plowman changed his plow bade and retraced his steps, shaping the plot into the rough form of rows.

All of this occupied the better part of a half-day.

The next order was for all available members of the family to take hoes and rakes in hand to break up the remaining clods, remove the grass and roots, and shape the rows into their final form, ready to receive the seeds and plants.

Mama was the principal gardener. Everyone said she had a green thumb. The men helped when they were home. I don't recall that my grandmother had much to do with the garden.

oooooooooooooooo

With an earnest presentation of how I could be of help to this important project, I could usually finagle my mother into letting me stay home from school for the afternoon to help hoe and plant.

I don't suppose Mama expected to get much work out of me, so she was not disappointed. But this rite of spring was a special time for us. She made me feel loved and important.

Part of the tradition was that I would set up a howl, as Mama put it, to go barefooted for the first time of the year. The negotiation varied little from year to year as if it had been scripted. I would ask to take my shoes off because my feet were hot. Mama would say, "No, Ramon, you will get a sore throat and catch your death of cold." I would counter that it was plenty warm and besides, every other boy in the neighborhood had already gone barefooted.

Finally, she would relent. Inevitably, I caught a cold and my throat got sore. She never said, "I told you so." Anyway, the absolute sensual delights experienced when my toes dug into the cool damp soil and when I felt the tickle of the grass on my feet made it all worthwhile.

My feet were tender in the early spring after being confined in shoes during the fall and winter. After a few weeks, the soles of my feet became as tough as leather. Rocks and hot sidewalks were no problem. The molten asphalt that boiled up in the cracks in the street was another matter. Stepping on one those spots was sheer torture. And I was certain to suffer wounds from encounters with one or more rusty nails and pieces of broken glass before I had to go back into shoes at the beginning of school in September.

After the first burst of my enthusiasm for the work in the garden subsided, I was easily diverted, running through the raw soil and throwing dirt clods at the birds that flew into the garden plot to feed on the worms and fresh roots that had been turned up by the plowing.

One of my tasks was getting water from the well to the garden, a bucketful at a time. The trick was to have one full bucket of water at Mama's side as she fashioned a hole in the ground, carefully dropped a fragile plant or seed in place, took water in a gourd dipper from the bucket and poured it over her planting as she gently tamped the soil back in place.

This job of hauling water always frustrated me. It was hard repetitive work that I tried, in various ways, to reduce or eliminate. Mama either ignored my ideas or declared, "I need more water."

When the planting was all done we had in place the making of rows of corn, greenbeans, butterbeans, field peas, greens and turnips, onions, tomatoes, bell peppers, hot peppers, cucumbers, cabbages, lettuce, radishes, squash, and potatoes, plus several hills of watermelons, pumpkins and gourds.

Within a few days, if the nights were warm, the delicate shoots from the seed broke through the soil and the tomatoes and peppers plants began to stand fully erect and grow.

oooooooooooooooo

Making a garden offered great rewards, but it was hard work and there was the constant threat of failure.

Varmints and plant diseases were a problem. Also, it was a given that rabbits would take their share of sprouting vegetables in the early spring.

A mysterious gray powder sprinkled on the vines usually controlled the wilt. What we later knew as pesticide drove away the black and orange potato bugs, but not always before they chewed their intricate patterns in the leaves on the vines.

But no matter what anyone did, the fate of the garden was ultimately in the hands of the water it received either from the heavens or from our well and the city water supply. Without water, the soil dried to the consistency of a brick, leaving the garden to literally die on the vine.

We hauled all of the water we could from our well, but when it began to run low we turned to a second source, the city's water supply. But we could barely pay for the water needed in the house, let alone for enough to save the garden. The meter to measure the use of water and thus the charges to be paid was located in the front yard. The men of the house turned it off after nightfall so we could run water to the garden without having to pay for it.

Many others families probably did the same thing. "Red" King, who kept the city water department going, just looked the other way.

Sometimes in the summer we went for weeks without rain. When we had all but given up hope, the clouds began to gather in the afternoons. After days of teasing with a drizzle here and there, a heavy downpour would finally come, turning the street curbs and little creeks into runaway torrents. We youngsters ran and played in the downpour, savoring the rain and making the most of the sense of abandon that came with the blessed refreshment. Eventually, we had to admit that the water had turned cold and that our overalls had begun to chafe. It was time to go in the house and put on dry clothes, which our mothers had been urging us to do.

When the sun broke through, the clouds dissipated, and a rainbow appeared across the horizon. It was said that a pot of gold could be found at the end of the arc of colors. Often, as if to put a finishing touch to that time of magic, a light shower would fall among the rays of sunshine. Raindrops in sunshine were really the tears the devil's wife shed because he was beating her, we were told.

The rain lifted everyone's spirits. The garden had been saved for the time being. The air was cooler and the heat wave was broken for a few hours. The grass and the leaves on the trees sparkled in their cleanliness. A special aroma filled the air.

ooooooooooooooo

_Ramon Greenwood_

If the weather had been kind to us we began to eat vegetables from our garden by early May.

First came the spring onions, bone white and marked by minute green stripes to match their dark green tops. We started to eat them when they were smaller than a lead pencil. By the end of the season they had grown into shanks with bulbs as big as eggs. Radishes came in two varieties and shapes, red bulbs and white tubular. We enjoyed tender turnip greens. Lettuce and spinach were rarities that were available for only a few weeks.

Mama didn't make salads as we know them today. Instead she placed whole spring onions and radishes on the table. We picked from the bowl according to our taste. As a special treat we sometimes had a delicious concoction of spinach wilted with hot grease from fatback and topped by pieces of the crisp meat.

There was more work to be done in the coming weeks to bring the garden to full bloom. The rows had to be hoed frequently so as to cut out the weeds, which otherwise would have crowded out the vegetables, and loosen the soil to give the plants breathing room. Tomatoes and pole beans had to be staked and tied up.

When the garden reached its peak from the middle of June to late July, we had more fresh vegetables than we could eat.

For awhile, we feasted two meals a day on vegetables cooked the same morning they were gathered from our garden 50 yards away from the kitchen.

We enjoyed fresh corn boiled on the cob when it was still tender and cut off of the cob after it got coarse to be made into a sort of stew. Potatoes boiled and eaten, jackets and all, to retain the flavor, peeled and mashed with milk and butter; fried, soft, never McDonald crisp. Greenbeans boiled until they were limp. Butterbeans and field peas. Boiled okra. Trays heaped high with sliced tomatoes, slices of bell peppers, hot peppers, onions and radishes, grown much larger and more pungent to the taste.

Most vegetables were cooked with a piece of fatmeat, cut in the style of an accordion, in a big cast-iron pot filled with water from the well.

Cornbread and rolls were our breads of choice. Somehow biscuits never made my preferred list. Although the self-rising rolls were delicious, especially with jelly or molasses, cornbread was always my favorite.

My mother and my grandmother each had her specialty in cornbread. Mama made hers with a combination of cornmeal, eggs and buttermilk whipped into a creamy mixture which she poured into a iron skillet in which lard had been preheated until it began to smoke. The result was a "pie" of cornbread, baked so that it came to the table moist on the inside of a crisp goldenbrown crust. She often baked cornbread in a set of iron cookware that turned out pones bearing some resemblance to small ears of corn.

My grandmother's specialty was the poor man's cornbread which dated from the impoverished days of the Civil War. The bread was in fact nothing more than cornmeal made into a paste with boiling water, cooked in an oiled iron skillet. It was known as "hot water bread," "dogbread," or "dodger." The names were not without reason. The "dogbread" name originated from the fact that it was sometimes cooked to feed hunting hounds. Some people referred to it as "dodger" because it was said that sometimes it was so hard that the dogs "dodged it" when it was thrown at them to quit their howling.

My grandmother didn't cook "dodger" very often. When she served it for lunch it was such a treat for me that I took a few slices back to school to eat during the afternoon recess.

We also relished another form of cornbread known as "cracklin' bread." It could be either of the cornbread recipes into which slivers of fatback or pork skins had been mixed.

167

Of course, whatever the form it took, we always slathered each piece with butter. We often finished our meals with a dessert of buttered cornbread and jelly or molasses. Another favorite dish was crumbled cornbread in a glass of milk—sweet or butter. The grown-ups often added chopped-up onion.

ooooooooooooooo

When the garden was producing at its peak my mother, with the help of my grandmother and sometimes my Dad and Uncle Jewell, began to can vegetables for the fall and winter ahead.

Somewhere along the way, Mama worked up her courage to buy a steam pressure cooker from the Sears Roebuck catalog. There was great excitement the day it arrived. There was also considerable concern that it might blow up when she started using it. My grandmother was against the whole idea.

The process involved placing five quart sealed jars, filled with a single vegetable or some mixture, in the heavy aluminum pot containing water, tightening the lid with several screws and placing it over a blazing fire. We stood there watching anxiously as the gauge showed the rising steam pressure in the pot. Was it about to explode? Soon the safety valve hissed out steam, and Mama assured us that according to the directions, it was cooking properly. When the process was completed, the jars were removed from the boiling water to cool off before being stacked in the pantry.

With her pressure cooker, she could also turn the toughest old hen into chicken that would melt in our mouths. Years later when she first tasted Colonel Sanders' chicken she declared, correctly so, that it had been prepared in a pressure cooker.

She was very proud to show the ladies in the neighborhood how the new utensil worked.

Mama canned just about every kind of vegetable that came from the garden. Sometimes she mixed green tomatoes, onions and peppers into a concoction known as Chow-Chow. She also combined ripe tomatoes, onions and peppers to make our version of ketchup which we called "chili sauce." She made jelly and jam when the fruit could be bought at the right price or when a neighbor gave us some from their trees. Best of all, someone would go to the river bottoms and gather scuppernongs or mayhaws which made splendid jelly.

My favorite of her canned food was the vegetable soup mix containing corn shaved from the cob, ripe tomatoes, okra, onions and peppers. Plain canned tomatoes were a close second.

During the winter we made many meals from the soup mixture, cooked with a soup bone or a bit of stew meat, and served with cornbread. Canned tomatoes were used for cooking other dishes. I always craved those tomatoes when I was recovering from one of my childhood illnesses. I ate them by the bowlfulls, heavily salted. We didn't know they contained the vitamins my recovering body needed. We just knew they were good.

Chicken was the mainstay of our meat menu.

We raised our own, sometimes from eggs hatched in our chicken house. Most years we ordered baby chicks from the Bradley Feed Store or from Sears Roebuck. I had great fun when the chicks arrived. They were soft and fluffy and yellow, cute as buttons, whether I had watched them crack out of their eggshells in our chicken house or had first seen them when I eagerly helped open the shipping crate in which they arrived. We carefully nurtured them in the chicken house. Once they were grown enough to sort of fend for themselves they were turned loose in the chicken yard. In spite of all we could do a mean rooster usually pecked one or two of them to death.

On the days we were to eat chicken my mother or my grandmother went to the chicken yard early in the morning to pick out the appropriate bird—a mature hen if we were to have baked chicken and dressing; a younger, more tender, bird for frying.

The targeted chicken was coaxed forward by scattering corn kernels in an ever-diminishing circle up the executioner's feet. My grandmother had a special knack for this process. With a quick swoop this frail little woman picked up the selected chicken by its feet. There was much squawking and flapping of wings, all to no avail. My grandmother put her hand around the chicken's neck as she released its feet. With a few well-practiced turns of her wrist the chicken's head was wrung off. Blood spurted from the stump of the neck as the headless body flopped around on the ground stirring up dust. I tried once or twice to wring the neck of a chicken, but I just didn't have the strength or the stomach to finish the job.

The carcass of the chicken was soaked in a pot of boiling water. for a few minutes so that its feathers could be easily plucked. Once the feathers had been removed, flames from a burning stick or a roll of paper were applied to singe the chicken and in order to remove the pinfeathers that protruded from the pale skin.

My grandmother sometimes wanted me to pluck the chicken, but I usually found some excuse to run away to play out of sight of the violence of the beheading and the stench that arose from the plucking of the wet feathers and the singeing that followed.

All of that, plus the butchering that followed, convinced me for the moment that I never wanted to eat chicken again. Fortunately, however, when the aroma from cooking chicken began to drift out of the kitchen, my memory faded. By mealtime, I had dismissed all recall of the preparations.

We ate chicken over and over again—fried, baked with dressing, boiled with dumplings, and sometimes under cover of a tomato and onion sauce. It followed that we usually had plenty of eggs, too. Fried or scrambled for breakfast. Hardboiled. One of my favorites was Mama's "deviled" eggs. She boiled the eggs and cut them in halves, then extracted the yellows which she mixed with mustard and refilled the sections.

oooooooooooooooo

In the very early years we "kept a cow." The truth is that our cow, Flossie by name, was more than a source of milk; she was a family pet. A beautiful tan and white animal, docile in nature, she had large, luminous eyes that seemed intelligent to me. She produced milk in considerable abundance. We had plenty of sweet milk to drink. What we couldn't drink or use with our oatmeal was churned into buttermilk and butter.

From time to time, Uncle Jewell and I tied a rope around Flossie's neck and led her to Grady Richardson's place just northeast of town. Mr. Richardson operated a dipping vat where people brought their cows to have the ticks and other varmints killed off them and their hides soaked so that more wouldn't gather.

There was much milling around and bellowing as the cows were lined up and prodded to make their way through a chute until they stumbled forward into and out of the narrow concrete vat filled with creosote and other noxious chemicals. I cried the first time I saw Flossie in that predicament.

171

Flossie came to a bitter and mysterious end. One of the family went to the barn early one morning to milk her, but found her lying on her side in her stall. Her breathing was labored, her eyes glazed over.

We sent word for Dr. Campbell, Warren's only licensed veterinarian, to come as quickly as he could. He took one look at Flossie and said she would not live out the day. He was correct.

There was much puzzlement about what had caused Flossie to die. Several days later Dr. Campbell said she had been poisoned or fed ground glass. I heard my parents voice their suspicions about who had killed Flossie, but they could not be certain. Better to let it drop, they said. We mourned as if she had been a member of the family.

Without butter produced from Flossie's milk we were introduced to oleomargarine, which was to always be known simply as oleo or margarine, as a substitute for butter. Oleo came in an unappetizing white block that looked and tasted for all the world like lard. It came with a package of yellow coloring that had to be worked into the glob to give it the appearance of the more expensive butter. Much to Mama's chagrin at the dinner table I insisted on asking that someone please pass the lard.

oooooooooooooooo

Putting red meat on the table was more of a challenge.

If nothing else quite defines the radical difference between those times and now, the horse-drawn meat wagon that made the rounds in our neighborhood does so sharply and clearly.

The butcher was a farmer who raised livestock for slaughter to supplement the income from his struggling cotton patch and thriving vegetable garden. He also sold wild game he and his family had killed in the stands of timber that dotted his land and the surrounding countryside. He brought the meat to town in his wagon covered with two or three bed sheets which arrived soaked through with blood.

It was up in the morning when he began his door-to-door rounds in our neighborhood. As the ladies gathered around the wagon, the butcher removed the covering sheets with a practiced flourish. The sight of the array of meats on display in the wagon bed was something to behold. A mound of homemade pork sausage, more fat than lean. Beef liver. Beef and pork roasts. Round steak. Sides of beef. Ribs. Calf brains. A hog head. Hog's Head Cheese. A whole pig.

In the fall and winter he offered dressed rabbits and other wild game. Rabbits were known as "Hoover Hogs," in wry recognition of the fact that many people during the Depression ate the animals, which they had hunted or trapped, because they couldn't afford to buy pork or other meat.

Even if they had the money to buy for days ahead, the housewives could purchase no more than the family could eat in the next day or two because of the likelihood of spoilage.

Each selection was weighed on a scale balanced on the tailgate of the wagon. Some of the ladies swore they had seen the butcher place an order of meat on the scale and then press down on the tray with his thumb to run up the price. No one could ever prove the charge, but the women watched him like a hawk.

All the while, the butcher periodically fanned the air to keep away the black flies and other winged pests that were attracted to the blood of the fresh meat.

There were no U. S. Department of Agriculture inspectors or representatives from the state health department to assure sanitation in his slaughtering and handling of meat.

173

The wonder of it is that we didn't all suffer from food poisoning. But then the meat had not been infused with chemicals to speed up growth and add weight. The air was not polluted. We had never heard of viruses, so they must not have existed.

All I know is the meat was delicious. I liked everything Mama cooked except calf brains scrambled with eggs.

ooooooooooooooo

With all of this, we still had to buy some of our food from the neighborhood grocery store and the Bradley Store up town where my father had credit on the books when he had an opportunity to work at the company's mill.

It seemed that every part of town had its own little grocery store. Blankenship's out on the Pine Bluff highway; Moseley's on the way to New Edinburgh; Mills' and Carmichal's on the south side; Curry's and Davis' on the west; Burns', Adams' and Roddey's in town.

The Corner Grocery down the street from our house was most convenient for us since we didn't have a car.

The store, owned and operated at various times by the Mitchell Godwin family and the Stells, was housed in a small oblong building of one room at the corner of East Church and Gannaway streets.

There was a refrigerator cabinet at the back of the store where an array of meat could be inspected. Orders were cut to request, handwrapped in white butcher's paper and tied with string unwound from a large cone standing upright on a pedestal.

"Weenies" had a prominent place in the showcase. They were joined together, end to end, in a long rope formed by their casing. We didn't eat them very often as hot dogs because it was believed that they would give us a stomach ache. But "weenies" frequently showed up on our table in a bowl of sauerkraut, served with mashed potatoes and cornbread.

The cabinet was also stocked with round steak, roast, hunks of baloney and wedges of "rat" cheese priced at a few cents a pound.

Fatback or sowbelly sold at 10 to 15 cents a pound. In the fall of the year when it was "hog killin'" time there was fresh sausage to be had. It was made from many parts of a hog, some we didn't want to know about, finely ground up and seasoned with hot peppers and other spices. The greasy patties served with fresh eggs from our own hens made for a treat to be remembered.

We were happy when we had round steak or a pot roast for supper. It was about 25 cents a pound. My mother pounded the meat with her meat hammer until it was tender, then she worked in flour and fried it crisp on the outside, tender on the inside. Sometimes she smothered it with sliced onions. On other occasions she added canned tomatoes, onions and bell peppers. For reasons I never knew, this dish was known as "Swiss Steak."

There were few canned goods available compared to today, and no prepackaged or frozen food in any of the stores. In fact, some of the old-timers were leery of food in cans. They had the idea that eating such concoctions was a good way to get poisoned, especially if food was left in a can for any length of time.

We did buy canned sardines, mackerel and sauerkraut. Before there was such a thing as "political correctness," we ate canned oysters under the brand name of "Nigger Toe." Mama mixed the oysters with milk and crumbled soda crackers to make oyster pie. I often made smart remarks about looking for the oysters among all those crackers. She combined the mackerel, at about a nickel a can, with grated onions and crumbled soda crackers, rolled them into patties which she fried to a crusty exterior. I never got tired of mackerel patties.

Some packaged foods offered bonus benefits. The cloth sacks in which flour was sold provided material for housewives to make dresses and aprons. Dishes were added as premiums in the packages of some foods such as oatmeal.

Foods such as flour, salt, sugar, cornmeal, dried beans and peas were sold by the pound, scooped out of large barrels and poured into brown paper bags closed with cotton string.

Pickles were speared with a long fork out of dark oak barrels. Hard candy and spices were presented in large glass jars. "Light" bread, baked locally, was sold unsliced. Soda pops were standing with the remains of a block of ice in very cold water in a horizontal metal icebox with sliding panels on top. The much-desired candybars, bubble gum and suckers known as "jawbreakers" displayed in a glassed-in cabinet could be looked at but not touched unless the shopper handed over money.

Most stores were glad to make home deliveries, no minimum required. The Bradley Store took this service one step further. Mr. Frank Meek made the rounds of the homes of the store's regular customers, and those he hoped to develop, to take their orders for the day. He showed up at our house at about daylight. "Anything I can get for you today?" he would ask my mother. When she gave him an order she was assured it would be delivered late that afternoon.

oooooooooooooooo

That time and place provided never-to-be-forgotten food for body and spirit.

We didn't count fat grams or calories, and they didn't count, because we never heard of them. Still there were fewer fat people then than now. Those who were fat seemed to thrive. Heart attacks were few and far between. High blood pressure must have been a rare ailment because we hardly ever heard of anyone suffering from it. Of course, the physical condition of the population had a lot to do with the fact that most people had to walk most everywhere they went, children ran and played outside from early morning until bedtime, and adults worked hard at physical labor.

Writing about his childhood growing up on a working Texas ranch of that era, Larry McMurtry, the highly regarded novelist, recalls that "Food has gone from what's good to what's good for you."

*Ramon Greenwood*

# *FROM WOMB TO TOMB*

Matters of birthing, illness, and death were family business to be taken care of for the most part at home. Participation of doctors, hospitals and drugstores was the last resort. There were no antibiotics, no miracle procedures. Undertakers were called in because they were necessary for the mechanics of death.

ooooooooooooooo

More times than I can count I heard my mother tell the story of my birth on January 14, 1927, in the front bedroom of the house where she spent most of her life and where I grew up.

She was 28; my father 41. Both were older than the norm for first births in those days. The saga she related importantly involved the fact that my cousin Robert Clary Reep, son of my mother's brother, Howard Reep, and his wife Maude, was born across the "dog trot" hall in the same house one week earlier.

My mother suffered a very difficult delivery. Doctor Herring did the best he could, the family always said, but nevertheless she experienced damage to her body that led the way to a hysterectomy some seven or eight years later in which she nearly died.

To make matters worse, according to my mother and others, I was probably the ugliest baby ever born. I was as red as a beet and bore many bruises and lacerations from the violent delivery.

Not only that, I learned later that she had wanted a daughter. It was ironic that she was to tell me stories of how her mother had wanted so fervently to have a girl, but her wish wasn't fulfilled until after she had delivered three sons. Mama declared that she couldn't understand why she had been saddled with such an ugly name as Ophie Mae, which she disliked all of her life, if her mother wanted a daughter so badly.

As luck would have it, my mother's discomfort was multiplied because Bob Reep was a fine specimen of a boy, born fair and without a blemish. Everybody said he was pretty. Furthermore, Aunt Maude had had an easy delivery. The family was surprised by this because the pretty, smallish woman frequently nursed some ailment or another that required pampering whereas my mother was always healthy and self-reliant.

Naturally in the small community the two sets of parents shared many friends. "To tell you the truth, those first few days when friends came to call on us and see our babies were not pleasant," my mother was to recall. "When they went to see Maude and Bob first I could hear them laughing and generally enjoying themselves, but when they crossed the hall and saw us they'd quiet down and become very proper. I was very sick and weak and you were not very pretty. I could tell our visitors were uneasy. It was downright embarrassing."

In later years, she was quick to say that it wasn't very long before she decided she really was glad I had been born a boy. She also insisted that within just a few days my looks began to improve, a process that continued she assured me, until I became, in her judgment, "the prettiest baby in town."

"I couldn't get down the street without people stopping me to say what a beautiful baby you were," she said. She also liked to cite the fact that I was judged the "healthiest" baby in Bradley County in a contest at the American

Legion Hut. When she got to these wrap-up points in her story there was a sparkle in her eye. It was no doubt pride, seasoned with a great deal of it-was-no-more-than-I-expected satisfaction. Shakespeare was right on target when he wrote that love is blind.

ooooooooooooooo

People must have been tougher in those days.

At any rate, less attention was paid to comfort. Recoveries were quicker, either by choice or necessity.

It seems unfathomable now that my father had most of the middle finger on his left hand amputated while he was stretched out on the front porch of the house where he lived.

His finger had become infected from a splinter of wood that he had picked up at work. He was on the verge of developing blood poisoning when Doctor Herring declared that his finger had to come off. Otherwise, he likely would lose his whole hand or arm. He might even die.

Doctor Herring laid him down on a pallet then poured some ether from a bottle into a handful of cotton cloth and held it over my father's nose. When he was "put under," the doctor proceeded with the surgery. All the while neighbors were standing around watching and speculating about the outcome as the children continued their games.

Dr. Joe Bond declared that all of my father's teeth had to be pulled, otherwise, the frequent pain and poison from them would ruin his general health.

Dad worked at the sawmill until noon Saturday, came home to eat his lunch and clean up before walking back up town to Doctor Joe's office. He was given gas to put him to sleep so he could tolerate having all of his remaining teeth pulled in one session. When it was over he walked back home and rested over the weekend before he went back to work Monday morning. He lived on mush, oatmeal and boiled eggs for a week until his set of false teeth was ready for fitting. There was more intense pain from the crude fit which was par for the course in those days. But Doctor Joe whittled away on the dentures until they fit properly.

Doctor Joe was one of my favorite personalities in town. I was never afraid when I went to see him. The fact was that I had few dental problems. My grandmother said my teeth would have been even healthier if I had followed her advice and brushed them with baking soda, using a good-size twig from a black gum tree as a brush.

Doctor Joe was a man of stocky build, short of six feet tall. He always wore a white headpiece that looked something like a baker's cap. Strangely enough, his teeth were stained. Too much coffee and too many cigarettes, I assume.

He was a great sportsman. We heard often about his bass-fishing exploits and his quail hunting. My Uncle Jewell built boats and iceboxes for him, but more about that elsewhere. We youngsters thought his daughter, Joy, was about the best-looking girl in town.

ooooooooooooooo

A great deal of our medical care came from my mother and grandmother.

They had a remedy for just about all ailments. Some potions they concocted at home, some were bought over-the-counter. Very little medicine came by prescription.

A medicine show came to town at least once a year offering miracle potions with exaggerated claims for cures of ailments of all sorts. The show's appearance was a much anticipated event. The promoter arrived the day before the performance to set up his tent and several rows of folding chairs on the lot across from where the public library now stands. He and his associates distributed flyers around town announcing the all-free show and the availability of the "miracle" mixtures.

Two or three cast members, wearing heavy makeup and colorful clothes, performed various routines of slapstick comedy, played several instruments and sang songs familiar to all of us. Between acts the master of ceremonies, a rascal with a silver tongue, used a combination of fear, humor and a slight hint of the risque to extol the virtues of his elixir, which was guaranteed to cure all ailments and restore "pep" to one's life. Cast members moved among the crowd offering the cure-all for a dollar or two a bottle.

Boxes of candy or crackerjacks were also made available. The sales pitch assured there was a surprise bonus gift in each of the packages. The master of ceremony underscored the promised by opening a box and displaying a very attractive prize. Never mind that with maybe one exception as bait the prizes the buyers actually received were the cheapest of trinkets, which were a far cry from those displayed earlier.

My mother and father turned deaf ears to the offerings, despite my plea that we buy a box of treats. My mother declared that the promise of a prize in the candy and crackerjacks was just a come-on. She also said she had heard that the so-called "miracle" potions were full of alcohol; they just made people feel better for a time, but they didn't cure anything.

ooooooooooooooo

Some of our medicines were calculated to prevent ailments.

At the first sign of spring we all had to take a "through" of liver medicine. This ordeal was faced with great dread.

The promise was that those who took the medicine would benefit because their bodies would be thoroughly cleansed, assuring protection against malaria and other ailments that had festered in our systems during the winter. "Cleansed" is the precise word to describe the result. Everything was purged from the body over the course of about 24 hours. This regime became doubly troublesome if one didn't enjoy the privilege of indoor plumbing.

If there was ever a case of the cure being worse than the ailment, this was it. Grove's Chill Tonic, the best known of the preventatives, possessed a vile odor. Moreover, it had the consistency and taste of sand mixed in motor oil.

Doctor Gannaway, the patriarch of local druggists, dispensed a brand of his own liver pills from his store across from the court square. They were sold beyond the borders of Warren and produced royalties for his descendents.

A wizened figure always dressed in black, Doctor Gannawy owned and operated one of the few, if not the only, X-ray machine in town. He had suffered extensive radium burns to his body from operating it, which people said had contributed to his death.

*The Eagle Democrat* advertised "Tedford's Black Draught...for constipation, indigestion, biliousness." In the ad a mother testified "I give it when any one of my six children complains of upset stomach or begin to look pale and sickly."

All of those medicines were expected to deliver positive results in direct ratio to the vileness of their taste and reactions they caused. The standard response when we complained was, "Well, it will either cure you or kill you."

For good measure, we also usually drank sassafras tea. We believed that it thinned and cleansed the blood, improving general health in many ways. It was about the only home remedy that did not smell bad, taste bad and cause unpleasant side effects.

It was fun to gather sassafras roots from which the tea was brewed. We went to the wooded hill over by the cemetery to dig out the roots with our hands from the banks of red clay we had scouted out earlier in the year. The broken roots we carried home gave off a sweet aroma of cleanliness.

The recipe for sassafras tea was simple. We put a handful of cleaned roots in a pan of water and boiled them until the water turned the proper shade of copper. Each of us diluted his tea and added sugar to taste.

We often enjoyed the tea in ways not envisioned by our parents. We took whiskey bottles, which we could always find in trash piles around the neighborhood, and filled them with the tea, which was about the color of bourbon. Pretending we were drinking whiskey, we staggered around as we had seen the men do on the sidewalks uptown on Saturday afternoons. We heightened the game by smoking "cigarettes" made from corn silks or dried leaves from magnolia trees in pieces of newspaper. Sometimes we smoked long brown beans gathered from a tree down by the town branch. While our sassafras "whiskey" was sweet, our smoking materials left nothing but blistered tongues and bad tastes.

ooooooooooooooo

Voodoo wasn't ruled out of the list of cures.

185

When I was about six or seven years old I turned up with several warts on my fingers. No one could figure out why. The old wives' explanation, offered by my grandmother, was that I had been playing with toads. I suppose it is possible that the creatures did spread some sort of unknown virus. There were plenty of them hopping around under our house, but I didn't relish picking them up, so that couldn't have been the source of my affliction.

The warts got to be something of a problem as they continued to spread over my hands. The cure came from an unlikely source, the Williams family who lived on the road that bordered the field behind our house.

When Mrs. Williams got word of my ailment she came immediately to advise a cure. I remember her principally as a rather smallish woman with long straight hair of a color between red and blonde, who appeared to be perpetually exhausted from corralling a house full of children and a husband who was known not to work very much at his trade as a blacksmith. He seemed to spend a lot of time drinking rot gut whiskey.

In any case, my need was urgent. My mother was instructed to use a sewing needle, the point of which had been burned black with a kitchen match for sterilization, to pick at each of the warts until it bled. She was then to take a dried kernel of corn, cover it with my blood and throw it out for the chickens to eat. We were skeptical about the potential results and I was not particularly keen about the idea of being probed with a needle. Nevertheless, the consensus was that the warts had to go.

With my buddies from the neighborhood gathered around and my grandmother and Mrs. Williams hovering in the background, Mama carried out the procedure. For the next few days I looked anxiously for the cure, but nothing happened. I forgot about it for a week or so until one day I looked and the warts had disappeared.

ooooooooooooooo

Despite our sassafras tea and the "through" of liver medicine we had a lot of ailments, particularly in the summers, that were attributed to "bad blood."

There was the dreaded, highly infectious skin disease, which we knew as "infantigo." It was to be many years before I learned that the proper name for this pesky ailment was Impetigo. There was no mistaking "infantigo." It was a repulsive ailment. The infection started with a multitude of small, pus-filled pimples that covered the victim's legs. These progressed to open sores and went on to varying degrees of scabbing before they went away.

It seems now that I had a bad case of "infantigo" each summer for several years. This frustrated me greatly because it interfered with my playing with my friends. It also was embarrassing, although many of my playmates were also afflicted.

When "infantigo" struck my mother washed my legs, the primary site of the infection, with a germicidal soap as soon as I got out of bed in the morning Then she spread on a heavy layer of a home remedy of turpentine and tallow that looked and felt like lard. Finally, my legs were wrapped in a heavy layer of cotton cloth which she had gotten from old bed sheets or flour sacks and boiled for sterilization. My friends teased me, saying I looked like a mummy.

I spent most of my recovery time sitting on the unscreened back porch. My main diversion was driving away the black flies that were attracted by my infection. My weapons were a fly swatter and a water pistol.

Mercifully, the "infantigo" began to dry up in 10 days or two weeks. The final stage included a spell of horrible itching.

My "infantigo" was the cause of a minor family riff one year. Clifford Reep, a cousin several years my senior, whom I admired greatly, said I looked like "Lazarus." I didn't know who Lazarus was until my mother told me that he was a character from the Bible who had suffered all sorts of afflictions including terrible sores all over his body. My mother was so outraged that she marched next door and lambasted Aunt Myrtle, Clifford's mother. No one was allowed to talk to her son like that and Clifford should be set straight. He made peace by allowing me to play with him.

ooooooooooooooo

Boils, carbuncles, or "risens," were on the list of nasty and painful ailments that came to plague us.

Thankfully, there were effective home cures to deal with them. The inexpensive cures also to heal the numerous cuts on our feet we suffered from running far and wide bare footed.

The widely used combination of turpentine and tallow was the treatment of choice. My grandmother made up a supply of this salve each spring in preparation for the infectious season ahead. She also prepared poultices of grated Irish potatoes and flaxseed as needed.

The drawing power of the poultices could be felt within a few minutes after they were applied to a boil or carbuncle. After several applications the offending site began to itch, which meant that the curse was headed toward a cure.

After the boils came to a head, a second and sometimes third step was usually required to finish them off. First a firm squeezing around the eruption was needed to force out the pus and bring the core, which was a firm piece of pus, to the surface. When the core rose above the surrounding inflamed skin, someone would stretch out a string or coarse thread on it. The next step was to roll the string back and forth until the core was caught up in it and could be pulled out. The procedure usually brought immediate relief and left a startlingly large hole which took a day or two to close.

Polio was a curse that came each summer, driving absolute fear into the hearts of parents and children alike. There were no treatments, preventive or curative, to deal with polio. Frightening imagines of the iron lung occupied our minds. Some said the disease was carried by flies; others were of the opinion that it was somehow related to swimming, so we couldn't go to the YMCA or to the Saline River. We knew one or two young people who had been struck down with the dreaded disease. Moreover, President Roosevelt had been paralyzed by polio. That meant that no one was safe.

ooooooooooooooo

Fall and winter brought on an entirely new set of ailments and specialized home cures.

Influenza could be counted on to run rampart every winter. It simply had to be suffered through with bed rest and plenty of liquids. Pneumonia, a regular visitor to the community, was greatly feared. The body was left to fight off the affliction pretty much on its own because doctors could not provide a cure.

The simpler ailments such as chest colds and sore throats called for Vicks salve which was put up the nose, swallowed and applied in copious amounts to the throat and chest. The chest application involved rubbing the salve into the skin and covering the treated area with a hot cloth, usually flannel or wool. The cloth was removed periodically and held in front of the stove to warm it up. More salve was applied to the patient's chest before the cloth was put back in place. The fumes from the salve caused a lot of burning eyes. It was another entirely uncomfortable cure.

But the worst cure of all was an offending mixture of fried onions and castor oil, which we had to hold our nose to drink. I have a keen memory of the horrible taste. I could not stand the odor or the taste of fried onions until I was a grown man.

A repulsive mixture of sugar and turpentine was another medication used for colds and coughs.

oooooooooooooooo

There was an ample supply of doctors and pharmacists in town ready to take over when things got beyond the health care experts in our homes.

The pharmacists, in addition to Dr. Gannaway, were Mr. Appleton and Mr. Pirtle. They ran fully stocked drugstores where the business was dispensing drugs by prescription as well as a plethora of over-the-counter concoctions and cosmetics. The exception was Mr. McCaskill whose store also provided a soda fountain with a jukebox that featured films of the performing artists.

The number of doctors was adequate for the town. They all seemed to work incredibly hard. Dr. M. T. Crow headed a practice with his sons Bruce and Merl. They had a hospital where the Warren public library stands now and later on East Church Street. Doctor Hunt had his office and hospital over the Ederington Cash Store. There were also Doctor Martin, a member of a pioneer family, and Doctor Snodgrass.

Medical care, like everything else in town, was strictly segregated. There were three "colored" doctors—Drs. John Brunson, John White and H.

H. Rhinehart—who treated only "their" people. Likewise, that community had its own funeral homes.

It was another physician, Doctor Ellison, with whom we had the most contact. He was the doctor for employees of the Bradley Lumber Company. Fifty cents or so per month deducted from my father's paycheck paid for the services he provided for us. Unbelievably, this included not only visits to his office, but house calls as well. He also frequently dispensed medicine from his office when we went there or from his satchel when he came to the house.

Doctor Ellison, who came to Warren from St. Louis, was redheaded and a bit on the chubby side. He seemed permanently exhausted, I am sure with good reason since, he took care of a huge patient load numbering in the hundreds.

When Doctor Ellison's services were needed, word was sent by using one of the rare telephones in the neighborhood or by having someone in the family walk over to his office at the mill. Sometimes we waited all day for him to come and he always did, even if it was after any reasonable hour, including in the middle of the night.

His carried a large black bag that he unfolded at the bedside to reveal a fascinating selection of instruments along with many bottles of pills. After he had tended to the sick at our house my mother would offer him a cup of coffee and perhaps a piece of cake. Most often he declined, saying he would just sit for a minute or two. He usually went to sleep in his chair beside the bed.

Dr. Ellison was a blessing to the families he served. He was a hero in our eyes.

After a few years of such backbreaking drudgery he moved back to St. Louis. We heard later that his son had become a doctor.

ooooooooooooooo

A life-threatening crisis in my mother's health nearly devastated our family in late 1934 and a good part of 1935 as I was turning eight years of age.

Not only did her sickness inflict a cruel blow to our spirit, it crippled our financial situation, which was already fragile.

My mother had never totally recovered from the damage she suffered at my birth. Her problems eventually worsened beyond the expertise of local doctors. She was sent to see a specialist in Little Rock, which in our view was about like being sent to another planet.

She made at least two trips there by Missouri-Pacific bus. I was permitted to skip school for a day during my second year at Miss Dot Martin's primary school to make one of the trips with her.

I was amazed at the crowds of people and the tall buildings we saw on our way to the doctor's office in the Donaghey Building in Little Rock. It was there that I had my first ride on an elevator.

It troubles me that one of my most vivid memories from that trip was a negative one for the wrong reason.

My mother and I stopped at Walgreen's drug store at the corner of Main Street and Capitol Avenue for lunch. She had brought sandwiches in a brown paper bag so we only had to buy two fountain Cokes. I was too embarrassed to look the waitress in the eye. I am sure my mother knew that and suffered a bit with me.

We came back to Warren on the bus late that afternoon after she had seen the doctor who declared that she needed a complete hysterectomy to repair the damage she had suffered during my birth.

Doctor Clark came from Pine Bluff to perform the operation with the assistance of Dr. M. T. Crow.

The operation was a disaster. As my mother recuperated at the hospital it was determined that her bladder had been punctured during the procedure. The constant leakage of urine made the normal healing process all but impossible. The prognosis for her recovery was not encouraging.

She stayed in Doctor Crow's hospital for weeks that spring and summer. There was no air-conditioning of hospitals in those days. Windows, covered with screens, were left open to draw in whatever breeze might be stirring. There was one "blow fan" in her room.

Dad left the mill at noon every day to walk to the hospital to see her. He ate his lunch from a pail as he hurried along. There was no rule prohibiting children from visiting the hospital, so I saw her most days. My father always went back to visit her after he ate supper.

I did not understand much about her condition, but I did know that she might not recover. I also overheard enough of the adult talk to know that we were in deep trouble financially and the charges from the doctor and the hospital kept mounting. My father was working for common labor wages and there was no such thing as health insurance.

We had no relationship with a bank. My father had borrowed all the money that his brothers and sisters had to loan him. I am sure my Uncle Howard, my mother's brother, had helped also.

My father turned to the only source of help that seemed to be available. That was The Bradley. There was a practice in those days that workers in need could plead their case to Mr. Baker Fullerton, one of the owners. The supplicants waited in line outside Mr. Fullerton's office. Each was allowed a few minutes to make his case for a loan.

My father told Mr. Fullerton of his problem and asked for a loan of $50. He had been a good and willing employee, he recalled; he would work out the loan by his labor at the mill.

Mr. Fullerton turned down his request. His explanation was direct and incredibly callous. "I am not going to let you have the money," he said. "If you people would try to save a little along the way, you wouldn't have to come in here asking me to loan you money." Our family felt the term "you people" was particularly degrading.

I don't know how my family got along, but we survived.

(Years later I was required to work with Mr. Fullerton in a public relations effort on the part of the forest products industry. Time had healed some of the wounds I felt, so I swallowed my pride and did not let him know that I knew of this incident, which I am sure he had forgotten. It was somewhat easier to work with him when I learned of his limitations and could guess at some of his burdens, although they were far different from mine and most people of less privilege. Over several rather strong belts of bourbon one night I heard him bemoan the fact that his grandfather had not bought more timberland when it was available at 50 cents an acre. "We could have owned this whole part of the country," he said. It was believed at the time that the Bradley Lumber Company owned some 350,000 to 400,000 acres of land in South Arkansas.)

Finally, after her stay of several weeks in the hospital I think the doctors about gave up on my mother ever recovering. They sent her home to let her body make a do-or-die effort.

The doctor stopped by occasionally, but he didn't know what to do. He recommended at one point that she eat dill pickles; they might help the healing.

The drainage and the infection from her incision continued. The family collected old sheets from the neighborhood to be ripped into strips and used as compresses and bandages to try to staunch the flow.

Neighbors and friends came to see her often, their worry and concern in plain view. They brought in food and helped wash and sterilize the bandages, which had to be changed several times each day. Our family was in the solid grip of fear.

But somehow over the course of the summer of 1935 she began to improve. The puncture in her bladder started to heal and the leakage stopped. The incision finally healed. She gathered her strength in the fall, and by Thanksgiving she was almost back to her former self, a happy and energetic woman. Everyone said it was a miracle.

ooooooooooooooo

Children in those times learned a lot about dying and death because we saw it up close at home.

Deaths at home always took on the programmed trappings of tribal rituals. The grim news of death spread instantaneously throughout the neighborhood.

The neighbors organized themselves quickly. They knew what needed to be done; they had experienced all of this before. The ladies who would put the house in order arrived first. They went about the house doing all sorts of things, depending on the fastidiousness of the homemaker involved. Their work might involve what was described as "turning the house upside down with a good cleaning from the front door to the back." Or it could be little more than dusting and straightening up. If an all out effort was called for, it would be duly commented on with clucking tongues then and later.

To avoid this ever happening at our house my mother always straightened up the house before she went to bed at night. "If I got real sick or died during the night I wouldn't want the neighbors to find my house in a mess," she said.

Pots of coffee and iced tea were made. Someone took on the task of managing the food that would certainly be brought in. The quantity and quality of the food were measures of the standing of the family and how active they had been in supporting grieving neighbors who had dealt with death in their own homes.

There were regulars caregivers who could be counted on. In fact, they wouldn't miss a good funeral. One old lady in the neighborhood never missed the occasion of a death. It was said "she never had a better time than at a funeral."

The preacher came to console the bereaved. He said a prayer for the deceased, the family and the good neighbors who were, he declared, steadfast in their Christian love and support. The pastor sat and rocked awhile. If pressed, he would take a cup of coffee and perhaps a piece of pie. Some pastors were known to always show up around mealtimes.

Meanwhile, some man in the neighborhood made up a roster and assigned shifts of those who would "sit up" all night with the departed once the Frazer Funeral Home had prepared the body and returned it to the home. The family compiled a list of pallbearers and the funeral director began calling the honored ones.

The casket was placed in the living room. It was positioned tastefully against a bank of white lilies. Usually it was left open so that all could see and pay proper respects to the deceased.

By now a full-fledged social event was in full swing. Soon after suppertime the first shift of those who were to "sit up" began to arrive in a properly somber mood. They took a cup of coffee and "just a small plate," and perhaps refills later, of food. There were expressions of sadness about the loss of a friend and neighbor who was almost always recalled as a "good" person who could be counted on for help through thick and thin. Stories of the deceased's life were recalled. It was better if some of the recollections were humorous. Now and then the men drifted outside to get a breathe of fresh air and to smoke.

Friends and neighbors came to call. They signed the registration book, extended their sympathies to the family and had a bit of food and a cup of coffee. Some mercifully came and left with due haste. Others, capitalizing on the chance to visit a bit, hunkered down to stay for an extended period.

There was a festive spirit in the air.

Sometime before midnight the bereaved family could go to bed, totally exhausted, overfed and overconsoled, drifting off to a troubled sleep. The men holding watch over the deceased could be heard engaged in gossip and light hearted banter as if they were gathered around a convivial campfire.

The day of the funeral was busy. Friends returned to sympathize still more. The men from the funeral home came to take away the departed and the flowers; the undertaker's big cars arrived to drive the members of the family to a church for the service. There was a certain amount of consoling satisfaction that came from being seen riding in such splendor.

Soon the funeral procession came back down East Church Street turning south on Cemetery Road, a narrow gravel way leading across the town branch and up the hill to the cemetery. The graveside service was mercifully brief. Contrary to the more sensitive practices of these days the casket was lowered into the ground while the mourners looked on. Soon the sound of dirt being shoveled into the grave provided a gruesome background beat.

Back home after the graveside service friends and relatives gathered to feast once again before they expressed their final sympathy with pledges to help the family and departed.

oooooooooooooooo

It was in this environment that I first saw dying and death as a reality.

My grandmother, Melissa Catherine Ashcraft Reep died on January 28, 1939 in her bed just a few months short of her 78th birthday. I was 12 years old.

She had taken to her bed with the flu just a few weeks earlier. Pneumonia followed quickly. I heard my parents say that the doctor didn't give her much of a chance to get well. When I came home from school one day I learned that she had died and her body had been taken away to the funeral home.

About a year later the family began to be seriously concerned over the health of Uncle Jewell. A prominent hard lump that had been on the back of his neck for years began to enlarge. Then lumps began to appear all over his body. He lost weight and became listless.

The doctor said he had Hodgkin's disease, a form of cancer. By the summer Uncle Jewell was bedridden most of the time. The entire family worked to nurse him. We brought his food to the bed. We bathed him there and helped him with the bedpan. The times he was able to get out of bed he could only stand and stumble along for a few minutes.

He recognized his impending death on a fall afternoon while sitting on the side porch with my mother. "Sister," declared, "I have never seen the color of the leaves as pretty as they are this year, but I will not see them change next year."

When the end seemed near, a special person in his life—a lady with whom he had enjoyed an on-again-off-again romantic liaison through the years—sent word she wanted to pay him a last visit. My mother and grandmother, as well as the other ladies in the neighborhood, had never approved of her. Her impending visit caused my mother considerable stress. When the visitor came to the front door my mother graciously invited her in. Mama told me that she and I should leave the house. "Your uncle needs time to visit with his friend," she confided. She did not need to explain to me, because even we young boys had heard the stories about our visitor and Uncle Jewell. I was proud of how Mama handled the situation.

Uncle Jewell died a few days later.

The funeral flowers and casket left a strange haunting odor in the house long afterward his death.

*Ramon Greenwood*

# CONNECTIONS WITH OTHER WORLDS

The radio and the movies connected us with places where people led lives far different from ours in Warren. Through these media we came to accept the idea that although Warren was the center of the universe, there was a far bigger world out there than we had imagined.

With a turn of the dial, static permitting, those who had radios could tune into programs of drama, humor, intrigue and strange doings created by professional actors, musicians and comedians. News reports came to us from pioneers in the budding specialty of broadcast journalism as they spoke from Washington, New York, Chicago, London, Paris and Berlin. The miseries of war and other forms of suffering were brought into our homes, making the universal human condition more real than ever before.

The big sports events, which we had only been able to read about the next day after they occurred or see in movie news reels a week or so later were now easily accessible in the real time of their happening.

At the same time motion pictures were completing the transition from silent films to the "talkies."

Some "hard-shell" church folks said the movies and all they showed were the work of the Devil; they would be the ruination of us all. Not the least of the evil was that the local theater screened movies at the late show on Saturday night and on Sunday afternoons and nights. The critics said keeping people out until after midnight Saturday would most certainly make them too tired to go to Sunday school and church on the Sabbath. The showings on Sunday afternoons and nights were, of course, in direct conflict

201

with the schedule of the church. However, the churches not withstanding, most people were greatly excited and welcomed these opportunities for entertainment and enlightenment.

ooooooooooooooo

At home, radios were the center for family and even neighborhood gatherings which usually began soon after supper and ended when folks started going home by nine o'clock.

Few people in our neighborhood owned radios, so possession of one conferred a substantial sense of social status. We were lucky that Uncle Van and Aunt Myrtle next door were among the first families we knew to own a radio. We couldn't understand how they could afford it.

It became a routine for my mother, father and grandmother, and sometimes Uncle Jewell, to go over to Uncle Van's house after supper to enjoy two or three programs with them. These nightly visits were great fun and they went along smoothly, at least in our opinion. To our surprise Aunt Myrtle made it plain one night that she had had about enough of having to rush through supper and clean up the kitchen so we could come over to listen to their radio. She said our visits disrupted their family time. It was past time, she said, for us to buy our own radio. My mother took considerable offense, unfairly in retrospect, at this position. I heard the adults in our home discuss this episode at great length. But it is an ill wind that blows no good. My parents bought a radio a few weeks later.

Little Jimmy Dickens was one of our favorites. He was staged as a cute little boy with a precocious talent for singing and playing his guitar in the company of older musicians. One of the supporting cast made it clear he thought Little Jimmy was just about the funniest, most talented youngster

202

around. The act lost a lot of favor with us—in fact, my grandmother was outraged—when we learned that Little Jimmy's most ardent admirer was his father.

Another of our favorites was Jimmy Davis, who was to become governor of Louisiana, due in no small part to his having written "You Are My Sunshine," a classic in its genre, which he sang day in and day out on his radio show. The Sons of the Pioneers, The Riders of the Purple Sage and Minnie Pearl always attracted us when they appeared on "The Grand Ole Opry" and "The Louisiana Hayride."

ooooooooooooooo

The broadcast of heavyweight boxing matches, featuring Joe Louis, and major league baseball with the St. Louis Cardinals, were major events.

On the night of a Joe Louis match we all gathered around the radio situated on the kitchen table to hear the hyped-up announcers report the matches blow by blow. We heard the roar of the crowd and the clanging of the bell to end and start rounds in such far-away places as Yankee Stadium and the Polo Grounds in New York, Washington's Griffith Stadium and Cominsky Park in Chicago.

The breathless reporting of the action by the broadcasters gave us vivid pictures of the action: "Louis hits with a hard left jab to the jaw, a quick left and right to the body. The challenger goes down on a dynamite shot to the head. One, two, three…"

Any racial bias took a second seat when it came to Joe Louis. Radio provided him with a national stage and he became a hero for the entire country. After a number of convincing victories even the most devoted white supremacist stopped claiming that "a good white man" would knock him out in no time. People were even willing to overlook his reported love affair with Sonja Henie, the dazzling blonde ice skater and film star from Norway, who was also said to be a sympathizer of Hitler and Nazi Germany.

Some wag said at the time that there were two things for certain— Roosevelt would probably always be president, and Joe Louis could knock out anybody. Sports writers bestowed all sorts of nicknames on Louis: The Champ, The Brown Bomber, The Dark Destroyer, The Chocolate Chopper and The Dusky David From Detroit.

Joe Louis took on a broader national meaning when he knocked out Max Schmeling, the pride of Nazi Germany, in two minutes and four seconds of the first round, in a match before 70,000 people at Yankee Stadium.

Other opponents fell in rapid order: Billy Conn, Jimmy Braddock, Max Baer and John Henry Lewis. Not the least of the opponents, figuratively and literally, was a bartender and brawler from New Jersey by the name of "Two Ton" Tony Galento.

ooooooooooooooooo

The broadcasts of "Amos 'n' Andy" provide a sharp picture of the contrast between now and those days, when no one had ever heard of political correctness.

The program was introduced on the National Broadcasting Network in 1929 and soon became the most popular radio show of its era. Forty million people were said to tune in to the program, which was sponsored by such household names as Pepsodent toothpaste, Campbell soup, Rinso soap, Rexall drugs and Chrysler automobiles.

The 30-minute show poked fun at the comedic cast of blacks who operated a taxi cab company in Harlem. The story line was explained as "The misadventures of Andrew Halt Brown, the naïve and dim-witted president of the Fresh Air Taxi Company of America, Inc.; Amos Jones, his level-headed partner and the cab driver; and George "Kingfish" Stevens, a con artist and head of the "Mystic Knights of the Sea" fraternity.

To make matters worse by today's standards for political correctness the leading roles were played by two white men, Freeman Gosden and Charles Correll.

It all seemed to be taken as good fun by both blacks and whites.

Imagine such a program ever getting on the air now. In the first place, no sponsor would be willing to risk the boycott of its products that would certainly come. Protesters, no doubt led by Jesse Jackson, would take to the streets.

No one was spared the barbs of humor stereotyping races, colors and creeds.

We heard Bob Burns rattle out his homespun comedy and play his bazooka, a Rube Goldberg sort of instrument fashioned from pieces of pipe and scrap metal. He made a career on the radio and in movies by ridiculing his home state of Arkansas.

Lum and Abner, who were our favorites, were doing the same thing. They were proprietors of a country store and post office. They, too, made a career of making fun of Arkansas, as Lum's grandiose schemes collided with Abner's down-home wisdom in the little mountain hamlet of Pine Ridge, Arkansas. In a way, they were hillbilly versions of Amos 'n' Andy in the good-natured conflicts between a know-it-all and his common-sense sidekick. We didn't realize that these buffoons with their radio programs and movies were solidifying and extending the negative image of Arkansas as a backward enclave for hillbillies which was started by a book detailing the adventures of a traveler on a slow train through Arkansas and the commentaries of others.

ooooooooooooooo

There was a great variety of entertainment to be found every night on radio. Sunday was an especially good time.

NBC's "Chase and Sanborn Radio Hour" featured the shenanigans of ventriloquist Edgar Bergen and his impish dummy, Charlie McCarthy, and sometimes Charlie's country cousin, Mortimer Snerd. It was easy to slip into the belief that Charlie and Mortimer were real persons.

We tuned in "The Maxwell House Hour," "Lux Radio Theater," "The GM Family Party," "The Ipana [toothpaste] Troubadours."

"Fibber McGee and Molly" came to us from their stage home 70 Wistful Vista. There was the goofiness of Ed Wynn as the Fire Chief on his own show sponsored by Texaco; the dry wit of Jack Benny and his driver, Roscoe, and their Maxwell touring car along with Dennis Day, the Irish Tenor; the repartees of George Burns and Gracie Allen and The Easy Aces; the goofiness of Abbott and Costello.

"One Man's Family" introduced us to the soap opera format. Father Barber, the wise grandfather, established a strong radio persona by virtue of a deep audible sigh and the ready dispensing of wisdom to his naïve and restless brood.

We were thrilled by the adventures of "The Lone Ranger" and his trusted partner, Tonto; detectives Sam Spade and Phillip Marlowe; Superman: and Tarzan, Lord of The Jungle.

We heard the big bands—Benny Goodman, Woody Herman, Artie Shaw, Tommy and Jimmy Dorsey, Kay Kyser, Gene Krupa, Harry James, Paul Whiteman, Louie Armstrong, Duke Ellington, Cab Calloway, Freddie Martin and the like—in broadcasts from the networks own studios and from some of the most sophisticated venues for dining and dancing around the country such as the Rainbow Room in New York City, the Skylight Room atop the Peabody Hotel in Memphis, the Blue Room at the Roosevelt Hotel in New Orleans, the Fairmont Hotel in San Francisco and the Edgewater Beach in Chicago.

Glenn Miller, with Tex Beneke, Ray Eberle and the Modernaires as vocalists, was by any measure our favorite orchestra. We rarely missed his daily 15-minute broadcasts beginning with his theme song, "Moonlight Serenade." No one protested that he might be leading young folks astray by advertising Chesterfield cigarettes.

It was a sad day when Glenn Miller announced he was going into the Air Force and closed his program with a new song, "American Patrol." We mourned later when we heard that his plane had disappeared over the English Channel.

We had crushes on beguiling female vocalists such as Helen O'Connell, Helen Forrest, Ginny Simms and Betty Hutton. While they didn't stir our glands, we thought the Andrews Sisters were cute.

The skinny guy with the bow tie, Frank Sinatra, was just launching his career and the girls were swooning. There were heated debates about who had the best voice, Frankie or Bing Crosby. Nat "King" Cole was still with his trio where he was clearly the star. The Ink Spots made one hit record after another.

The music these bands and vocalists performed clearly reflected the mood of the times as the country marched off to war. "I'm Making Believe,"

"He Wears A Pair of Silver Wings," "I'll Be Home For Christmas," "Don't Sit Under The Apple Tree With Anyone Else But Me," "I'll Walk Alone," "I'll Be Seeing You," "Praise the Lord and Pass the Ammunition," "Goodbye Mama, I'm Off to Yokohama," "The White Cliffs Of Dover." There were songs of romance: "At Last," "Serenade In Blue," "Moonlight Serenade," "Skylark". We knew for certain that these songs, especially "Star Dust," our favorite, would be popular forever.

oooooooooooooooo

Radio cultivated and stimulated the imagination of listeners with sound effects and compelling stories that amused, aroused and frightened massive audiences.

Of course, there were no facial expressions or body movements to be seen. Actors relied on their voices to express sorrow, joy, mystery, excitement, whatever emotion was called for by the story. The sound effect of a creaking door in a haunted house raised the hair on the back of our necks. Claps of thunder, galloping horses, racing cars formed vivid mental pictures. Background music enhanced most situations.

Any doubts about the power of radio to stimulate and manipulate the imagination of its audience came to a conclusive end on Sunday night, October 30, 1938.

My Grandmother Reep and I settled in to listen to the radio after my mother and father had gone to church. As she turned the dial we heard a program of music interrupted by a hysterical man sobbing out a news bulletin as if he were taking his last breath. "Ladies and gentlemen." he gasped," this is the most terrifying thing I have ever witnessed. There, I can see the thing's body. It's as large as a bear and it glistens like wet leather.

The eyes are black and gleam like a serpent. The mouth is V-shaped with salvia dripping from its rimless lips."

Total fear and confusion gripped my grandmother and me.

Within a few minutes another reporter came on to explain that Martians had landed on Earth and were already occupying a large portion of the United States. Using their heat-ray devices they had routed the Army and Navy.

A reporter in St. Louis said the city had been destroyed and that people were fleeing as best they could to the countryside. He said the Martians were headed south.

My grandmother sent me out in the front yard several times to see if I could spot anything in the sky toward the north. My imagination was running wild. Still, things looked normal to me, except I did see some stars that I would have sworn looked as if they were turning red. My grandmother insisted that the reports wouldn't be on the radio if they weren't true.

About this time my mother and father came in the door; they had hurried home, having heard some talk of the panic when they came out of church. They tried to reassure us that all was well, although they seemed to have some doubts.

An announcer closed the program in a normal tone of voice, expressing apologies and disclaimers. He said that what we had heard had only been a presentation of H. G. Wells' science fiction thriller, "The War of The Worlds," adopted for broadcast on Mercury Theater by the brilliant young director Orson Welles. The announcer said there had been all sorts of proper disclaimers at the beginning of the program explaining and assuring that it was all fiction.

Nevertheless, there had been widespread hysteria. Radio stations were swamped with calls. People overflowed train and bus stations trying to get away from the invaders from outer space. Roads were jammed with people fleeing the cities. A startling number of people committed suicide.

The New York City Police threatened Welles with arrest, although he had not broken the law. Agencies of the government and the nation's press reprimanded him and the Columbia Broadcasting System.

ooooooooooooooo

Radio was soon to demonstrate another kind of power—its capacity to inform and to shape public opinion and events with its coverage of politics and international conflicts.

Sitting at home we heard Hitler's voice as he raved his madness. Edward R. Murrow and his comrades took us to the scene with his nightly broadcast, beginning "This is London..." We heard the wail of air raid sirens in the background. Live reports brought us the sound of Nazi troops goose-stepping through one captured European capitol after another. The world was reassured for the moment when Neville Chamberlain, the British Prime Minister, went on radio to report that Czechoslovakia had been ceded to Hitler, guaranteeing "peace in our time."

We heard the dive bombers attacking Pearl Harbor and President Roosevelt calling for declarations of war against Japan and the Axis nations.

The President had used the same media—his voice and radio—to lead the country out of the Great Depression.

ooooooooooooooo

Radio, with relatively little regulation and a largely unsophisticated audience, was a breeding ground for all sorts of charlatans.

210

There was no better example of this brand of hustlers than "Dr." John Brinkley, commonly referred to as the "Goat Gland Doctor," who operated out of Arkansas at the height of his career.

Doctor Brinkley, who had no known medical credentials, began his career as a hot check artist. At some point he claimed to have developed a surgical procedure by which he could transplant the gonads of a goat into an aged human male, and thus restore him to a vigorous sexual life.

Radio was his key to success. Using a 50,000-watt station that he operated in Kansas, he inundated a good part of the nation with his message and testimonials from satisfied customers. "Why be a capon?" he challenged in his commercials.

After his shady past began to catch up with him Doctor Brinkley moved his enterprise to Little Rock. It was a good move, he said, because he had determined that the glands from goats raised in Kansas imparted an unpleasant odor to the resurrected patients whereas those in Arkansas did not.

He was soon to relocate again, this time in the wake of the chilly reception he received from the city fathers in Little Rock. The location he chose for his home and clinic was a sylvan setting on the highway between Little Rock and Sheridan. It had been the site of a nightclub and retreat for Shriners. With his typical hype Dr. Brinkley labeled it the "world's most beautiful hospital." From there he kept blasting away with illegal signals from super clear channel radio station, which was by this time relocated in Mexico. And men seeking to recapture their youth continued to flock to his clinic.

Medical professionals and government officials finally cracked down on Doctor Brinkley and his kind of radio station.

Yet he left a legacy of sorts. There were people who maintained that he had been on to something. Others were fond of describing an event that took place in a hurry as "Faster than a goat going by Doctor Brinkley's clinic."

ooooooooooooooo

Radio provided us with the opportunity to hear about the rest of the world; the movies let us see what that world looked like.

Almost always the view was through rose-colored glasses.

Warren was fortunate to have a movie theater from the earliest days of talking pictures. Mr. Wharton and his family came to town in the early days of the 1930s to own and operate the Pastime Theater. Later they opened the Avalon Theater near Hughes Café on Main Street. The Wharton's picture business thrived until television virtually killed the medium.

The talking picture shows were a fascinating new medium that had its commercial beginning in 1927, the year I was born. The idea that audiences in our town could actually see and hear Al Jolson perform in *The Jazz Singer*, the first feature-length film with spoken dialogue, was mind-boggling. It was equally amazing that people could see live moving pictures and hear the sounds from people and places around the world.

Mr. Wharton's Pastime Theater soon became the entertainment and social center in town for people of all ages who could scrape together the few cents a ticket cost.

The theater was "integrated" to the extent that blacks could enter by a side door and sit in one-half of the balcony, next to where Mr. Joe Griffin ran the projector.

Later, when Mr. Wharton air-conditioned the theater, a lot of people went to the movies on summer nights just to avoid the heat. (It was the first air-conditioned building in town.) It was quite a sensation to go from waiting in line outside in 100-degree temperature in to the comfortable seats in the cool, airy theater.

ooooooooooooooo

Saturday matinees at the Pastime Theater were special times for my friends and me in our pre-teens.

Those were our opportunities to enter a wild world of adventure. Week after week, we returned, drawn by our addictions to the bill that opened with a short feature, known as the serial, that unfolded a story over several weeks like so many chapters in a book. To miss an episode was to be out of the loop among one's friends who had been there to see it.

The settings varied from the jungles of Africa, populated by ferocious beasts and spear-carrying natives, to some far-away planet where a rocketship landed, leaving its crew to deal with evil rulers, to westerns where heroes on white horses shot it out with sneaky Indians and outlaws. But the story lines were always the same. The good guys, who were on a mission to rescue someone or something, confronted the bad guys, who were determined to stop them by fair play or otherwise.

Each installment ended with the hero or heroine in grave danger. In one typical serial, the hero was tied down in a run-away canoe going over a waterfall. There seemed to be no way for him to escape. We were left to debate all week whether the hero had reached the end of his valorous life. The next week's episode began with a replay of the harrowing scene. Only this time the hero was able to struggle out of his bondage just in time to flip out of the canoe and grasp an overhanging tree limb as the fragile vessel hurdled over the falls. Somehow we failed to catch on to the weekly pattern of danger and ultimate survival or maybe we didn't want to destroy the illusion. In any case, the hero's fate was discussed often during the following week.

ooooooooooooooo

Exciting as they were, the serials were only the warm-ups for the features.

We found our true heroes in these movies which were almost always "westerns." There was no confusion between the good and the bad. The "good guys" wore white hats and rode big stallions of uncommon intelligence. The "bad guys" wore black hats and rode smaller horses not nearly so splendid as the steeds the heroes mounted. The heroes played by the rules and suffered big but temporary setbacks as the results of the villains' underhanded dealings. The Indians almost always sided with the outlaws. There were rare exceptions to this rule such as Tonto, the Lone Ranger's sidekick. The heroes were often seen chasing down runaway wagons and stagecoaches. These scenes usually included attractive young women dressed in long gingham dresses, swooning in the drama of it all. You could bet the rescuers always got the girl to the extent that holding her hand constituted "got." To be seen kissing would have destroyed the rugged hero persona.

Sometimes a "good guy" like Gene Autry, Dick Foran and Roy Rogers picked a guitar and sang along with the perfectly pitched voices of a backup group of vocalists. Their songs were about campfires, roundups and sagebrush. Many of us thought that "singing cowboys" were too sissy. The only exception was Tex Ritter, who really couldn't sing anyway. I particularly didn't like Roy Rogers. His palomino horse Trigger was all right, but he spent too much time with his girlfriend, Dale Evans. Some comedian said that Roy Rogers kissed his horse, but never Dale.

Although the roles of the heroes were the same we had our favorites among the actors. Each of them brought enough differences to the screen that we could argue endlessly about who was the best shooter, the best horseman, the bravest among a list that included William Boyd, (aka Hopalong Cassidy,) Jack Holt, Johnny Mack Brown, Hoot Gibson, Tom Mix, Tim McCoy, Ken Maynard, Harry Carrey and Buck Jones. Bob Steel was on and off the list because for a while he was a "good guy," but then he turned bad. Nevertheless, he made 180 westerns.

Most of the leading men had sidekicks for comic relief. We were greatly amused by Andy Devine and his strained voice and "Gabby" Hays, a smallish man who wore an unruly graybeard and a bedraggled hat.

The moviemakers were careful to go only so far with the violence. When there was "gun play" the shooters were only wounded in the shoulder or leg. We never saw blood. If we did, it was only a dark splotch seeping around the bandana used to bandage the wound. Arrows were quickly pulled out. The heroine soothed the hero's fevered brow with cool water from a nearby spring. Injuries were always borne with gritted teeth and a weak smile.

It was not unusual for the audience's fascination with the suspense of the unfolding plot to be so intense that someone called out a warning to the hero to avoid an ambush clearly seen by those watching.

We went with Tarzan, who was Olympic swimmer Johnny Weissmuller in real life, to his tree house in the jungles of Africa where he resided with his wife, Jane, "Boy," their precocious offspring, and "Cheeta," their pesky but often helpful chimpanzee. We didn't complain when the setting inexplicably switched from the deepest jungles, where the enemies were blacks armed with spears and bows and arrows, wearing bones in their noses, to desert settings where evil rulers lived in elaborate caves and cavorted about in flowing robes and strange headgear that looked a lot like that those worn by the Martians that battled "Flash" Gordon in other films.

We were engrossed and happily entertained so long as Tarzan outswam the alligators in the swamps, manhandled the lions, stood off the fierce natives and glided from tree to tree on long vines that were always conveniently in place.

Excitement was added to the afternoon when we agreed with some of the girls to meet inside the theater and sit together.

The Saturday matinee cost only a dime, but that was not always easy to come by. I was stunned one Saturday when Mama said she didn't have a dime to spare. No movie. I threw a crying fit, which lasted most of the morning. The world, as I knew it, was crashing around me. Finally, my mother came to me where I was sitting under the Cape Jasmine bush by the side of the house, no doubt pouting. She handed me a dime, hugged my neck and said that I should enjoy the movie. I was not proud of my behavior, but not too remorseful to turn down the trip to the movies. I hope she knew I appreciated what she and my father had done.

ooooooooooooooo

The movies provided a brand of humor and young romance just right for youngsters.

We thought The Three Stooges, who appeared in "shorts," and The Marx Brothers, who made feature-length films, were the funniest people in the world. Stan Laurel and Oliver Hardy movies kept us in stitches as the mournful Stan always got in a jam trying to extricate Oliver, his buddy, from some self-inflicted problem. Martha Raye, a singer and comedienne who had the biggest mouth in Hollywood, was right up there with them. Joe E. Brown made comedic history with his goofy grin that stretched from ear to ear across an incredibly funny face.

We all wanted to be a member of *Our Gang* so we could consort with Spanky and Buckwheat as they held meetings in their clubhouse, a setup we all envied and tried to duplicate in the playhouses we built.

As we got older and our libidos began to take over we felt pure envy, relieved only a bit by the entertainment of it, over the Andy Hardy movies. Mickey Rooney, Judy Garland and Ann Rutherford, teenagers so glamorous, wise and foolish, sophisticated and innocent at the same time, brought a hint of romance, pathos and comedy to their stories. Judge Hardy, portrayed by Lewis Stone, was a wise and patient father figure who was head of the household that lived in the clapboard house behind a white picket fence on a shady street in their picturesque hometown.

Mickey and Judy are best recalled for their staging of elaborate musical variety shows in a barn. Their schemes began with someone's bright idea to put on a show to raise money for one good community cause or another. Swept up in it all, we didn't stop to wonder how they came to have costumes, lights and an orchestra for their staging. But they did, and put on a full-blown play right there in the barn.

oooooooooooooooo

Movies were never more popular than in the years when the 1930s were winding down. The country was still in the grips of a depression. People sought something to take their minds off the grind of making a go of it in a hard-knock world.

We had never seen anything to match the excitement and anticipation that accompanied the making of a movie from the hugely popular 1936 novel, *Gone With the Wind.*

The country was enthralled by this story of a willful woman and the people around her as they fought to survive the Civil War and the Reconstruction at Tara, the heroine's family plantation. The book sold a million copies in 31 printings during its first year. The movie was to be even more popular.

Hollywood worked the country into a high pitched excitement with announcements about which stars would make up the cast. Vivien Leigh, an English actress, was a surprise selection to play Scarlett O'Hara. Clark Gable was cast as Rhett Butler, a cynical rogue turned into a reluctant hero. Leslie Howard became Ashley Wilkes, a Southern aristocrat, and Olivia de Havilland was to appear as Melanie Hamilton, a sugary, see-no-evil plantation lady. In a departure from the customs of the day two black women had prominent roles: Butterfly McQueen became the giddy Prissy, a domestic at Tara, and Hattie McDaniel played the strong role of Mammy, Miss O'Hara's confidant, dresser and handmaiden.

The film debuted in Atlanta in 1939. It was not long in coming to Warren. The school officials and city fathers deemed it of such historic and social importance that we were let out of school one afternoon to see it.

Before our very eyes we saw Tara fall apart when the men went off to battle on the Confederate side and the carpetbaggers rode through. We saw a few kindly Union officers, such as portrayed by Ward Bond, act on their concerns for the ladies and children left behind to keep the plantations going. We saw the carnage of war and scenes of Atlanta being burned.

Many of the scenes were made even more realistic because we had heard people who had lived in those times tell stories of what they had seen and felt.

Some were shocked, others were titillated, when they heard Rhett leave Scarlett with the immortal line, "Frankly, my dear, I don't give a damn" at the end of the film. It was not the fact that he was leaving. Many people thought he should; a few in the audience applauded. It was his use of that word "damn" that stirred the emotions. Such language simply wasn't used in movies back then. We heard that the "damn" had barely cleared the Hayes Office, which protected the morals of the country. The censors wanted him to say, "Frankly, my dear, I don't care." The producer successfully argued that such tepid words hardly fit the image of a hard-driving soldier of fortune such as Rhett Butler. We looked forward to hearing the actual words come from Clark Gable.

It is amazing to contemplate how much emotion was generated by *Gone With The Wind*. The movie was actually a fairly balanced presentation between the North and the South, each with its share of villains and heroes. But to put it in perspective there were still many people around Warren who lived in those times or who had heard, as I had, first hand stories of the War Between the States from those who had lived it. Any attempt at balance in the story was rejected. The North was wrong; the South was right.

ooooooooooooooo

Those were the times of the big full blown movies—musicals, dramas and comedies.

As we grew into our mid-to-late teens, the late picture show on Saturday night became the event not to be missed. The line for tickets started to form soon after 9:30 when the stores on Main Street began to close. We were excited by the prospects of the film we were about to see and tantalized by the aroma of Doc Powell's fresh popcorn. The program began sharply at 10:20 and we were back out on the streets by 12:30 or so.

Sunday nights were the time to take a date to the movies.

Fred Astaire and Ginger Rogers, he in his tuxedo and she in her flowing evening grown, danced in lavish settings of waterfalls, swirling lights and elegant stairways. A big orchestra, the members dressed in tails and stuffed shirts, provided the fullest of music. There were usually massive white pianos with candelabra atop them.

Ester Williams combined sex appeal and athleticism as she performed her water ballets in perfect unison in pools filled with bathing beauties in demure bathing suits as handsome men in white dinner jackets looked on.

Nelson Eddy and Jeanette MacDonald were both just plain pretty. He most often was dressed in tails and a sparkling white shirt. If these weren't the costume and setting he was probably in the uniform of the Northwest Mounted Police or cowboy garb. She was customed in flowing gauzy gowns or impossibly chic buckskin. They were elegant and romantic as they sang in ballrooms or on balconies in the moonlight or by campfires along side waterfalls deep in a Canadian forest.

There was never much plot to the films which their promoters called "extravaganzas." But no one cared.

We saw a lot of gangsters in such movies as *Little Caesar*, featuring Edgar G. Robinson and *Dead End* with Humphrey Bogart. Paul Muni had the lead in *I Am A Fugitive From A Chain Gang*. As if to prove his versatility, Muni also starred in *The Story of Louis Pasteur*, the French chemist who founded modern microbiology and developed vaccines for anthrax, rabies and chicken cholera.

As bad as the hoodlums might have been, the roles often evoked some empathy from the viewers as the outlaws fought against the bankers and land barons who frequently were reviled by the public for causing the Great Depression. Those who produced the movies knew how to connect with their audiences.

Horror movies scared the wits out of us, but we never wanted to miss them. *Dracula* starred Bela Lugosa at about the time Boris Karloff was making the first of several Frankenstein pictures. We were chilled to the bone by *The Hound of The Baskerville*, set in the foreboding fog of the moors of England. *The Invisible Man* with Claude Raines was no less frightening.

We enjoyed the great stars like Jimmy Stewart, Gary Cooper, Clark Gable, Charles Boyer, Sidney Greenstreet, John Wayne, Tyrone Power, Wallace Beery, Chill Wills, Peter Lorre, Richard Widmark, Gene Tierney, Joan Crawford, Lana Turner, Rita Hayworth, Betty Grable, Marlene Dietrich and Bette Davis.

Some were best known as couples: Spencer Tracey and Katherine Hepburn in sophisticated social commentaries; Lauren Bacall and Humphrey Bogart portraying characters barely on the right side of the law in tense thrillers; William Powell and Myrna Loy as super sophisticates who seemed always to have a chilled straight-up martini and cigarettes in their hands. Their dog, Asta, joined in as they solved crimes in *The Thin Man* series.

Although no one seemed to be aware of it, we now know that as we neared the end of the 1930s and entered the 1940s the movies were increasingly used to prime the country for the prosecution of a war. Newsreels showed the atrocities of war as committed by the Nazis and "yellow hordes" of Japan. We hated Erich von Stroheim when he portrayed a Nazi officer. His stiff uniform, shaved head and monocled eye personified evil. The "Japs," as we knew them, were often shown burning villages. Scenes of bayoneting innocent civilians were not actual shown but we somehow got the message that it was commonplace.

We saw a lot of flag waving, people marching in patriotic parades, war plants operating around the clock and brave men assaulting beaches.

Our boys were pictured in one heroic deed after another: flying fighter planes, manning machine guns, steering warships through hails of gunfire and withstanding torture rather than revealing the secrets of our armed forces. The loyal sidekicks, usually plain boys from Brooklyn or farms in the Midwest, were odds on favorites to be killed, leaving behind a message to their buddies and families back home to keep up the good fight.

The newsreels showed several of our favorite movie stars enlisting in the services. We heard that some of them had gone immediately into combat. We saw clips of those who stayed behind and went on national tours to sell war bonds and encourage the collection of scrap metal.

Movies ended with a stirring picture of the American flag waving in the breeze and patriotic music filling the theater.

The starlets and female leads had their wartime movie roles to play. They were hostesses at USO clubs where servicemen were entertained before they went off to battle. They also portrayed loyal brides and mothers waiting anxiously at home for their men to return. In the meantime, they took up jobs in the war plants, knitted sweaters or rolled bandages at the local church. The actors who portrayed children of the servicemen were seen variously with stiff upper lips and tear-filled eyes, but always brave about the situation.

Some of the most memorable movies of the time concerned men and women stealing a brief time of love from the massive upheavals of a world at war. The classsics of these movies were *Casablanca* and *For Whom The Bell Tolls* made from Ernest Hemingway's legendary novel about the civil war in Spain.

No one who saw such films could forget the drama surrounding those great love stories and the struggles against evil.

In *For Whom the Bell Tolls* Gary Cooper played Robert Jordan, an American hero fighting in the mountains with the guerillas against the tyrannical government during the Spanish civil war. The dashing soldier of fortune falls madly in love with Maria, a gypsy girl played by Ingrid Bergman. In one scene, very spicy for those days, little doubt was left that Robert and Maria had made love in his bedroll under the stars as a light snow fell.

The same Ingrid Bergman, turned up as Ilsa, an entrancing figure of intrigue, playing opposite Humphrey Bogart, as "Rick" Blaine, a hardened expatriate, in the movie *Casablanca.* The movie was also populated with such stars as Paul Henreid, Sidney Greenstreet, Claude Raines and Peter Lorre.

Bogart outwits the Nazis so that he, Ilsa and Laslo, her husband, a leader of the freedom fighters, can escape from the Moroccan city to continue the war against evil. Ilsa is torn with regret in leaving Rick, her true love, but he assures her she has to go because, in a world with issues so much larger than their love they must sacrifice and continue the fight for peace.

We left the theater thrilled and humming the theme song "As Time Goes By" sung by Sam.

But none of these classics enthralled me like the drama of *Laura*. It is my all-time favorite motion picture. The setting was in New York City, which I envisioned as the most romantic place in the world where I wanted to live one day. There were scenes of the heroine's luxurious apartment, a

223

country cottage, night clubs and restaurants, swank cocktail parties, and the offices of an advertising agency.

The stunningly beautiful Gene Tierney, who portrayed Laura, led the cast along with Dana Andrews who played Mark McPherson, a hardened blue-collar, New York detective. Clifton Webb was masterful in his role as Waldo Lydecker, an egomaniacal, sarcastic New York elitist gossip columnist who falls madly in love with Laura, whom he had adopted as his protégé. Vincent Price was Shelby Carpenter, an insipid gigolo who lives the good life thanks to the generosity of the women he charmed. Laura and McPherson fall in love. Lydecker is gunned down by the police.

There was never more than a kiss between McPherson and Laura, but the sexual tension vibrated right off the screen, exceeding anything in today's see-all, do-all films.

The background music, the haunting melody and lyrics of the theme song "Laura" transported the story and the sense of it all to another level.

"...and you see Laura on a train that is passing through...those eyes how familiar they seem...that was Laura, but she is only a dream."

ooooooooooooooo

It was easy to romanticize about the adventurous lives we heard about on the radio and saw in films.

Big-game hunting; undercover agents working behind enemy lines; brave men assaulting the beaches in the Pacific Islands; cowboys defending a surrounded wagon train; explorers fighting off the natives in remote jungles; scientists subduing monsters in laboratories; sleek women in perfect clothes and handsome men in tweed jackets and trench coats living dangerous lives in foreign cities; beautiful people dancing in night clubs; lovers and soldiers traveling across the country by train.

The radio and motion pictures of those days fired my imagination and had a great influence on my life.

## THE HAND OF LAW AND ORDER

Maintaining law and order was a rough business in that time and place. The hand of the law was usually swift, sure and often harsh in the style of the frontier. The lines were clearly fixed between the law enforcers, who wore big badges and carried billy clubs and six-shooter pistols, and those who broke the law.

There was crime in Warren, but still it was a safe place in which to grow up. No one ever locked a door or window at night. Young and old alike had free run of the town day and night. If on the rare occasion something was stolen the thief was usually arrested within hours and the item was most often recovered. Violence, when it did occur, was an isolated incident. Citizens knew the difference between right and wrong, between guilty and not guilty, because they were on a first-name basis with the human beings involved and the issues at stake.

Most people believed that criminals should be held responsible for the crimes they committed rather than society being responsible for the actions of those who broke the law. Public opinion exerted a powerful influence on the execution of the law.

Still, many thought the law was often unfair, with the balance tipped in favor of the "haves" over the "have nots."

It was widely believed that the law took the side of the Bradley Lumber Company when workers went on strike in the traumatic birth of a labor union for local workers. Some said the offices of the marshall and sheriff were strengthened by tough goons hired from out of town by the company to keep the striking workers in line.

The gossip was that a local druggist was a "dope fiend," but the law looked the other way. On the other hand, a mill hand or a farmer who got drunk and acted up on Saturday would be hauled off to jail.

Proprietors of business were empowered to protect their own establishments. Some of them kept a billy club or the big end of a pool cue under their cash registers. Guns for self-defense were not unusual.

While the law seemed to give a wide berth to the goings on out at the Airport Inn. The owners, Rex and Ollie Fraser, assured that those who went there for a few beers or swigs of bourbons chased with Coca-Cola behaved themselves. Rex had his pool cue ready and he was willing to use it. Still, the place was known as the "Bucket of Blood." The Frasers were particularly vigilant on Saturday nights when people came to dance and blow off steam from the week's work. I was glad to see Rex in action one night when I foolishly tried to stop a fight between a man and his wife on the dance floor only to have the man pull a knife and chase me out the front door.

One of the older boys in the neighborhood told of being taken by an adult to a beer joint where he saw a scene straight out of a western epic when one of the owners of the place brought a gang fight to an early conclusion and cleared the house when she took a rifle from under the bar and began firing into the ceiling while she ordered everyone to settle down.

ooooooooooooooo

It is easy to see now that little attention was paid to the balance of justice between the blacks and the whites.

While law officers kept a heavy lid on crime in town, they did little more than contain "Catfish," the blacks' business section, an enclave with its own rules and customs. The town heard about bloody knife fights, icepick stabbings and Saturday night shootings, but the white lawmen seldom ventured there except in the case of murder. It was thought to be better to let "those people" take care of their own problems.

However, if one watched his step, "Catfish" could be a relatively safe place for whites to go. R. P. Dial sometimes took members of his high school band there to hear live jazz from a reserved section in the balcony of one of the nightspots.

Adventurous boys were known to go to the alley behind "Catfish Row" to buy a bottle of cheap wine or bourbon.

A black man who talked back to a white, especially a lady, or crowded a white off the sidewalk was likely get a hard slap with a billy club or blackjack, no questions asked. I saw a lawman beat a black man mercilessly with his billy club in front of Shorty Montgomery's barbershop. Someone said the drunk black had staggered into a white man and failed to apologize.

oooooooooooooooo

While Warren was a peaceful town, the law was frequently challenged for real or imagined crimes and threats of crimes.

Lawmen and townspeople went on special alert when the gypsies made their annual pilgrimage in the spring to their campground at Hi-Y Hill across from Joe Griffin's pasture.

The gypsies, short of stature and dark of complexion, dressed in clothes garnished with beads and spangles. They traveled in a caravan of good automobiles and trucks followed by a few garish buggies and wagons drawn by finely groomed horses with decorative harnesses.

It was just a "known fact" that these foreigners did all sorts of evil things. They were said to be dope fiends who smoked Mary Wanna, as people pronounced it, and sacrificed animals in secret rites when they gathered at night around their campfire. It was believed that these wandering tribes would steal anything from chickens and pigs to valuables from the house. Someone said they might even kidnap children and force them to become members of their brotherhood. The word went out to keep everything under lock and key. At best, people said gypsies were known as sharp traders who would skin your eyeteeth.

The truth was that no one really knew how they lived and what supported them other than their selling trinkets, telling fortunes and sharpening knives and scissors.

The king of gypsies paid a courtesy call on the mayor and officers of the law when the band came to town. All parties agreed on the rules by which the visitors would conduct themselves during their encampment. When they were ready to leave town the king stopped by to inform the officers that his band was departing and to settle any differences that might have come up.

ooooooooooooooo

During the hard times of the Depression, many houses and small businesses burned to the ground.

The common explanation was that the owners "had sold out to the man up north." That was to say the owners had set fire to their own property in order to collect the insurance from the big companies who issued policies from the big cities "up north." The local law looked the other way when these reports surfaced.

A feud between two farm families over a property line erupted in violence when a pair of brothers in one clan burned the barn of their neighbor.

A boy in our neighborhood stole a shotgun from a car parked on Main Street. He was arrested and put in the local jail, tried in a court of law within days and immediately sent away to the state penitentiary for 18 months. There was no talk of leniency for a first offense, nor were there excuses that he was a victim of society. He served his time and came home a hardened, intimidating man.

A hoodlum on the run from lawmen in Louisiana robbed a filling station when passing through Warren. In the course of the theft he shot and killed a local boy by the name of Kelly who was working there. Rumors swept through town that the killer was either John Dillinger or "Pretty Boy" Floyd, the notorious outlaws who were rampaging through the region at about that time. The killer was quickly tried and convicted in the local court.

A local boy capped his career in crime, during which he was repeatedly in and out of prison, with a conviction for kidnapping one of the state's leading industrialists.

Two brothers were widely thought to have shot their abusive father to death. If they ever stood a real trial the proceedings were over before they got started. It was as if the community had made a judgment that the father deserved what he got so the boys should be let off for cause.

oooooooooooooooo

Public drunkenness was one of the main problems dealt with by the law, especially on Saturday afternoons.

National prohibition was repealed in 1933 and the country was adjusting to the fact that liquor was widely available by the bottle. The people of Warren who had a thirst took full advantage of their new freedom to visit anyone of at least seven liquor stores and countless beer joints in town. Bootleg whiskey continued to be readily available on the sly because some people simply liked its taste.

Carl "Peanut" Hughes ran a liquor store next to Hughes Café operated by his sons, Grady and "Skeeter," across Main Street from the Bradley Store.

Mr. Hughes had lost an arm in a sawmill accident after which he turned to selling parched peanuts on the streets. He accumulated enough money to open his café and then the liquor store. The Hughes enterprises prospered.

Both Hughes Café and The Wonder Bar, operated by the Herring brothers just a few storefronts south, did a big business in beer, served ice cold in tall brown bottles, and hamburgers. Hughes's place also featured pies topped with towering layers of meringue baked by Grady's wife, Mamie. The Herring boys' place provided pool tables and dominoes.

I went to Hughes's once with my father. We ate hamburgers. I drank a Coca-Cola while Dad had a Jax beer. I was fascinated to see him sprinkle salt down the neck of the bottle, creating big bubbles and a lot of foam. He let me have a sip of the frothy brew which I found to be a bitter concoction. The fact that my father had let me taste a beer must have worried him because he told me more than once on the way home that I was not to tell my mother. I felt important sharing the secret with him.

Drinking men gathered around "Peanut" Hughes's liquor store every Saturday afternoon.

Most of the liquor business was transacted with Mr. Hughes through a sliding window at the front of his narrow space, which was known as the "Hole In The Wall." He also did a brisk business out the backdoor with those patrons who didn't want to be seen buying a bottle.

Mill hands worked until noon on Saturday then came to town to let off a little steam. The first stop for many of them was The Bradley Store, where they bought several cartons of cigarettes against the credit they had earned working at the mill. They took these across the street to the liquor store to trade them at a deep discount for a bottle of liquor. Farmers brought chickens and eggs and other produce to swap for liquor.

Just as surely as a man had bought a bottle of liquor he was bound to drink all of it. Most of the drinking was done in the alleys and in the wagon lots behind Main Street during the early part of the afternoon. But by the time we came out of the Saturday movie matinee, a lot of the drinkers had gathered on the sidewalk from Hughes down to The Wonder Bar. Ladies and children were expected to avoid that area. Still, we youngsters hung around on the edge of the crowds to see the action. No one tried to interfere when an irate wife, who braved the embarrassment of it all, stepped in to pull her husband away from the drinkers and haul him home to sober up.

As surely as night follows day, some men, having put away most of their bottle by mid-afternoon became boisterous, staggering, fall-down drunk.

When there were outbreaks of loud cursing and fighting either Marshall Trav Beard or Marshall Jess Crawford showed up to corral the troublemakers.

Each lawman had his own style and methods of law enforcement. Marshall Beard was an imposing figure of a man. His bearing, set off by a full head of snow-white hair, spoke authority. The impression he created

233

was enhanced by the oversized six-shooter, silver with a heavy bone handle, that he carried on his hip in a hand-tooled leather holster. He reminded me of the hero in one of the shoot-em-up picture shows.

The drunks and the crowds of amused hecklers and irate family members usually calmed down when he arrived on the scene. Most offenders were willing to let him walk them off to jail where they could sober up. He rarely had to club a man unconscious with his blackjack. But when force was necessary he administered it with a minimum of show.

Jesse Crawford was a man who enforced the law with a heavy billyclub that evoked fear and intimidation. A staunch member of the First Baptist Church, he was viewed as a pious administrator of the law. He looked the part, dressed in navy blue pants, a white shirt and sometimes a suit coat to match. He wore a badge that seemed to be as big as a saucer. The tension increased when he arrived at the scene of a disturbance. It was almost certain that one or more of the offenders would resist him. The drunks ended up being knocked down and beat up by Marshall Crawford before being dragged off to the city jail. The same went for the man's drinking buddies who might be foolish enough to try to help their fallen friend. Wives and children were left wailing on the street, appealing the offender's case.

The same kind of conflicts took place in the wagon yards and on Myrtle Street beside the Southern Hotel.

By late afternoon the heavy drinkers had thinned out.

Those who had wives and children at home staggered away to receive their punishment in the form of reprimands from their wives and children. Some of them had managed to buy a half-pint of bourbon to help ease themselves through the sobering up that night and the next day before going back to work on Monday.

The hard core, those who couldn't face going home or had no real home and family to go to, hung on till sundown. The stragglers made their way back across the street to the meat market at The Bradley Store. There they used up some of their credit to buy chunks of baloney and "rat" cheese, along with loaves of bread or sacks of soda crackers for their evening meal. One of the heavy drinkers, a fellow by the name of McCain, was widely known for buying a pint of raw oysters. He said oysters sobered him up and kept him healthy. A few of them bartered more cigarettes for a supper of sausage and eggs or hamburgers at Hughes's Café.

These scenes were repeated Saturday after Saturday. No lessons were learned and best intentions were soon forgotten by men looking for escape from the hard times.

ooooooooooooooo

No event enhanced the image of early-day law enforcement in Warren as much as the legend of the Ricks-Hoyle shootout.

Walter Ricks was widely known around town as a tough bully. Bob Hoyle, a short, unimposing figure for a lawman, was night marshall. His detractors said his ego was bigger than he was.

There was bad blood between Ricks and Hoyle. The hard feelings began to boil on the morning of the fateful day. By the time Marshall Hoyle came on duty at noon Ricks had been seen carrying a pistol. When citizens complained, the lawman went to take Ricks to jail, but the attempted arrest turned violent. It was quickly reported over town that Ricks had wrestled Marshall Hoyle's gun away from him and rubbed the barrel over his face and head, threatening to shoot him if he ever came again to arrest him.

235

For the next several hours Ricks and his cohorts rode about town flaunting their pistols and generally disturbing the peace. Along the way they sent word to Marshall Hoyle that they were coming to get him. Rumor had it that Mr. Hoyle called for help from other lawmen, but they were afraid to come to his aid. By this time Mr. Hoyle had retreated to the sheriff's office in the small redbrick building on the northeast corner of the court square.

That night Ricks drove a car up over the curb onto the courthouse grounds and headed for the marhall's retreat. Mr. Hoyle was to relate that he felt he had but one chance and that was to hide in the bushes outside the building out of range of the headlights of Rick's car. It was there that he heard Ricks call for him to step outside and shoot it out.

According to the marshall, Ricks fired the first shot into the windows of the little building. The marshall returned the fire with one or more blasts from his shotgun, killing Ricks and wounding his sidekick.

Marshall Hoyle stood for a perfunctory court hearing. He was not indicted. But the story was told and retold in many different versions for many years. The reputations of the city's other lawmen who were thought to have turned coward and failed to answer Mr. Hoyle's call for help were tarnished. Mr. Hoyle was a town hero for a time.

ooooooooooooooo

As a boy I was fascinated by the drama of the conflict between the law and the community.

I begged my parents to let me go to the courthouse to see trials in process. I imagine they must have thought I would grow up to be a lawyer. In any case, they encouraged me in my interest, and what they took to be my ambition, so they let me go to the courtroom, although my mother was concerned that I might hear and see some things a bit risqué for a lad of my age.

I was greatly impressed by what I saw—Judges Bradham and Perkins in their black robes sitting above the hushed courtrooms; lawyers in their business suits trying to make their cases before juries. When I heard the prosecutor charge the accused with the worse possible behavior I just knew he was guilty as sin. I soon changed my mind when I heard the defense.

I wonder how the lawmen and the citizens of those days would react to the resolution of issues of law and order that plague today's world.

# THE POWER OF READING AND WRITING

An insatiable compulsion to read, along with the ambition to write, made a crucial difference in my life.

Reading, beyond the narrow confines of classrooms, has been the primary tool of my education. It has taken me to places I could never have gone otherwise and opened my eyes to the possibilities the world has to offer. Writing has given me an outlet for whatever creativity I possess and has provided me with the basis for a rewarding career.

ooooooooooooooo

I believe I inherited my love of reading from my father.

Although the economic conditions of his family and the dictates of the time prevented him from going beyond the sixth or seventh grade in a one-room schoolhouse, he was an avid reader within the limits of his opportunities. His favorites were the daily *Arkansas Democrat* and pulp magazines which featured a variety of stories ranging from "The Spider" and "The Batman" to westerns and the saga of gold mining in the Far North.

He had the opportunity to read an occasional book, too. I was told that the spelling of my given middle name, Ramon, unusual as it was for our time and in our part of the country, came about because at the time I was born he was reading a book about the adventures of a Spanish nobleman bearing that name. My mother insisted that I be named Charles in memory of her father. My father held out for Ramon as my middle name. Somehow

239

he even convinced my mother and my grandmother that I should be addressed by my middle name.

My long-running love affair with books began when I was a very young boy. It continues today. It is difficult to pass a bookstore without going in and browsing the shelves and tables. I am always behind in reading the books I have bought. But no matter, I take great pleasure simply in owning books. Libraries attract me like honey draws bees. In short I am a compulsive reader, a bookaholic. If I go many days without reading I feel withdrawal pains. I have a hard time watching an entire television program without picking up a book, a magazine, a newspaper or whatever has print on it to read for awhile.

ooooooooooooooo

In the home in which I grew up there were no books to speak of beyond a family bible.

My parents more than made up for that condition when they gave me what was surely the most important material gift they ever provided. It was a membership in the Warren public library. I think it cost $1.00 a year. I must have been about 12 years old.

Lesley Conger expressed my feelings about libraries when he wrote: "The best of my education has come from the public library... You don't need to know very much to start with, if you know the way to the public library."

The library occupies a colorful and critical place in the history of Warren. In 1926 the Warren Woman's Club took on as its main project the establishing of a library. The club was not able to secure a permanent place because it couldn't raise enough money for rent. Mrs. Lee Martin assumed the chairmanship, a position she held for 14 years. The position included the responsibility of keeping the library's hand full of books, in the sunroom of her home on Hankins Street. Her front door was left unlocked, so anyone wanting a book could go in, sign a card and leave a dime for rental. A few months later S. B. Meek, one of the town's leading citizens, donated space in one of his buildings in the business district. The library officially opened there in mid-1927 with 449 books, most of which had been donated by Warren citizens.

This was to be the home of the library until 1931 when it was moved to the little red brick building that sits on the northeast corner of the court square.

The books which still numbered only in the hundreds were displayed on shelves running from floor to ceiling in the poorly lit one room library. The books were mostly bound in dark covers; there were no dust jackets. The aroma of old books was at once comforting and inviting. The ambiance of it all whispered "come in, spend some time, read a book and take one home."

Some of the leading ladies of the town supported and operated the library as members of the forerunner of what is known today as Friends of The Library. They kept the library open two afternoons a week. I particularly remember Mrs. Louis Ederington, who served as chairman from 1940 to 1956, Mrs. H. D. Wharton, Mrs. Hugh Moseley, Senior, and Mrs. Karl Neal, who earned a library degree from a college in Oklahoma and served for many years as head librarian for the State of Arkansas. They were very kind as they encouraged my reading habit and guided me in my selection of books. I have especially fond memories of Mrs. Ederington.

It was there that I became acquainted with books featuring Tom Swift and Nancy Drew. I read every book I could get my hands on that featured Horatio Alger, the young man of bulldog determination who proved that by pure grit and honesty of purpose one could rise from rags to riches against all odds and villains. I also found *Northwest Passage* by Kenneth L. Roberts. This story of the French-Indian War and pre-Revolutionary days in our country is perhaps my all-time favorite book. I have read it as many as a dozen times. The saga of those rowdy Americans dressed in buckskins fighting the uniformed and decorated European soldiers and the treacherous Indians while making their way through the virgin forests has remained vivid for me these many years later.

When I read book after book by Zane Grey, I was transported to the Wild West where I sat around campfires and hunted own badmen. My dreams of seeing the sights of the world went into high gear when I read *I Married Adventure* by Osa Johnson and her explorer husband. My fantasies seemed all the more attainable when I realized that the Johnsons were from Memphis.

Each time I visited the library I took home as many books as the librarian would permit. My excitement about reading them sometimes exceeded my ability to resist playing outside. I am glad now that neither my parents nor the library ladies forgave the fines I owed when I failed to return books on time, because I learned an important lesson from having to come up with a few pennies to pay for breaking the rules.

At about the same time I started going to the library, my parents also gave me a subscription to *Boys Life* magazine. I could hardly wait until my copy came in the mail each month. Outdoor adventure appeared on every page, including the advertisements for all sorts of equipment and books required to face the challenges of the forests and streams.

There were stories of intrepid boys finding adventure in the wilds in Canada. They pitched their tents beside waterfalls on roaring rivers and built perfect campfires over which they cooked the huge trout they had caught in the pristine waters. One could count on stories of rampaging grizzlies or badmen and Indians who prowled through the forest. Wandering trappers stopped by just in time to share their expertise in wilderness living to help the boys solve some dark mystery and avert the direst of consequences.

*Boys Life* was also the place to read about making a canoe from birch bark, never mind there were no birch trees in our part of the world. The magazine included explicit instructions for starting campfires by rubbing two sticks together or striking flints. For some reason none of us ever pulled off that feat.

The publisher's advertisements lured me to try to sell enough subscriptions to *Boys Life* to earn a bicycle or at least a hunting knife. While the come-on advertisement made it all seem so easy, I don't think I sold a single subscription.

I also started reading *The Grit*, a national tabloid. It, too, came in the mail. There were tales of all sorts of oddities along with heavy doses of success stories, which surely proved that with a little effort anyone could win fame and fortune.

The advertisements were almost as fascinating as the stories. There were sure-fire remedies for hair loss, trusses for hernias, liver medicine to guarantee healthy blood. My father, who had lost most of his hair while in his twenties, often clipped the advertisements for saving hair and left them in prominent places around the house for me to see that I could ward off my impending baldness.

The regular advertisement I liked best was the cartoon of several panels that showed a skinny weakling named Charles Atlas being run off the beach by a bully who kicked sand in his face and took away his girlfriend. Not to be undone, Atlas went home where he began using exercise devices (available for purchase) to develop perfect muscles and Herculean strength so that he could come back and recapture his place on the beach and the attention of the fairer sex.

Predictably, I also tried to sell *The Grit*. The promise of easy success was more than I could resist. Just a few visits around the neighborhood would insure a steady cash income, plus all sorts of prizes. Unfortunately, I learned again that "sales" was not my game.

It was ironic that years later I would sell a story to *Grit*. It was about an old man I knew who claimed to have died and come back to life just as the undertaker was beginning to prepare him for the grave.

ooooooooooooooo

I was also fortunate to be able to borrow books from two of our neighbors.

There were a number of books in the Hammons' house next door. They must have belonged to Doctor Hammons, the dentist, who died young. No one in their house seemed to be interested in the books, but I was, and they were glad to let me borrow them.

It was at the Hammons that I discovered W. Somerset Maugham, the noted British author, waiting in their glassed-in bookshelves. I thought Maugham's writings, in the ironic style, represented the best of the world of romantic adventure and sophistication.

Just down street at Mrs. Beadie Stell's house, to the side of The Corner Grocery, which she and her family operated, I was free to borrow more books. I particularly remember their several volumes of Sherlock Holmes' adventures. The mind mind-boggling sleuthing of Holmes and his sidekick, Dr. Watson, held me spellbound as they thwarted the evil designs of Professor Moriarty and other equally villainous characters. Could there be better stories for a boy to read than *A Study In Scarlet*, *The Hound of the Baskervilles*, and *The Red-Headed League*?

ooooooooooooooo

In addition, there was a treasure-trove of pulp magazines around town that I could dip into by borrowing, scrounging and trading.

After I had acquired and read a few copies of "pulps" I was able to go to a grocery store near the Fullerton's home on South Main Street which featured a trading post for these publications. We traded two of our copies for one of the proprietor's.

Pulp magazines represented a distinct era in American's reading. The "pulps" were usually in a small format, seven inches by 10 inches. They were printed on a grade paper, somewhat like newsprint only coarser. Occasionally, a hint of bark from the pulpwood from which the paper was made showed up to mar the print. They had titles like *Argosy, Dime Detective, Big Chief Western, and Ranch Romances*. My father's favorite bore the simple title *Short Stories*. When times improved Dad usually bought a copy each month. What great pleasure we for 25 cents!

In the "pulps" we could read stories heavy on adventure in many climes. Good guys and bad guys were pitted against each other in clearly defined conflict. Cliches were plentiful. Such characters as The Shadow, The Spider and Doc Savage always lost in the beginning but triumphed in the end.

ooooooooooooooo

The summer of the year I turned 12, I spent long hot days mowing lawns or sprawled out on a daybed in the entry hall of our house reading "pulps."

Later I was to read a passage by Cynthia Heimel that must be descriptive of how my family saw me that summer:

"Your family sees you as a lazy lump lying on the couch, propping a book up on your stomach, never realizing that you are really in the midst of an African safari that has just been charged by elephants, or in the drawing room of a large English country house interrogating the butler about the body discovered on the Aubusson carpet."

"Reading is an escape, an education, a delving into the brain of another human being on such an intimate level that every nuance of thought, every snapping synapse, every slippery desire of the author is laid open before you like, well, a book."

ooooooooooooooo

It followed as surely as night follows day that as addicted as I was to reading, I would become enamored with the idea of writing.

From the stories I read and the movies I saw, I concluded that writing must be a very easy, glamorous life. Mainly it seemed to require sitting in a cozy den before a fireplace, pen or typewriter at hand, composing stories that brought attention and adulation to the author. There were occasional trips to the English countryside for long weekends with intriguing people; big game to be bagged while on safari in Africa. War correspondents, wearing trench coats and walking about in the fog of some city in Europe personified a life of adventure. Of course, there was also always plenty of time to don the tweed jacket, tamp the briarwood pipe and assume the wise demeanor of a literary figure at cocktail parties.

My heroes included journalists Ernie Pyle, the GIs' war correspondent, writing from the blood and fear of the foxholes, and Edward R. Murrow, the suave trench-coated radio correspondent filing his daily radio reports from London under siege.

There were others in my hall of fame, men who became icons of the war as they created radio news as a new form of journalism. Winston Burdett, Eric Sevaried, Charles Collingwood, Howard K. Smith, William L. Shirer, Richard C. Hottelet, Larry LeSueur, and Ned Calmer.

Known as "The Murrow Boys," in honor of their leader, these newsmen seemed so worldly and wise, although as I was to learn later, most of them were still in their twenties and thirties. They had come, for the most part, from ordinary beginnings in the Depression years to provide first-hand news and offer their opinions of the battle for the future of the Free World.

Paulette Presson (Culpepper) was the first teacher to really encourage my aspiration to write. I wrote a story for a class assignment about a drifter and a tarnished young lady brought together on a South Sea Island in a monsoon. Admittedly, my writing style and even the story line borrowed heavily from W. Somerset Maugham, particularly his story, "Rain". But, nevertheless, my story was good enough to be singled out for praise by Miss Presson. It is an understatement to say that it was a rare occasion for any of my classroom efforts to draw favorable attention.

ooooooooooooooo

Early in my senior year high school Ross Adams, a year behind me in school, and I concocted the idea that our school needed a printed newspaper.

With encouragement from Miss Mary Sue Walsh, who became our sponsor, Miss Presson, Miss Mary McDermott and Mrs. Helen Smith, we organized a staff, laid out a plan and asked permission from the faculty to proceed. There was just one hitch that almost sank the enterprise as far as I was concerned. The staff had elected me to be editor. The problem was that some members of the faculty saw me as quite a troublemaker in the classrooms and a poor example of scholarship. From the vantage point of time, I have to admit that their assessment was not far off the mark. I learned much later that Miss Presson and Mrs. Smith led my defense. They declared that I would most likely be driven from of school if I were denied this opportunity on the heels of a major disappointment in athletics which I will get into in another essay.

When the smoke cleared, I became editor of *The Tall Timber_Times*. Ross Adams, who went on to earn a good career in journalism and public relations, was named assistant editor. It was a great experience. We had to earn the money to pay for the printing at *The Eagle Democrat*, so we organized an advertising sales staff headed by a rabble-rouser, Orville Arnold, and Cherie Harrison, a popular girl of sharp wit.

Ross Adams reported sports. I wrote editorials and an occasional front-page story. Harvey Donegan, a boy who later would have a fine career in journalism with the Time-Life organization and as something of a playwright in New York City, authored an occasional feature story.

Others on the staff included Pat Ellen and Pat Ball, co-society editors; Billy Frank King, assistant sports editor; Bob Moseley and Jean Riley, alumni editors; Fred Holt, art editor; Harold Porter, circulation manager; and Jean McClendon and Juanita Atkins, typists.

Without question Bill Frazier and Charles Temple were stars of the staff. They wrote a gossip column titled "Through the Knot Hole." It sparkled with wit and a sort of sharp edged sophistication that set tongues wagging happily among students and sometimes caused concern among parents and teachers.

*The Tall Timber Times* experience was a pivotal point in my life. It went a long way toward keeping me on track and saving my high school career. It also convinced me that I would make my way by some sort of writing.

Writing has compelled and thrilled me through newspapering in the Army, earning a degree in journalism from the University of Arkansas, working as a reporter political writer for the late, lamented *Arkansas Democrat*, earning a living in a career based on writing and finally authoring books.

As a writer I have been enabled to play a pivotal role in setting policy and strategies in major corporations and framing decisions in public policy. To this day there is no greater thrill for me than seeing something I have written appear in type or hearing a speech I have written being delivered by a client.

## THE SCHOOL YEARS

September 1933 was not a promising time for parents to be entering their children in school for the first time. The Great Depression was in full swing. Families were having a hard enough time putting food on the table much less coming up with money or credit to buy school clothes and supplies.

But some how they sent us off to primary school, a small frame building, painted white with green trim, which sat on the large block where the post office now stands. Excited about the adventure of it all, but fearful of the unknown, our worries, cosmic to us, were as specific as how to avoid the bullying of older kids and make our way back and forth across town from home to the school; survive the watchful eyes of teachers, and get along with a largely new set of youngsters, to say nothing of learning readin', writin' and 'rithmatic.

What a motley bunch we first graders must have been when we reported to Miss Dot Martin's, our first grade teacher who was also the principal of our primary school.

We were sons and daughters of prosperous main street merchants and clerks, laborers and bosses at the sawmills, farmers, tradesmen, absent fathers, widowed mothers, law officers and city employees, the employed and those on relief. One boy came from a family we heard were millionaires. He was in and out of our class for the first few years because he and his mother, who had health problems, spent most of the winter months at a resort in south Texas. When he was a bit older he went away to

251

military school, but we always claimed him as a classmate. Another boy was enrolled with us when his mother chose to stay in Warren rather than move on with the carnival which brought them to town.

Some wore clothes and shoes just arrived from Sears Roebuck; a few were dressed from local stores, others even had furnishings from Pine Bluff or Little Rock. The popular dress for boys was corduroy knickers with knee-length socks that always collapsed around the ankles. The knickers were called "whistle britches" because of the sound the corduroy material made when the wearer was walking. Many wore frayed hand-me-downs and came to school barefooted during the hot days of September. A few badly needed soap and water. Skin infections were not uncommon. During the winter there were always "runny" noses and hacking coughs. The entire classroom often smelled like Vick Salve or turpentine. Parents were warned to be on the lookout for lice in our hair.

Most of us started off with new book satchels, crayons, jumbo pencils, big red erasers, tablets of lined coarse paper, snub-nosed scissors and little pots of paste, but some had next to nothing. Our heads were busy with the idea that we would learn most of what we needed to know in a short while. If we thought about it at all, we couldn't fathom 12 years of such servitude.

Miss Dot, an "old maid" descendant of an aristocratic physician and entrepreneur, ran the school as a benevolent dictator. No one was excluded from her firm, caring embrace. While we had a crush on her we held her in awe.

There was no doubt that Lloyd McCann was the star of the class for the first few weeks. He assumed that position because he could recite the alphabet in reverse. But Lloyd did not maintain his zest for academics throughout his school career. Meanwhile, the remainder of us were challenged to our limits just to learn to read and write and add and subtract a few numbers.

○○○○○○○○○○○○○○

I decided I'd had about enough of education by the time I reached the second grade and school became an all day affair.

My relationship with my classmates was not enhanced when Mama coerced me into demonstrating my skills with the violin before the entire class. Never mind that I could only finger a few cords and saw away with the bow in some remote semblance of a rhythm. This was in spite of the fact that I had been taking lessons for about a year. Truth be told, I didn't improve my abilities with irregular practice, but my family refused to face the fact that I did not have any talent. Some of the boys in my class nailed me with the ultimate insult at that age; they called me a sissy. That was about as bad as it could get.

My violin lessons were only an adjunct to regular school. My violin teacher was Professor Bird, an itinerant musician, who appeared in Warren out of nowhere. Tall and thin, dapper in dress, his face adorned with a moustache, he appeared as if he had just stepped out of the stage setting of an English drawing room. He took room and board in the home of a prominent widow on Pine Street. It was there in her living room that he gave violin lessons to the sons and daughters of hapless parents who envisioned careers in music for their youngsters or at least a social skill that would serve them well.

Professor Bird soon had a full roster of students, young and old alike. Toward the end of his stay in Warren, I heard the adults whispering that he might be practicing more than music with some of the ladies in town who

253

had developed quite a yearning to play the violin. There was also some gossip over the fact that he was the sole boarder in the widow's home.

Anyway, Professor Bird disappeared from town as quickly and as mysteriously as he had appeared, leaving some used violins behind, as well as a number of unpaid bills.

I was to be embarrassed again that year. Along in the spring I decided that if I couldn't quit school entirely, I could at least shorten the day. Providentially, I began to develop, or imagine, very bad headaches soon after lunch each day. They were worse on days when storm clouds gathered. I begged to go home because I was "sick." I suppose Miss Emily Carter, our teacher, saw through my scam, but what was a teacher to do?

My scheme worked for a few times until my mother got over her initial worry about my health and put her foot down. I had to stop that nonsense, she declared. I just couldn't believe that she was practically turning me out in my time of need.

Within a day or two, I pleaded my case to Miss Carter again so earnestly that she let me go home again. This time I was in for a surprise when I got home. Mama saw me coming. She went to a shrub at the corner of the house and ripped off a long, tough switch. Before I got into our front yard she began whipping me about the bare legs below my short pants. She didn't quit until my legs were laced with red welts. As was her practice, she said it hurt her more than it did me. I didn't believe that at all. Then she carefully explained that there was nothing wrong with me and that whether I liked it or not I had to go to school. She promised me that she would come to visit my teacher the next day to see what the problem was with me and school.

By early afternoon on the day of resolution I felt another headache coming on. Where was my mother? Why had she not come as she had promised? I could not stand the suspense any longer, so I asked the teacher to let me leave.

I had walked no farther than the court square when I looked up and saw Mama marching down the sidewalk on her way to school. She saw me at about the same time. When we met she simply took my arm, turned me around and marched me back to school. I was not gone from the classroom for more than 15 or 20 minutes. Miss Carter, did not seem to be the least bit surprised to see me. Mama directed me to my chair and took a seat in the back of the classroom where she remained until school was out.

Thus, my scheme to cut short my formal education was brought to a decisive end.

ooooooooooooooo

I was introduced to the swift and sure hand of corporal discipline at the hands of teachers in the third grade.

The law of the classroom was simple. Misbehave; get punished with a spanking or be sentenced to sit in the corner facing the walls for what seemed like an eternity. Worse still, an offender could be forced to sit next to a teacher on the school steps during recess.

The teachers' judgments were absolute. No turning to higher authorities; no probations unless one was a real "teacher's pet." It was not wise to appeal one's case to parents because that course would likely result in another spanking at home or at least a tongue-lashing. We never heard of parents protesting a teacher's discipline.

And most of us deserved what we got. That was the case with my first spanking.

We were in some sort of arts and crafts class under the tutelage of Mrs. Helms. I was chewing a big wad of bubble gum, which, of course, was against the rules. When Mrs. Helms saw me she ordered that I dispose of the gum immediately. She didn't say how I was to do that. Noma Anderson, a very pretty girl with long blonde hair, sat innocently with her back to me in the chair just ahead. Evidently, some evil spirit took over my brain, because I proceeded to remove the gum from my mouth, pick up a handful of Noma's hair and wrap it around the offending wad. I thought it made a neat ball.

I should not have been surprised when Noma screamed and began to cry. Mrs. Helms demanded to know what I had done. I answered truthfully. "Get that gum out of Noma's hair this instant," Mrs. Helms ordered. Then, compounding my offense, I took up my little craft scissors and cut off a large section of Noma's hair where I had wrapped the gum.

Noma cried even louder; bedlam seized the classroom. I got my first spanking with a solid oak paddle with holes bored in it to make it a more efficient instrument of pain.

Although I didn't set any records in school for punishment, I managed one way or another to earn my share.

Mrs. Botts, an intense woman who taught music in elementary school, introduced us to her own form of corporal punishment. Those who misbehaved had their hand turned palms up and bent backward so that she could strike the open palm with a long wooden ruler. That hurt a lot.

I had my experience with Mrs. Botts' punishment when I attempted to argue with her that there was not much point in our learning the scales by do, re, mi, fa when nobody knew what those words meant or sang like that. She explained to me that they were Latin words, and besides that was just the way it was. Foolishly, I persisted in my argument; predictably, I got the ruler.

Punishment by Mrs. Sharp, who taught mathematics in junior high school, included its own brand of discomfort. This little lady with the barest cover of white hair on her head had been born with a left arm that ended with a pointed nub at about where her elbow should have been. But that didn't handicap her when it came to dealing out punishment. Offenders, always boys, were ordered to bend over her desk; she held the victim in place by boring the nub of her arm in the middle of his back. In this commanding position she was able to pound away with the paddle in her good hand. After she administered a spanking a faint odor of body sweat and talcum powder lingered in the room.

My last spanking came when I was a junior in high school. I had sassed a teacher and been sent to the office of Mr. Herring, the school superintendent. After expressing his abject sorrow and disappointment that I had been sent to him, he proceeded to whack me 10 or 12 times across the butt with a stout wooden paddle and sent me back to class. I denied it hurt, but it did. My classmates thought that was funny; I didn't.

ooooooooooooooo

Our teachers took it as part of their mission in life to introduce us to the arts.

I learned early on that acting and singing on the stage were not to be in my future.

A stage production was a key part of graduation from the third grade to elementary school. For reasons that escape me now our play included a flock of birds of some sort, singing and making chirping sounds.

Bird costumes were a problem. The mothers and teachers had a conference to see what could be done to make us look at least a little bit like birds. Mama, always creative, ended up with the assignment to make a prototype. She managed somehow to concoct a sort of cape and head cover out of brown wrapping paper to which she laboriously sewed layer upon layer of individual "feathers" she had cut from crepe paper. She fashioned the eyes and beak from a mixture of paper and homemade paste.

The bird suit was an instant hit with the teachers and other mothers, several of whom paid Mama to duplicate the costume for their youngsters. I was conflicted with feelings of pride in my mother's accomplishment and embarrassment at wearing the outfit.

There was no escaping the annual pageant of spring rites when we neared graduation from the sixth grade and elementary school. To our great embarrassment we were required to dress in costumes as elves and sprites, despite the fact that we were sure we were quite grown up. The starring role was reserved for Bob Moseley, whom we always thought was a special favorite of the teachers. We all shared his horror when he was required to fit his pudgy adolescent form into a skintight leotard, fashioned from pink satin, and carry a wand, while the rest of us had to endure only slightly less offensive dark green-tights and tops with the pointed hats, complete with a feather, such as wood elves wore. We sang and danced about among garlands of crepe paper.

When we finished the pageant that spring of 1939, where we had been caught in the awkward crevice between being a child and being a teenager, we could hardly wait to move on to the adventure of being in junior high school.

The physical plants of junior high school and high school were separated by only a few yards from Miss Allie Mae Colvin Temple's elementary school. Still, this was an entirely new world, with a new pecking order, ruled from the top by young men and women in high school we would have described as "sophisticated" if we had known that word then. We were mightily impressed by girls who looked very grown up and the boys who appeared to be so big and strong. We were anxious to grow up to be like them.

oooooooooooooooo

Playing football and basketball in junior and senior high school taught me a great deal about teamwork and competition, while allowing me to earn some status in a status-conscious school and community and to make priceless friendships that have endured through the years.

We took pride in the fact that Warren was among the smallest communities in America to have a YMCA. The "Y" was housed in a large three-story structure built in 1920 from lumber and other materials donated by the Bradley, the Southern and the Arkansas lumber companies and various merchants and public spirited citizens. We saw it destroyed on a Friday night in 1944 by the most spectacular fire in Warren's history.

The third floor was occupied by a large meeting room and a kitchen. The Rotary Club and various youth groups such as the Hi-Y Club, the Girl Reserves and the Friendly Indians met there.

The ground floor, actually it was more like a dark and dank basement, featured showers and lockers and dressing rooms for both boys and girls. It also contained what had to be absolutely the coldest swimming pool on the planet and a bowling alley with a single lane. The odor of disinfectants and Life Buoy soap was always present.

The middle floor was the heart of the "Y." At its center was a large room furnished with comfortable chairs where we could sit and read a meager selection of outdated newspapers, magazines and books of the Tom Swift variety. Ping-Pong and pool tables were available for those willing to wait their turn.

An undersized basketball court with a small raised stage at one end, which I never saw anyone use, was located behind swinging doors leading from the lounge area. There was a narrow balcony. A meager set of lifting weights and tumbling mats were scattered along one side of the court.

There were two pairs of boxing gloves and a mat for the more aggressive among us. They didn't get much use except when Mr. Robert L. Newton, who was manager of the "Y," once in a great while organized a match.

When I told my father about the boxing gloves and the implied opportunity to learn the manly art of self-defense, he was greatly disappointed that I hadn't stepped up to the challenge. When I expressed some curiosity as to his unexpected interest in boxing he said that every man should learn to defend himself from bullies. I never took up boxing and he never gave up trying to persuade me.

There was a single tennis court to the rear of the three-story building on the banks of the Town Branch. We thought it was a game for sissies.

oooooooooooooooo

Mr. Robert L. Newton presided over all of this from behind a high counter and swinging gate that stood as a barrier to his office in the corner of the lounge on the second floor.

Autocratic in style and demeanor, he was of a decidedly unlikely athletic build, and it was rumored that he smoked cigars. However, when he blew his ubiquitous whistle none of us questioned that he was in charge.

My defining moment with Mr. Newton came when I took swimming lessons in the ice-cold pool. The graduation exercise required that each of us jump off into the deep end and paddle across the pool and back. Mr. Newton stood by with a long pole which he promised to extend to us if we got in trouble. When it came my turn I plunged in feet first and promptly sank to the bottom. I made it back to the surface, and flapped my arms about, but I wasn't able to kick my legs up so as to make my way to the side. I went down again and panic set in. I never knew whether it was the cold, or fear or simply that I hadn't really learned how to swim. When I made it back to the surface the second time, I knew I needed help. There was no room for pride. I called for Mr. Newton to reach out with the pole. He stood there looking at me. After what seemed to be an eternity he reached out with the pole which I seized to be pulled to the side. He shook his head in disgust or dismay and walked away. I made my way to the dressing room, humiliated and convinced that my life was crashing around me. The experience left with me with an unpleasant memory.

I took what I had learned at the "Y" and went to a sandbar on Saline River where I entered the much warmer water and a friendlier environment and on my own finished the challenge of learning to swim.

Basketball kept me going to the "Y." I spent many hours on the court there the summer before I entered the ninth grade and became eligible to play junior high school basketball. I enjoyed pick-up games with boys of all ages and skills. A star of those games was Glenn "Bud" Robinson from next door who had been named an All-American player among the nation's schools for the deaf.

We played without benefit of referees, unless we could persuade one of our peers to stay out of the game to carry the whistle, so things were a bit loose and often rough and tumble. One admonition, posted at the entrance to the gym, guided us: "Play hard, play clean, and don't spit on the floor."

I learned many lessons about the game and the nature of competition from basketball at the "Y." Those games began to enlarge my world of friends in school and supporters in the community.

It seems strange now that I hardly knew the boys from the "Y", one and two years ahead of me in school, who were to become my teammates and lifelong friends: Jim Hurley, Sonny Morgan, Bobby Galloway, Lawrence Derby, Jimmy Dowell, among others.

These boys, known at the "Y" as the Friendly Indians, were the heart of a fine junior high school basketball team a season ahead of me, which eventually made its way to the state tournament. I would not have admitted it then, but I can say now that I thought they were "hot stuff", especially after I saw them wearing their orange sweaters featuring the large black "W" as recognition of their having played enough time to "letter."

I had my chance when I entered the ninth grade and they went on to high school. At a tad under six feet tall and 165 pounds I was one of the larger boys on the team, so I played center, the position to which I had aspired. Our coach, Elton Gray, had under his charge youngsters of various levels of skills and ambitions—Billy Lee Denton, "Marty" Hoyle, Buddy Mhoon, Harry Denson, James Pennington and a boy named Lancaster. Although my memory fogs over a bit here, I believe we won the district tournament, but missed the opportunity to play in a state tournament because that event had fallen victim to wartime rationing of gas and tires. However, ego being what it is, my memory clears up at this point, because I do remember being named to the all district team. I am not proud of the fact that I can't recall whether any of my teammates were selected for that honor.

The rewards of playing ball as a Lumberjack became readily apparent. Not the least of these was that the girls in school, even the "older" ones, including senior cheerleaders, came down off their pedestals, where we had placed them, to pay some attention to us. We were titillated in the extreme by the older girls such as Pauline Thurman, Helen Moseley, Miriam Ball, Wilda Mecham, Mary Elizabeth Apple, Margaret Garrison and Helen Herring. They sort of took us under their wings to advise us on matters of the heart while flirting with us just enough to throw us into a dither. I'm sure it didn't hurt my position to have two cousins—Shirley Broach (Godwin) and Pat Murry (Walker)—just ahead of me in school. I finished junior high with my head, at a considerably expanded size, high in the sky.

oooooooooooooooo

My eyes were firmly fixed on the next level of basketball, but what about football?

I knew I wanted to play if it was just half as rewarding and anywhere near as much fun as basketball. Besides, it was clearly the macho thing to do.

My mother swore that she would never permit me to risk injury by playing that brutal game. Never mind that she had never seen a game, but the ladies in the neighborhood "knew all about it."

My mother and I began a test of wills. My father stayed out of it as far as I knew. I begged and cajoled. I tried reason as well as emotion. "They want me to play. They need me." "I will be embarrassed because they will think I'm a sissy." She didn't budge. Finally, I proposed a deal that she accepted. Just let me go out for practice. If I didn't like it, I would quit. The chance of that happening was just about zero.

In mid-August, I quit my job making pallets at The Bradley and reported for practice under Coach Ned Moseley. It was an unlikely crew that showed up that first day. Big, little, fat, skinny, muscular, wimpy, graceful, clumsy, meek and nervous and self-assured. The best of the equipment went to the returning lettermen; the leftovers were distributed to the rest of us. At best, the equipment for lettermen and neophytes alike was a disaster by today's standards. It was rare for shoes to fit. The sole of one of mine was broken under the arch. Thigh pads often had to be taped in place. Straps were missing from shoulder pads. Many helmets, in various stages of disrepair, offered scant protection. There was no such thing as a faceguard.

Open cupboards for our clothes and belongings lined the walls of the small dressing room. There was one toilet and five or six showerheads. Lukewarm water was available sporadically. Drains were stopped up more often than not. Open burning gas stoves, one in the dressing room and one in the coaches' locker room, provided the only heat. It was a feeding ground for virulent fungi; athletes' foot and jockey itch were usually on the rampage. It didn't help that despite frequent reminders from our coaches and the dismay of our mothers we didn't keep our socks and jock straps as clean as we might. After all, we were tough, at least in our minds.

Such conditions today would send parents and fans into a frenzy of outrage and protests, but we were happy, glad for the opportunity to earn the right to wear the orange and black of the Lumberjacks.

The ranks of candidates for the squad were soon reduced as practice in pads began in the blazing heat of August. Ill-fitting equipment rubbed raw spots. Bones and muscles were bruised and ached. Wind sprints left a few behind most days.

I was sorely tempted to keep my bargain with my mother and quit. I am thankful to this day that I didn't.

Things improved after two or three weeks of practice. We got some better equipment and we began to get in shape. We thought we were ready for the first game to be played at Monticello. I was slotted in at second string right tackle behind a young fellow named James Sanders. Of rangy build, with long muscular legs and arms, he could run faster than any of the linemen. We called him "Racehorse."

Much to my disappointment, "Racehorse" started the game against Monticello's Hillbillies and played all but the last three or four minutes, when I finally got in the game. It didn't help my morale when we lost.

Vowing I was going to change that lineup, I went to practice the next week and tried as I had never tried before in football, or in much else. Coach Moseley must have recognized that he had the kind of challenge for a position going on that any coach would like to see.

In the middle of the week, the coach told Sanders and me to face off, blocking man on man. Others from the squad gathered around to watch. We hit and hit, head to head. Most licks were harder than anything I ever experienced in a game.

Winning that contest was a rite of passage for me. I started the next game at right tackle, all 165 pounds of me, and played almost every minute of every quarter, offense and defense, the remainder of my sophomore and junior years.

I can see us now, lining up over the ball. To my right at end, Bobby Galloway; to my left at right guard, Bobby Gene Richardson; Rufus Johnson, center; Harry Hargis, left guard; Odys Lyons, left tackle; and Ernest Sangster, left end. Regulars in the backfield were Sonny Morgan, Lawrence Derby, Billy Lee Denton and Jimmy Dowell.

We lost more games than we won. To tell the truth, we weren't much of a football team. However, we did set a record (not to be proud of) in 1943 that holds to this day. It came at Smackover, a small town located near El Dorado in Arkansas' oil belt, that was a football powerhouse.

We had lost to Smackover in 1942 (20-0). But we had an excuse. The star of the Buckeroos was a boy by the name of Clyde Scott who would go on to win All-American honors in college football and an Olympic medal in track. It was the first match to be played on the Lumberjacks' new field. Following a daylong rain, the field was a quagmire of red clay mud and pebbles, relieved here and there by a clump of whatever grass had cropped up.

Although Scott had graduated, we heard the Buckeroos were awesome in 1943 We rode the bus to Smackover, full of dread, thinly masked by bravado.

Our worst nightmare was realized once we took to the field. The Buckerroos started their second team and led us 25 to 0 at the end of the first half. To add insult to injury, their first team came on the field to play the second half. The final score, 71 to 0.

ooooooooooooooo

The Big War took its toll on high school athletics, as it did on all other aspects of our lives.

Transportation for team and fans alike for out-of-town games was hard to arrange because of gas and tire rationing. A number of schools curtailed or cancelled their programs. Players and would-bes came and went as their families were uprooted by military service and opportunities for jobs in defense plants around the country.

When we lost Ned Moseley, our regular coach, to the military two coaches, Perry Herring, our school superintendent, and Corbun "Cooney" Curry, a young man whose regular job was as an accountant at the Bradley Lumber Company took over.

It is "Cooney" Curry that I remember most fondly. His qualifications for coaching were that he had been quite a high school football player. From time to time at practice he would remind us of this fact by running with the ball and daring us to tackle him. Never mind that he was dressed in khaki pants and a cotton sweatshirt with neither pads nor helmet.

Being both young and realistic, "Cooney" looked the other way when he caught us smoking cigarettes. Neither was he up in arms when he heard that any of our numbers had been seen sneaking a beer at The Topper drive-in.

"Cooney" announced at the end of one of our practices that he and the entire team had been puzzled as to whether Odys Lyons or I was the slowest running lineman. He said that the question would be answered by the two of us running the full length of the field and back.

Ready, set, go, Odys and I took off. With the entire squad cheering us on as we circled the far goalpost and headed home in a dead heat. As we made it back to the 50-yard line I looked down and saw the green of folding money lying on the field. It didn't take me more than two or three more steps to determine that spending money in hand was more important than the possibility of winning a footrace against Odys. I stopped, went back and picked up the money. It was a $5.00 bill. When I finished a distant second in a two-man race there were hoots and hollers from "Cooney" and my teammates, that is until I displayed my find.

That was to be my last season of high school football.

ooooooooooooooo

Our reputations as athletes were salvaged by our winning ways on the basketball court.

We had an unusually good high school team. I have always taken great pride in the fact that I was fortunate enough to play my sophomore and junior years on the starting team with four boys who were one year ahead of me in school. I have missed few opportunities through the years to remind them of my precociousness. Our first team was composed of Jim Hurley and Lawrence Derby, guards; Bob Galloway and George C. "Sonny" Morgan, forwards. I played center. The sixth man was Jimmy Dowell, a muscular young fellow we nicknamed "Sleek." I was known as "Stick" in an obvious reference to my last name. Rounding out the squad were more fine fellows such as Ernest Sangster, Harry Hargis, Jim Blaine Fullerton, Harry Denson and Gordon Apple, a hirsute lad we referred to as "Monkey."

I don't remember our record my sophomore year, but it was far better than okay. Our second year together was an outstanding 21 wins and four losses.

Ned Moseley taught me a lesson about discipline I have never forgotten.

Foolishly, some of us on the basketball squad smoked cigarettes. I suppose Coach Moseley knew that; after all, no doubt he could smell the foul odor on our breaths. But he failed to catch us in the act until one day when the squad gathered in Wayne's poolhall waiting to make the trip to play our arch rival, the Hermitage Hermits.

Intent on watching a game of snooker and enjoying my last cigarette before heading south to Hermitage, it was some time before I became aware of a sudden stillness in the room. I looked up to see Coach Moseley glaring at me from across the hall. I dropped the cigarette butt as he walked up and declared for all to hear, "Greenwood, we won't need you in Hermitage." I would not have been any more shocked or hurt by my stupidity and his action if he had hit me between the eyes with a pool cue.

I rode with some of the scrubs in Harry Hargis's car. We made the 15 miles over a gravel road to Hermitage in less than 15 minutes.

Coach Moseley ignored me most of the next week at practice where I walked a straight line and worked very hard. I must have impressed him with my work and improved attitude because he let me start the game the next Friday night.

With the regular coach away in the military, Mr. Perry Herring, the school superintendent, doubled his duties to include overseeing practice. He could devote little time to us. Most practices we showed up early to sweep the gym floor before playing scrimmage games, first team against second team. Mr. Herring made the road trips with us and handled what few substitutions were made.

ooooooooooooooo

My career as a high school athlete came to a bitter, crashing halt in the early fall of 1944, the beginning of my senior year.

I had made one of the biggest mistakes of my life, and it torments fleetingly in my memory to this day. The foolishness of youth and the breakdown of adult guidance came together in a force that nearly threw me off the track.

Those being the war years, colleges were lowering their bars as they went about desperately recruiting enough athletes to field teams. For this reason and in the atmosphere of accelerated lives generally, the University of Arkansas and others established a program whereby a student could skip his senior year in high school and enter college as a freshman. If he could complete the requirements of the first year of college, a high school diploma and one-year college credits would be granted.

A recruiter from the University of Arkansas offered me a full football scholarship. He was looking at 165 pounds, six feet of not a great deal of muscle and slow of feet. Incredulous? This has to be put in perspective by remembering that the military was calling up able bodied men as fast as they could be processed. That left the young, not-yet-developed ones, the 4-Fs and the veterans who had been discharged for one medical reason or another.

I guess I didn't give it much thought. Most of my teammates were graduating from high school and either going to college or into the military. Bob Galloway and Harry Hargis, graduating seniors, had accepted offers of scholarships at the University of Arkansas. Most of the girls in my social circle were graduating. By accepting the scholarship I could get my way in college paid for and relieve my parents of a load they could not have carried. I was restless with the feeling that by staying in high school I was missing out on the adventures and mobility of the times. All of this was underscored by the fact that the scholarship to join the Arkansas Razorbacks gave my ego a mainline jolt.

Mr. Hargis drove his son, Galloway and me to Little Rock where we boarded a train for a daylong ride through the unfamiliar Ozark Mountains to Fayetteville and Razorbackland. Most of my clothes, bed linens and the like had been shipped ahead in a secondhand steamer trunk. The remainder I carried in a tin suitcase my mother had painted Razorback red and decorated with team decals.

I soon found that the boys at the University were bigger and stronger than all but a few I had faced in high school. The coaches weren't nearly as caring as "Cooney" Curry or even Ned Moseley. Practice was grueling, but I hung on long enough to know, for reasons that I could never quite believe, that I could make the scholarship squad.

But reality began to dawn. What had I done? Left home a year before I had to. Missed my senior year in high school where I still had friends. Joined a football squad where I most likely would only serve as a practice tackle dummy for those who would actually play in games. I had no taste for that life. Why not go home where I could rejoin the football and basketball squads? I likely would be a leader, maybe even a star. Certainly, I would earn my third letter in both football and basketball. That would be no small achievement.

Two weeks after I arrived in Fayetteville I threw my things back in the steamer trunk, shipped it off by rail, packed my red suitcase and headed out with two or three dollars in my pocket to hitchhike home.

The first car to drive by was loaded with five ladies from Warren, all friends of my mother, who had been to Fayetteville to attend a conference of home demonstration clubs They dropped me off at my front door late that afternoon. I was mistaken when I took the ease with which I had caught a ride home as a good omen.

The next day I was welcomed at high school football practice with open arms by teammates and a new coach, Charles Baker.

My euphoria was short-lived. School Superintendent Herring called me in to explain that although he was sure there would be no problem with my eligibility it would still be a good idea to report my detour through The University just to be sure. I urged him to not do that, but he insisted there would be no problem. Well, there was. The state board that ruled on such matters declared me ineligible for all high school athletics. My friend, Mr. Jim Hurley, drove me to Little Rock to appeal the ruling. Such was his reputation for influence we had no doubt that somehow he could persuade the board that they had made a mistake. Instead, we met a stonewall of resistance. No exceptions to the rule that if a boy even practiced with a college team he was ineligible to participate in high school athletics.

Discouraged, bitter, angry, are words that do not begin to describe how I felt. I thought my world had come to an end. My parents and adult friends must have read my mind because they went all out to dissuade me from leaving home to join the military.

The faculty members who talked their colleagues into approving my serving as editor of the school newspaper saved my high school career.

ooooooooooooooo

Disappointments aside, I would not take any amount of money for the bittersweet memories of going to school, playing football and basketball and enjoying friends in that time and place.

In the relative scheme of things those recollections could seem foolish and irrelevant. But I know they were not, then or now. It was good to be caught up without reservation in serving what we conceived to be a noble cause—wearing the Orange and Black and winning for the Lumberjacks.

How could one duplicate the thrill of going to school on Friday morning knowing there would be a pep rally for the entire student body in the auditorium just before noon? There were cheerleaders dressed in saddle oxfords, white sweaters with orange Ws on the front and pleated black skirts, on the stage leading the fight songs and cheers. We players were called on to stand as we were admonished to go out and win for the honor of the school. We walked mighty tall the rest of the day, sort of gliding through classes with our mind on the battle to come.

Those of us who were fortunate enough to play very much had a sort of celebrity status. Football and basketball games were a big deal around town, especially along Main Street where many of the stores had window displays featuring Lumberjack orange and black. How sweet it was to have people call out "Good luck tonight...hope you win" as we walked along the street. Former players would pull us aside to offer advice and recall their days in the spotlight.

We gathered at a classmate's house on Wednesday and Thursday nights to build a class float for the homecoming parade on Friday. The hosting parents sometimes served hot chocolate, candied apples and popcorn. Those of us who were to play in the game did not work on the float, but we were expected to show up and visit with our fans.

Pretty girls in fancy dresses rode on the floats decorated with orange and black crepe paper and sporty men drove convertibles with gleaming whitewall tires in the homecoming parade. Vehicles were shined to such a high tone that the people who lined the street could see their reflections in the sheen. There were hand-painted signs that foretold of a certain victory for the home team. The band high-stepped at the head of the parade.

A special excitement filled the air at Wayne Wisener's soda fountain and poolhall. The jukebox blared when anyone had nickels to feed into it. If it stayed silent too long, Wayne would "trip it" to play several records free of charge. Those who would play in the game strutted abouts. Steady couples filled the booths.

When we gathered in the poolhall, there was always someone there to give us cigarettes. Our principal suppliers were Buddy "Catfish" Davis, whose parents owned a grocery store out on the west side of town, and Bill Bates, our team manager, who worked in a local grocery.

Boys and girls with cars were eager to give us a ride around town before dropping us off at our homes.

I don't know about the other boys, but the fare on our supper table on game days would give today's trainers and coaches a seizure. Mama had the idea, I suppose, that if I was going to play a strenuous game I needed to eat plenty of heavy food so I ate what our family ate. A typical menu included Lima beans, some kind of potatoes, fried baloney and cornbread. I don't remember any bad side effects. However, who is to say, I might have been a much better athlete if I had eaten lean beef and a baked potato or pasta.

Friday game days ended with a dance at the American Legion Hut, across the street from the YMCA. It is a misnomer to say they were "dances." They were really stand-around-look-and-talks. The boys lined up along the south wall eyeing the girls who stood across the floor to the north while the jukebox wailed away before a dance floor that was mostly empty.

Most of us didn't dance because we didn't know how and we were too shy to let the girls teach us. But what an ego trip it was when the girls, especially the older ones, tried to coax us out on the dance floor for a lesson. When we did venture to try we soon learned that with our awkwardness the anticipation of dancing was more fun than the actual dancing.

The best of all nights was when one had suffered a slight injury in the game; enough to be noticeable, but not enough to do lasting damage. A sprained ankle was first choice. That meant the wounded hero limped in—a little showboat exaggeration never hurt. This sure to draw the sympathetic attention of cheerleaders and other attentive girls. Some of the limping could be extended over into Saturday on the job or while hanging around at Wayne's. One of our number had it down pat; although he rarely played more than a few minutes in any game, he milked it for all he could. If the sympathizers ever figured out his scam they never let on.

274

The chaperones remained unobtrusive. In fact, I never saw the ladies do more than sit and chatter among themselves. The men spent more time furtively eyeing the girls.

It was not unheard of for some of the boys to drift outside to take a drink from a half-pint of grape wine or bourbon someone had managed to buy on "Catfish Row."

After the last game of the season in my sophomore year three of us managed to buy a pint of grape wine and sneak into to the coaches' locker room at the high school gym. We quickly consumed the bottle in the stifling heat of the room and became violently ill. We swore never to drink alcohol again.

A more normal night found us staying at the dance until the last record had been played and then drifting away. The boys without dates made their way to Wayne's or to a bench on the court square. The boys and girls with dates and cars went to less public places.

oooooooooooooooo

Our social lives in high school consumed a lot of time and energy.

Then, as now, having access to an automobile made all of the difference, but those vehicles were few and far between. My grandchildren have as much trouble finding a parking place when they drive to school as we did finding a car in those days. My parents hadn't owned a car since the earliest years of my childhood. That didn't cramp my style in romance when I was in junior high school because no one was allowed to drive, but it became a big time problem when I got to high school. I wasn't helped along in my social life either by the fact that there wasn't a telephone in our house. That meant, of course, that when I was arranging a date I had to use the telephone at a neighbor's house or at Wayne's. Or worst of all, I had to walk by the girl's house or send word by one of her friends.

But I was lucky to have a friend like Jim Hurley, whose well-to-do family owned a big black Cadillac. Jim saw to it that I had transportation for dates, at least on Sunday night.

We had a regular threesome for dating. Jim and Joyce Moore; Bob Galloway and Francis Horne, Marinette Thornton and me.

The Sunday night show at the Pastime Theater played a critical role in the ritual of dating. That was the time we took our girlfriends to the movies. There was usually a fair amount of commentary among adults and youngsters alike about who brought whom and which couple had split up and came to the movie as singles or was missing altogether. All of this attention was not lost on the young couples so there was a good deal of strutting and preening around.

The price of admission was 35 cents. A bag of popcorn was a nickel. Those lucky enough to have a car or, as in my case, have a friend like Jimmy Hurley who was always willing to share his car, took their date out to Bill Harding's drive-in after the movie for a hamburger and a coke. It seems to me that stop cost about 25 cents per person. So a Sunday night movie date ended up being about $1.50 for a couple. That was about one-half of what I had earned by clerking all day in the men's department of The Bradley Store or at Ederington's Cash Store.

After the trip to Bill's place, we usually drove around, making stops at the North Steel Bridge and the grove of pine trees that stood out south of town on the highway to Hermitage. Whatever togetherness there was had to be accomplished with five other people wedged into the car.

We imagined we were in love. But I think we were more in love with the idea of being in love. Mama called it "puppy love." She said our "sap was rising."

Hanging out with my friends often took precedent over dating. There were my teammates. Then came Jimmy Sanderlin, Bob Moseley, Buddy McCaskill, Orville Arnold, sBuddy Anderson, "Red" Robertson, Harry "Haywire" Denson, Jack Hammons, Billy "Garmouth" Frazier, Ross Adams, Marty "El Lobo" Hoyle, Charlie Temple, Harvey Donegan, Ross Broome and many more.

Our "gang" of girls included Joyce Godwin, Francis Horne, Marinette Thornton, Peggy Beard, Mary Francis Hurley, Mary Lillian Waites, Billie Clowers and Betty Jo Wardlaw. The wider circle of girls that I claimed as friends included Juanita Atkins, Noma Anderson, Pauline Guice, Nettie Jane Haygood, Hazel Hightower, Jean McClendon, Jean Riley, Sara Baker, Mable Jean Williams, Joanne Ederington, Mary Eberle and Cherie Harrison.

ooooooooooooooo

I was not a good student.

I did not apply myself. I had a bad attitude toward the entire idea of the authority and regimen associated with going to school. At best I was most often indifferent to studies, frequently rebellious and usually bored, given to arguing with teachers. I wasn't wise enough or disciplined enough to act on the reality that my high dreams and ambitions required that I do well in school.

I realized what a dismal academic record I had left behind in the Warren school system when I acquired a copy of my grades from high school with the idea of showing my own children what I had done. My C-minus average was so bad that I immediately destroyed the paper so that my son and daughter wouldn't see it.

Not that it absolves me, but I had plenty of company. In fact, the politically correct thing to do was to act dumb and rebellious. Working hard and getting good grades was to put one's popularity at risk.

It is amazing that some of the teachers remained patient with me. In another chapter about my interests in reading and writing, I recount how I was almost denied the editorship of our school newspaper *The Tall Timber Times*, because of my lack of scholarship and my general demeanor.

My supporters did not include Mrs. Robert L. Newton, who voiced what may have been a substantial opinion among teachers when she told me one day that I "was going to end up in prison if I didn't change my attitude."

Another matron, welcoming me into her home for her son's high school graduation party, assured me that I should have a good time because I was as "good as anybody else."

Years later when I was the featured speaker at one of our class reunions, Mr. Bledsoe, who had been our high school principal before entering the ministry, no doubt driven in part by his experience as a school administrator, told the group that hearing me speak on such an occasion was nothing short of a miracle considering my record in school.

ooooooooooooooo

I am no doubt rationalizing but I do recall that I was in school in a time of turmoil which was not conducive to scholarship or good behavior. However, that doesn't explain why some students achieved good grades and I didn't.

School looked awfully dull compared to the romantic ideas of joining the armed forces, defending freedom and seeing the world. Teachers were coming and going—men to serve in the armed forces, women to marry their sweethearts or to join their husbands before they shipped out to battlefields. I had seven different English teachers during my sophomore year.

My parents, who loved me and supported me without reservation, let me go my own way in school. Perhaps they relied on my common sense too much. I never brought schoolwork home. If I didn't do it in the classroom or in study hall, which was a barely controlled bedlam at best, I didn't get it done. My parents never asked about my homework; I never told.

With deep regret I recall that instead of staying home at night to do my schoolwork, read more books and enjoy the company of my parents, I almost always rushed home from one sort of ball practice or another, ate my supper and walked back to town to sit around the court square or in the poolhall until it was time to come back home, after my mother and father had gone to bed. I always listened to the Glenn Miller band broadcast on the radio and fantasized a lot about what my life after school would be like.

Apparently, I totally ignored or failed to see the irony in my running an editorial in *The Tall Timber Times*, railing against the general lack of scholarship in school which would handicap us in ridding the country of "crooked" politics when we took over "the wheel of our nation."

"Some day in the future," the editorial declared, "the student who is wasting his time now will realize that he should have taken advantage of his high school education. By studying hard we have nothing to lose and an abundance of knowledge to gain." To make matters worse, chances are I wrote that editorial.

I only found the so-called "soft" subjects such as history, literature and social science to be of interest. I simply couldn't handle mathematics and science. Or at least my teachers and I were convinced I couldn't. It became apparent when I was only able to eke out a "D" in the first semester of algebra, or maybe it was geometry, that I would never be able to do much better in the more advanced teachings of the second semester. I needed a "C" in that course for a full year in order to graduate. Someone, no doubt anxious to see the last of me in school, concocted a solution. If I would repeat the first semester and pull my "D" grade up to a "C" I would get the credit I needed for a diploma. I barely made it.

Putting modesty aside in order to provide some balance to my reporting I am compelled to record that my classmates saw me in a different light than did my teachers. I still take pride in the fact that my fellow staff members on *The Tall Timber Times* voted me Best Boy Athlete and Best Boy Personality. I was listed in the yearbook at the end of my senior year as Most Valuable.

ooooooooooooooo

We graduated early in June 1945.

Fifty-six of us, we were one of the smallest classes in the history of the school.

The high school yearbook for 1945 featured a U.S. flag in full color and listed 17 boys who had lost their lives in World War II. We knew that list would grow.

The annual declared in full-blown language that we were leaving "with sorrow the halls that have echoed for twelve years with the sound of (our) erstwhile happy voices." It was said that our "last words to (our) friends and their school are: 'Hail to the Warren High—long may she reign supreme'."

280

The class resolved "To follow knowledge like a sinking star; beyond the utmost realm of human thought."

My paragraph in the class will bequeathed to Ross Adams "(my) editorship, long line of lucky breaks, sartrical (I think the writer meant 'sarcastic') disposition and high ambition."

My senior year was a near-disaster. Without athletics, I lost much of my sense of identity and self-esteem. Only my editorship of *The Tall Timber Times* anchored me. Everything was distorted by the fact that I knew I had to wait until June before I could go into the armed forces. Thirteen days after I was graduated from high school I boarded a bus at the court square and left for the Army. I was glad to go.

ooooooooooooooo

Still, September never would come for me again but that I would recall in a complex of feelings—much pleasure, some sadness and longing—the first days of school each year.

I recall the tinge of regret that the free-ranging times of summer were being lost to the confines of the classroom. We came back to school with enthusiasm and commitment inspired by new clothes; fresh tablets and pencils; unmarked books, some with their covers protected by brown wrapping paper, new relationships and worlds of fresh possibilities that we surely could realize. It was a time for resolutions. We swore that we would do better in school. Homework would be done as it was assigned so that we would never get behind. We would make the team. But other things commanded attention, foreordaining the best intentions to failure.

There were the first sights of the new boys and girls who had moved to town over the summer. There were delicious flirtations with the new girls.

Meanwhile, we checked out the new boys to see if they were going to fit in with our crowd. This macho tradition for establishing the pecking order often resulted in fistfights. In fact, fights were not uncommon among the high school male population.

Boys and girls we had last seen in May came back to school, suddenly no longer children. The girls had filled out, as we said; the boys voices had changed while they had grown taller and more muscular.

We tested the teacher in the first few days to understand the limits of what we could get away with. There was a perverse pleasure to be found if we could reduce one of the new teachers, fresh out of college, to tears.

It was time for football.

I now know I was simply going through the trying process of growing up. There were many more good times than bad, times in which we led as carefree lives as we could have expected in an era of depression and prosperity, war and peace in a world expanding beyond anyone's wildest imagination.

I did not know it then, but those were golden years. I wish I had made more of the opportunities that were there for me.

# NO TIME FOR BOREDOM

My friends and I had little time for boredom when we were growing up.

There was an endless number of games to be played when we were children, and as we grew up there was always work to be done.

Our playgrounds were in our backyards, in the field behind our house and on the streets where few automobiles ran. There were acres of woods nearby, ours to roam about in, building lean-to shelters, hunting elusive rabbits and squirrels and plentiful birds. The river, not far away, invited us to fish and swim.

Our time was not commandeered by activities organized by adults determined to keep us busy as if free time was indeed the devil's workshop.

The neighborhood was full to running over with playmates. Someone always had an idea for a game we could play. When we tired of the traditional games passed along to us by the older kids, we invented new ones. Few of our games required much by way of equipment. When they did we were able to make most of what we needed.

oooooooooooooooo

Many of our ideas for games came from things we had seen at the Saturday movie or from the annual visits of airshows, carnivals and circuses.

A day or two before an airshow went on at Joe Griffin's cow pasture, which served as Warren's airport, a lone plane flew over town dropping leaflets advertising the wonders of what was to come. We walked out to the airport to see up close the daring pilots and the frail contraptions they flew. They were enough to stir the heart and imagination of any youngster who dreamed of adventure and faraway places. Rarely have I ridden in an airplane since those times that I did not think of the men and their crafts.

The airmen wore coveralls oil-stained from their constant tinkering with the mechanics of their planes. When they prepared to take off they donned leather helmets. Some even wore long flowing white scarves, just like in the movies. Brave or foolish, they were care-free, wind-burned heros in our eyes.

We envied the nerves and the purses of the few locals who bought rides with them.

There was, as advertised, a thrill a minute. The planes, usually two of them, swooped back and forth over the field, dipping their wings and banking into sharp turns. The engines were deliberately stalled in midair then restarted to power the planes into steep dives that appeared certain to plunge them into the ground. We held our breathes as they pulled up at the last moment. The grand finale came when a daredevil walked the wings of a plane while it cruised above us and then parachuted out over the field, firing off a smoke bomb while he floated to earth.

I was inspired to make my own parachute and jump off some high place. Not having any white silk at hand for the chute, I decided that Uncle Howard's wool blanket from his days as a U.S. Marine would be good enough. I attached a short piece of rope to each of the four corners which in turn I fastened to my belt. Thus equipped, I proceeded to the hayloft of our barn, which was some 10 or 12 feet off the ground. The outcome was predictable. I bailed out of the loft, my parachute never opened so I hit the ground with a hard thud. My ankles and feet were so sore that I could hardly walk away from my disaster. My playmates, who had been so excited in urging me on, thought it was funny. Shaken and embarrassed, I had had enough parachuting to last a lifetime.

ooooooooooooooo

We carried the spirit and excitement of the movies home with us where we acted out our versions of the stories.

If we had seen a movie about Robin Hood or some noble knight we fought duels with swords and joustling poles we had fashioned from sweet gum saplings. We strapped on our "cap" pistols or we used our rubber guns to recreate shootouts like the ones in the cowboy movies. After a Tarzan movie we climbed trees and competed with each other to imitate the famous call the hero had used to signal the wild beast to come to his aid.

Recess periods at school were often devoted to our versions of the actions we had seen the past Saturdays. Sara Baker and Jean McClendon, pretty and vivacious girls, were always the leaders and heroines, so they got to choose their followers. We were perfectly willing to be their toadies.

Saturday mornings were often spent gathering on the railroad tracks behind the Hoyle's boarding house to do combat with rival gangs. Swords and jousting sticks or rubber guns were our weapons against our main "enemies," the "Butcher Boys," led by Marty and Billy Bob Hoyle.

When Robin Hood or Indian fighting was in season, we made bows from hickory sticks or rattan cut in the thickets that grew in creek bottoms; arrows were fashioned from weeds that thrived in the field behind our house. The more advanced craftsmen among us made shafts for arrows from the sides of apple crates. Nails were driven in one end of the shaft and the head filed off to create a needle-like point to make an arrow for hunting birds and snakes.

Edwin Hickman, a bully who was not the brightest light in our neighborhood, had such a weapon with which I had a painful encounter.

We were playing in my cousin's front yard. It was summer and I was of course barefooted. Edwin declared that he wanted to shoot his nail-tipped arrow into the ground where I was standing. Being a hardheaded cuss, I refused to move despite his repeated threats.

To my surprise, and probably his, he fired the arrow, embedding it in the top of my foot. I looked at my foot in a sort of out-of-body trance as the shaft wobbled back and forth.

I ran home with the arrow still stuck in my foot. Of course, I was screaming like a wounded banshee so that my mother heard me coming. She sat me down on the front steps and pulled the "arrowhead" from my foot. She didn't miss a beat before she started berating Edwin in a voice that could be heard far and wide. Only when her immediate anger was vented did she turn to cleansing and dressing the wound, which after all was quite small.

By that time, we heard Mrs. Hickman calling, "Francis Edwin, you come home this very minute."

oooooooooooooooo

Baseball was a perennial favorite.

Our diamonds were open fields; our bases were bare spots where we had scraped away the grass or a tow sack filled with sawdust. Bats, gloves and mitts were few and far between.

We made most of the balls. The process started with a small rubber ball, such as was used in playing "jacks," which we wrapped with yards of white string that our parents had saved from their grocery shopping. We covered the ball, which was never perfectly round, with black friction tape such as electricians used. Hitting it was like striking the bat against a block of concrete. The surface of the ball, sticky from the adhesive on the tape, picked up pieces of grass and dirt each time it touched the ground.

After a lot of high-pressure salesmanship on my part my parents bought a glove for me. I think it cost less than $2.00. It was little more than a large leather handglove with a skimpy padding of horsehair which soon packed into the heel of the pocket. But I was lucky. Many of the boys played barehanded.

To tell the truth I never cared much about playing baseball because I didn't like someone throwing a hard ball at me when I was at bat or having my hand hurt when I caught a ball in my rag-tag glove.

There were only one or two footballs in our neighborhood. But that didn't hold us back. If the owner of the ball didn't show up for a game or had gone limping home in a huff or tears we made a ball out of a cloth bag stuffed with old rags. Of course, there was no padding nor were there helmets, but we played hard tackle or a rough brand of "touch," that term meaning "knock down."

We played an game known as "shinny." By today's standards it was dangerous. In fact, it bordered on violent. The equipment was primitive: a crushed tin can served as the puck; sweetgum saplings or limbs from hickory trees were our sticks. The playing field was simple; any flat surface a few yards across would do. The goal was a hole dug in the ground in the middle of a large circle. Other holes, or "homes," were spaced around the circle. We drew straws to determine the "out man," the one who faced the challenge of using his stick to maneuver the can (i.e. puck) through the circle into the goal.

The "out man" stayed in that position until he could get the puck in the goal. When he did we drew straws again to determine a new "out man." Or the "outman" could work his stick into a defender's "home" and force a trading of positions.

The rules allowed just about anything the defenders might do to keep the challenger at bay. So there was much thrashing around with our sticks. Of course, we were supposed to concentrate on knocking the puck away, but there was no avoiding hitting shins and ankles with those heavy sticks. It was a rare game when one or more combatants didn't go hobbling home.

oooooooooooooooo

Slingshots and rubber guns were always at the top of our list of playthings.

We made slingshots out of scraps of pinewood scavenged from apple crates and carpenter's cut-offs, rubber bands cut from ruptured inner tubes picked up a filling stations, and pieces of leather saved from old belts or the tongues of shoes.

For ammunition, we went to the town branch or to nearby gravel roads to gather the smoothest and best-shaped rocks we could find. Some of the boys developed amazing skills in killing birds with their slingshots. I had difficulty hitting the side of the barn.

Apple crates were our favorite wood for the stocks of our rubber guns. Sometimes we found longer pieces of pine lumber from which we could make rifles. Clothespins were mounted on the handles of the pistols and along the sides of the rifles to hold the ammunition which was bands of rubber cut from our scavenged inner tubes. Clifford Reep broke the mold when he came up with a board long enough to make a machine gun. He secured a string at the front of the notches, laid it along the top of the barrel and secured the stretched rubber bands on top of it in the notches. He got off an impressive number of shots by pulling up on the string; but, of course, he wasn't very accurate.

We waged many hard battles with our rubber guns. An up-close shot could raise a whelp.

ooooooooooooooo

We had our special games for the spring season.

Every year when it began to turn warm we bought a sack of marbles at Morgan and Lindsay's to add to the leftovers from the past season. Most of the games we played with marbles involved a mild form of gambling—the winners claimed the losers' marbles. It usually wasn't long before the experts such as James Wiggins and Bob Moseley had most of the marbles in their bags. One or two of the boys could shoot their taws so hard that they occasionally cracked an opponent's marbles. I tried to shoot like that, but all I got was a very sore thumbnail and I lost my marbles.

Spring was also the season when we played with yo-yos and tops. We were never successful in making those toys at home. However, I have a top in my office that Uncle Jewell made by hand, a job that required a great deal of craftmanship in order to achieve the necessary balance.We had to come up with a quarter or less to buy one of either.

Many of our games seemed to be concerned with simply running about pushing or pulling something.

We ran "hoops" —small iron wheels found in the junkyard and in worksheds in the neighborhood. We used a strip of wood to which we attached a tin can, flattened and formed into a "V" or "U" shape to guide the hoops as we ran around aimlessly.

Used automobile tires were highly prized. We rolled them by hand up and down the street. It followed that we engaged in combat in which we tried to knock over the opponent's tire. Boys with strong stomachs curled themselves inside tires and let playmates roll them about.

There must have been a special attraction to induced dizziness because we had another game in which we turned about rapidly with our arms outstretched like wings until we lost all equilibrium and collapsed to the ground on the verge of vomiting.

Building and walking on stilts, as we had seen clowns do in the circus, held our attention for awhile each year. The taller the stilts, the braver the walker. A few show-offs could trot on their stilts. There was a thrill to being up in the air looking down on our playmates even if we could only stumble about.

Making and flying kites was a family effort each March when the spring winds blew. I usually bought one kite a season. It was made of papers of brilliant colors with slender lightweight strips of wood for the frame. I think it cost about fifty cents. We had to come up with the tail, which we usually dug out of Mama's treasure of cloth scraps saved from her sewing.

We flew our kites at great heights in the open field behind our house and the Hammons. The winds were strong and unpredictable, making the little crafts difficult to get up and even harder to bring down. Absent considerable skill and more luck, it was inevitable that our kites would eventually get caught in tree limbs or the string would break and they would float away.

When I lost my store-bought kite, Mama and Uncle Jewell helped me make another one. We used slender weeds from the field back of the house and string to form the frame which we covered with newspaper stock. Mama made the necessary glue from flour and water. The entire contraption was a cumbersome thing that seemed unlikely to fly, but it did, albeit often off balance.

Uncle Jewell sometimes helped me launch my kite or retrieve it out of a tree. His participation came with a great deal of "cussing" at the ineptness of boys in general, the vagaries of the wind or the foolishness and frustration of it all. But he didn't mean it. He was just as excited and dumbfounded as I was that the kite we had made could in fact fly.

There was hide-and-seek, a game we often played at night in the fall around bonfires. We also enjoyed a form of dodgeball we called "Red Rover Come Over." Basically, one team chased another team around the house trying to hit one of the opposing players with a large rubber ball.

Mumblety peg was a game that required skill with a pocketknife. We challenged each other with various ways to throw a knife so that it firmly stuck in the ground: arms across the chest, the left hand holding the right ear, the right throwing the knife and vice versa; throwing the knife over the back or flipping it off the fingers one by one; flipping the knife in the air so that it turned over and over, arriving point down.

ooooooooooooooo

The diversions youngsters turned to at Halloween bore little resemblance to the innocence of costumes and "trick or treat" of later years.

In fact, Halloweens were often destructive. Soaping merchants' windows and turning over trash barrels were the least of it.

A group of the older teenagers from our neighborhood melted tar scrounged from a road crew and smeared their initials and other graffiti on the stark white concrete fence the Louis Ederingtons had erected around their new brick home on South Main Street. The rowdies were hauled before a judge who ordered them to remove the tar from the fence. Their attempts at cleaning the fence using gasoline and kerosene with rags and brushes only made it worse. The stains showed for years.

At least once each Halloween some bunch dismantled a wagon and put it back together on top of a church or some public building.

One year a flock of geese was put inside the high school building. They left behind ample evidence of their being caged inside overnight. Livestock was turned out of pastures. Air was let out of automobile tires.

ooooooooooooooo

On the wet cold days of winter we turned to indoor games that we usually played at our house.

Checkers was a favorite. Sometimes we had a board and pieces that someone had received for a birthday or Christmas gift. Often we used a board that had been laid out on a square of cardboard. When the regular red and black checkers were not available, we used soda bottle caps instead. The "checkers" of one player were turned upside down; the opponent's were played corkside down.

Bottle caps had another purpose. We carefully removed the cork, then affixed the metal part to a shirt or cap and secured it from the backside with the cork. We pretended they were badges.

We played games of monopoly that lasted from early mornings to late afternoons on rainy days.

Someone came up with a deck of cards, and we learned to play blackjack. One of the older boys suggested that we play "strip poker," which he explained in titillating terms. Four boys and a girl from the neighborhood gathered at our house one night after supper in a state of high naughty excitement. Every time we lost a hand we were to take off one article of clothing. My parents probably understood what was going on and knew our nerves would fail before we went very far. Sure enough they were correct. I don't recall that anyone ever removed more than his or her shoes and socks or sweater.

ooooooooooooooo

We could always find something to do in the woods and on the river.

There was one game my parents warned me about when I was a very young boy. They said, "Don't go snipe hunting with the older boys." They explained that the game involved teenagers taking a younger boy into the woods at night, leaving him to man the post to which they promised they would drive the snipes, described vaguely as big birds that roamed the fields and woods after dark. The unwitting youngster was to remain at his crucial post, no matter what, until a snipe was captured. Of course, the pranksters went home and left the victim waiting in the dark, no doubt scared out of his wits.

But hunting rabbits on cold winter nights was real. There was the sport of it, but we also knew our families would have welcomed a fresh rabbit to eat. The older boys wore caps bearing headlights fired by the gaseous flumes produced from a mixture of carbide and water. The result was a flickering light and a terrible stench. The hunters were armed with shotguns, most of them single-shot .410s; the rest of us carried heavy sticks.

We went across fields where the walking was made difficult by the rows of chilled, hard-packed soil and spiked stubble left from cornstalks or cotton plants.

293

We never saw, much less killed, a rabbit, because they were heavily hunted by men with more skills than we possessed. But we collected memories to remember.

As I grew into a teenager I spent many hours in the woods on Cemetery Hill and in Carmical's pasture with my .22 rifle hunting rabbits and squirrels. I never found either, but I report with regret that I usually shot one or more of the birds that flew about in great abundance.

After reading in my *Boy's Life* magazine about the rewards of trapping I begged my parents to get a steel trap for me so that I could bag valuable pelt-bearing animals along the creek bottoms. Fortunately, they resisted my nonsense. However, I did build traps for rabbits and birds from scraps of lumber and limbs cut from trees in the woods. Nothing came of my efforts.

We made lean-to huts from saplings and pine boughs in the woods where we built campfires over which we roasted birds we had killed and boiled ears of corn we had picked without permission from a nearby field. The meat of the scrawny birds was bitter to taste; the corn was tough.

The only time we cooked decent food was when Mama gave us a quart of her soup mix.

ooooooooooooooo

We went to the Saline River, out past the Airport Inn, to swim in clear blue-green water and play on sandbars bordered by willow trees and high clay banks variously shaped by the river's current.

We found mussels which looked like oysters and dug into them because we heard that sometimes they yielded pearls, if not fine enough for necklaces, good enough for buttons. We saw lily pads in still backwaters and dark green vines fluttering underwater in the shoals.

Two or three times each summer we went on overnight fishing trips. My companions always included Jim Hurley and often Gordon "Monkey" Apple and Glenn "Bud" Robinson. We camped among willow saplings on sandbars. Our beds were quilts spread on the sand around a campfire which we kept burning all night.

Before nightfall we seined the shallow water for minnows, which were in plentiful supply. These small silver fish were mixed with chunks of beef liver we had brought with us for baiting our sethooks and trotline.

As the sun went down, the mosquitoes came out. Despite all sorts of repellents and the smoke of our campfire, they swarmed about, inflicting their misery.

We cooked our meals over the campfire. The menu never varied—fried potatoes, swimming in grease; baloney and white bread—for supper and breakfast. We had stand-by supplies for frying fish, but we never caught any.

Several times during the night we went out in our boat to check our sethooks and trotline. The spotlights we wore on our caps penetrated the darkness so that through the swarms of moths and mosquitoes and the mist that rose from the water we saw the bright eyes of animals on the riverbanks and frogs sitting near the water's edge. Snakes lay on stumps protruding from the water and in the low-hanging branches of willow trees. Every log was covered with turtles. If we made that trip now we would not see such abundant wildlife. It has been mostly decimated by pollution of the river and the air.

Bleary-eyed from the smoke of our campfire and the lack of sleep, covered with grit and sand and countless mosquito bites, we must have made for a sorry picture when we went home at mid-morning.

It was on these trips that my friendship with Jim Hurley was cemented. We had a partnership for those excursions. He had an outboard motor and much of the equipment we used. I knew how to seine, paddle a boat and put out the sethooks and trotline. Also, I could cook.

Jim and I enjoyed our friendship from those days until his death in 1994.

I spent many happy hours in his company. I often stopped by his house on Pine Street after school. He had his own bedroom, equipped with a record player and a stack of the latest records. We played Glenn Miller, Woody Herman and other favorites of the day until it was time for me to go home for supper.

Most days with decent weather we got in a few shots at the basketball hoop mounted on his garage.

I never knew a more honest and decent man or had a better friend.

ooooooooooooooo

By the time I reached junior high school, organized athletics and part-time jobs left little time for pick-up games and expeditions to the woods and river.

From my early childhood, I worked, never very seriously or successfully, I must admit, at various schemes that I concocted.

My resume even includes a one-day stint at picking cotton. I had heard that John, a one-armed black man, was hiring men, women and children to pick cotton in the field he leased on Dr. Fike's property in the town branch bottom near us. With visions of making a lot of money at 35 cents per hundred pounds I showed up not long after sunup on a late August morning and convinced John that I could pick cotton. He handed me a picker's sack made from heavy canvas about eight feet long, took a few minutes to show me what he expected and sent me to a row. By the end of the first two hours the sun was heating up the field, my hands were raw from sharp cuts of the bolls into my fingers, my back and legs hurt from the constant bending and reaching and I had barely put enough cotton in my sack to be worth weighing. The older pickers had already begun to make noticeable progress in filling their sacks.

It was readily apparent that picking cotton was not for me. I turned in my sack and ate the working man's sandwich Mama had packed for me. I was back home before ten o 'clock. I think John paid me a dime for my effort, which I spent immediately for a candy bar and a soda pop at the neighborhood grocery store.

We scrounged through junkyards and old workshops for bits and pieces of scrap metal we could sell to Mr. Reppon, the local junk dealer, for pennies per pound. Discarded electrical wire yielded pure copper, which was the real payoff. Cashing in on scrap iron was harder work and paid less, but it meant money, too.

I delivered the afternoon *Arkansas Democrat* for Mr. and Mrs. Wentz. My route covered our side of town and Goatneck, the "colored" section, with 60 or so papers. Despite the fact that serving my route provided opportunities to be outside riding my bicycle, I didn't like the job, perhaps because it cut into my free time in the afternoons. But it was the Sunday mornings that really got to me. It wasn't just that the papers were thicker and heavier. It was that I had to get up before daylight in order to cover the route in time for my subscribers to read their papers before Sunday school and church. That made for a short night, since I almost always went to the late show at the Pastime Theater on Saturday night and didn't get to bed before one o'clock in the morning.

Hiring out to mow lawns in the neighborhood at 25 to 35 cents each provided a job for the last year or two before I was old enough at 15 to start working during the summers at the Bradley Lumber Company. World War II was well under way; the draft and the attraction of jobs in defense plants had cut deeply into the local labor force so jobs were plentiful.

We were paid a common-labor wage of 35 to 40 cents per hour which meant I took home less than $16.00, after deductions, per week in the paycheck the foreman handed out late Friday afternoons.

My first job was in the pallet factory. We spent the day driving nails by hand into strips of rough oak lumber laid out on two by fours to make pallets used for storing and moving materials about in warehouses. Safety on the job was not a high priority, so we didn't wear gloves or eye-protectors. Fingers were regularly smashed and splinters were embedded in hands. It was a wonder that no eyes were put out, since mishit nails flew about like hail.

During the summers of my high school years I worked at various other jobs at the Bradley and the Southern lumber company.

The mill whistle blew at seven o'clock to signal the start of the workday; we punched out to end the shift at five o'clock. The day was broken by two 15-minute rest periods and an hour off for lunch.

I hated every hour of those jobs. The monotony of feeding raw lumber hour after hour into a planing machine that made ear-splitting sounds and always demanded more fodder; loading boxcars; stacking lumber a board in a time in a warehouse that held thousands of pieces; seeming to work for hours only to discover that it was just a little past mid-morning; thinking on Monday mornings that quitting time Friday would never come.

Things were better during one summer when I worked with the carpenter crew at The Southern maintaining company-owned homes and helping with the construction of a huge lumber storage shed. My experience with Uncle Jewell, who was a carpenter by trade, equipped me with some skills.

The best summer was working with Bob Galloway, my friend and teammate, on Mr. Treavor Beard's crew that surveyed and ran property lines in the woodlands owned by The Southern Lumber Company. It was good to be working outside away from the sounds and bluster around the mill, although we did have to put up with stifling humidity in the deep woods as well as wasps, ticks, snakes and mosquitoes. One of the benefits was that we could sleep in the backseat of Mr. Beard's car as we traveled to and from the job site.

I always worked weekends and during the Christmas shopping seasons at either the men's department of the Bradley Store or Ederington's Cash Store. Saturdays meant being on hand for the store's opening at eight o'clock and closing the doors as the last customer finally left a little before ten that night, just in time to stop by Wayne Wisener's place for a coke before the late show.

In addition to earning spending money on these jobs I learned a lot about what I did and did not want to do with my life.

It was on this point that my father and I had our only serious misunderstanding. In the presence of my Greenwood kinfolks I announced that I did not intend to work for a living. Outraged, my father demanded to know what I meant. "I am not going to work at the sawmill," I answered. Imagine the reaction of my father and the family who had never known anything but sawmill work. I had thought that my father would be proud of my ambitions. Instead, as my mother relayed it to me, he thought I meant that I intended to con my way through life. It took a while for the rift to heal.

# THE END OF THAT TIME AND PLACE

From the perspective of this day, it is clear we should have known that our special time and place could not last. There was no escaping the inevitable and irrevocable changes that were taking place all around us as the world went to war. But for awhile we could not or would not let ourselves see beyond our insolated island.

Civil wars had been raging in Spain and China. Combatants on all sides had used those conflicts as laboratories in which they could perfect their weapons and rehearse their strategies. The war in Europe was spreading relentlessly from country to country. Mussolini was running amuck in his murderous campaign against the hapless Ethiopians. It was certain that the whole world would be drawn into the conflict.

Even in Warren where we thought we were far removed and insulated from the machinations of world powers, we began to feel the tremors of war as they reached across the protective oceans to sweep over the United States. The economy heated up as our country began to provide the materials of war to those nations that were soon to become our allies on the battlefields. Shipyards were hastily erected and put in to service. Steel mills were going back into full production. Detroit began to convert its production lines from automobiles and trucks to tanks and military vehicles. New army bases were being built; old military installations were being modernized and enlarged.

The melodramatic voices of foreign correspondents came into our homes on the radio each night from London, Berlin and Paris. They took us to the front lines of battles in Europe and the terror of the air raids on London.    The daily *Arkansas Democrat* brought stories of stirring in Washington as Congress, at President Roosevelt's urging, passed "lend-lease" legislation that allowed the United States to become the arsenal of democracy.    The paper carried Ernie Pyle's daily column reporting on his travels across the country. He told the stories of how communities like ours were already succumbing to a veritable upheaval of priorities and lifestyles.

There were notes of excitement and apprehension in the air. Times were improving in Warren. The Bradley and Southern Lumber companies, as well as many little sawmills in the area, were running all out to help meet the need for great amounts of lumber to build new military installations and rehabilitate many that dated back to World War I. The Bradley even served an overseas market by producing hickory stock from which skis were to be made for snow troops in Finland.

ooooooooooooooo

In 1940 Congress passed the Selective Service law, which provided for the drafting of 900,000 men each year.

Everyone assumed we would soon be in the thick of the war, but no one was really prepared for the shock of Pearl Harbor on Sunday, December 7, 1941.

I was loafing around the poolhall waiting for the matinee to begin at the picture show when I heard the radio reports that the Japanese had attacked Pearl Harbor, headquarters of America's Pacific fleet, at 7:55, Pacific Time, that morning. As background to the reporter's coverage, we heard the screaming dive of Japanese warplanes and the sporadic fire being returned by the U. S. forces.

The sneak attack by carrier-based airplanes and submarines lasted two hours. Some 3,000 military personnel plus 60 civilians were killed or injured. Eight battleships and 13 other naval vessels were sunk or damaged; 200 American aircraft were destroyed, most of them as they sat unprotected on the runways.

I hurried home to be with my family, hoping in vain that they could explain what it all meant.

The next day radios were provided to the schools by local merchants so that we could hear President Roosevelt address a joint meeting of Congress. As we listened raptly, he spoke his memorable words: "Yesterday, December 7, 1941—a date which will live in infamy—the United States of America was suddenly and deliberately attacked by naval and air forces of the Empire of Japan." The Japanese, he said, had also attacked many of our bases across the Pacific, and numerous of our ships had been torpedoed "on the high seas between San Francisco and Honolulu."

He concluded, "I ask that Congress declare that since the unprovoked and dastardly attack by Japan…a state of war has existed between the United States and the Japanese Empire."

Declarations of war against Germany and Italy followed quickly.

Americans came together as one to win the conflict.

Suddenly all of our bravado and the delicious excitement of gearing up for a war that someone else was fighting turned to the sobering reality that men we knew from Warren would soon be in harm's way, fighting battles against fearful enemies in places that had been just names on maps.

Our world became bigger than Warren.

The tides of war seemed to run against America and its allies in the early days of the conflict. Families began to receive dreaded messages of wounded, killed or missing in action. Our neighborhood was hard hit. Nolan

Williams, a boy from across the street, was captured at Bataan. Months passed before his parents heard from the Red Cross that he had survived "The Death March." "Red" Reynolds, who grew up near the Corner Grocery was held in an enemy prison camp. Luther Swan, a youngster barely out of high school died at Pearl Harbor. Cone Stell, an ordained minister, perished in action when the bomber he was piloting was shot down. James Berry and Gordon Norman were killed in battle.

More young men were called to duty. Men in uniform were seen everywhere. Young women joined the military and the Red Cross. Rationing was imposed on gasoline, tires and sugar. Merchants' shelves were stripped of some items. Black markets emerged.

Rumors spread that the Japanese would bomb California and that German U-boats would shell New York City. Axis soldiers captured by American troops in the war in Europe were interned in a prisoner of war camp at nearby Monticello. Japanese-Americans were relocated from their homes on the West Coast to a camp in southeast Arkansas. These camps became attractions for tourists who wanted to see what the enemy looked like.

Frightened, but at the same time excited, in a universal spirit of patriotism, everyone stood united, ready to do his or her part. Men and boys, some underage, rushed to enlist in their favorite branch of the armed services before their draft number came up. Volunteers on the home front manned emergency squads. There was a home guard with the responsibility to watch for enemy aircraft and foreign agents. Women knitted sweaters for servicemen and wrapped bandages. Youngsters collected tinfoil, scrap metal and old tires and inner tubes.

Families and friends got reports from young men sent to military bases as far away as California, New York, Washington State and all manner of places. Soon these messages began to arrive from Hawaii, North Africa, Italy and London and even from ships at sea. Many were sent from obscure islands in the Pacific or undisclosed places. Men and women who had never been outside Bradley County were experiencing the far reaches of the world.

A few young women who had married their sweethearts before they left for the service were fortunate enough to join their husbands at military bases before they were shipped overseas. Some of these war brides stayed away from Warren until their men were shipped back to the States, but most came back home to wait out the war.

Families left Warren to go to such places as Detroit, Houston, Kansas and California to work in the shipyards, aircraft factories and armament splants. Others found work at the arsenal less than 50 miles away in Pine Bluff and at the munitions plant in Camden.

Often the men went away alone to take jobs for several months at a time building and expanding defense facilities. Confident they could always find another job, perhaps at a higher wage, they would quit to come home to be with their families for awhile and leave them again in a few weeks to go to another job.

Men who had no real trade and women who had never held a steady job somehow acquired the skills to be welders, pipefitters, sheet metal workers and carpenters. Most who left home, some without two nickels to rub together, came back better fed and better clothed. Some who left on busses drove back in their own cars.

Most of those who went away returned with prosperity of pocket and mind they had not known before. They told us how they had been rewarded in a new world of opportunities.

I was envious of them and could hardly wait my time to be drafted for military service.

305

ooooooooooooooo

Just as individuals and families were going away from Warren, new people were moving in.

Dick Warner came from Minnesota to run the Southern Lumber Company. He brought in a tough Texan by the name of Ernest Gibbs to be plant superintendent. Ed Ives came back to Warren from the Dierks milling organization in western Arkansas, to head up a substantial portion of the Bradley Lumber Company operations. A man named Eberle and his family moved from St. Louis to take a top, but somewhat nebulous, job at The Bradley.

New ideas and new attitudes came with this influx of new people.

When the atom bombs ended the war, most of the men and women who had been away to fight or to work in the war industries came back to Warren at least for a little while. But others went in all directions, never to come back to stay. One young man from our neighborhood married a girl in Maine and worked the rest of his life as a lobster fisherman. Another hoboed around the country until he met a violent death up north. Others settled down all over the United States—Texas, California, North Dakota, Washington, D. C.

Many of those who came back to Warren were scarred by the horrors of battle; others were jaded by the romance of travel and the glamour of big cities. Some brought home new spouses from dissimilar backgrounds and cultures. Many who had expected to work all their lives at the mills and on surrounding farms suddenly had the opportunity to earn college degrees with the benefits they had been awarded for service in the armed forces. They would be doctors, CPAs, lawyers, engineers, teachers and coaches.

Those who came back to Warren found a town that had changed. And they and the relentless tides of events would change it still more.

For a time there were parades and speeches to honor the victory and those who won it. People pledged to never forget those who had served, especially the men who had paid the ultimate price. But other issues took over our lives and memories faded. The dates of Pearl Harbor, V-E Day and V-J Day gradually became for many no more than numbers on a calendar.

Years later Jeffrey Hart could have had Warren and those times in mind when he wrote eloquently:

"The last year of the old America, secure in its isolation, the last year of those lazy summers and provincial slumbers, that last year, 1940, had now vanished like the morning mist. Things would never be the same again. In the phrase of Yeats, a terrible beauty had been born."

**—XXX—**

## ABOUT THE AUTHOR

Ramon Greenwood began his career as a newspaper reporter upon his graduation from the University of Arkansas with a degree in journalism. He soon moved into the field of public relations and communications where he served as Senior Vice President of American Express and a member of the boards of directors of American Express Publishing Company and other subsidiaries of the worldwide corporation. He has also held senior executives positions with other "Fortune 500" companies and in President Ford's Administration. Greenwood has been Chairman of the Board of Children On The Go, Inc. and Career Counselors, Inc. while serving as a member of the boards of directors of a bank holding company, a chain of supermarkets and an advertising and public relations agency.

He has authored four books and has written a syndicated newspaper column.

Printed in the United States
5111